SEARCH THE SCRIPTURES

SEARCH THE SCRIPTURES

A systematic Bible study course

General Editor:
THE REV. ALAN M. STIBBS, M.A.
Oak Hill College, London

INTER-VARSITY FELLOWSHIP
39 *Bedford Square, London* WC1

First Edition in one volume 1949
Second Edition 1951
Third Edition (revised order of study) 1955
Fourth Edition 1960
Fifth Edition (completely revised) 1967
Reprinted 1969

STANDARD BOOK NUMBERS:

One-volume edition (casebound): 85110 613 7
Part 1 (limp): 85110 562 9
Part 2 (limp): 85110 563 7
Part 3 (limp): 85110 564 5

Printed in Great Britain by
Staples Printers Ltd., at their Rochester, Kent, establishment

PREFACE

This course of Bible reading was first issued in 1934 in response to a widespread demand from Christian students and others for a systematic plan which could be used daily. Its aim is to guide the reader through the whole Bible in three years of regular daily study.

The General Editor of the original edition was G. T. Manley. In 1949 a new and revised course was prepared by H. W. Oldham and others. The present fresh and thorough revision has been undertaken by a large team of helpers, each of whom has worked on an allotted section. These include G. L. Carey, D. Catchpole, M. J. Cole, J. C. Connell, P. A. Crowe, A. E. Cundall, D. R. J. Evans, M. R. W. Farrer, P. K. Finnie, R. T. France, P. H. Hacking, A. R. Henderson, J. B. Job, Dr. and Mrs. A. Johnston, F. D. Kidner, G. E. Lane, Mrs. A. Metcalfe, H. Peskett, Mrs. M. Roberts, Miss E. M. Scheuermeier, J. A. Simpson, J. K. Spence, Miss M. Sugden, J. B. Taylor, Miss R. E. Wintle, D. R. Wooldridge and D. F. Wright; with A. M. Stibbs acting as General Editor.

As G. T. Manley wrote of the compilers of the earlier editions, all who have shared in preparing this revision 'know well the difficulty of sustained Bible study, and how many a hindrance Satan will put in the way. But they pray that the guidance here given may, by the grace of God, stimulate such a taste for His Word as to make the time daily spent upon it a delight as well as a source of strength'.

OVER-ALL PLAN OF THE COURSE

PSALMS 1–12	7	35		
PSALMS 13–29	14	70		
PSALMS 30–41	14	119		
PSALMS 42–51	7		232	
PSALMS 52–72	14		239	
PSALMS 73–89	14			379
PSALMS 90–106	14			409
PSALMS 107–138	27			436
PSALMS 139–150	8			478
PROVERBS	21	88		
ECCLESIASTES	7			456
SONG OF SOLOMON	7			459
Prophets				
ISAIAH 1–39	21		277	
ISAIAH 40–66	21		294	
JEREMIAH 1–25	16			331
JEREMIAH 26–52	19			348
LAMENTATIONS	5			359
EZEKIEL 1–32	21			367
EZEKIEL 33–48	14			385
DANIEL	14			469
HOSEA	7	63		
JOEL	2			314
AMOS	5	63		
OBADIAH	1			323
JONAH	2			312
MICAH	5	131		
NAHUM	2			318
HABAKKUK	4			321
ZEPHANIAH	3			315
HAGGAI	2			415
ZECHARIAH	9			417
MALACHI	3			423

NEW TESTAMENT

Gospels

MATTHEW 1–7	10			307
MATTHEW 8–18	18			325
MATTHEW 19–28	21			341
MARK 1–9	19		170	
MARK 10–16	16		189	
LUKE 1:1 – 9:56	25	3		
LUKE 9:57 – 19:28	22	18		
LUKE 19:29 – 24:53	16	30		
JOHN 1–12	25		252	
JOHN 13–21	17		270	
ACTS 1:1 – 12:24	20	38		
ACTS 12:25 – 28:31	34	51		

Letters

ROMANS	28	94		
1 CORINTHIANS	14	111		
2 CORINTHIANS	14	123		
GALATIANS	7	84		
EPHESIANS	7		217	
PHILIPPIANS	7			362
COLOSSIANS	6			396
1 & 2 THESSALONIANS	8	74		
1 TIMOTHY	7	136		
2 TIMOTHY	4	142		
TITUS	3	140		
PHILEMON	1			399
HEBREWS	21		152	
JAMES	7			425
1 PETER	8		202	
2 PETER	5			465
1, 2, 3 JOHN	7		289	
JUDE	2			467
REVELATION	28			480

SUGGESTIONS ON METHOD OF STUDY

Aim of the course

The aim of this course is to help Christians young and old in their daily study of the Word of God. It differs from other schemes which have a similar aim in a number of important respects. First, the whole Bible can be covered in a period of three years. Second, the method employed is to set a number of questions on the content, meaning and application of each passage to be studied. These are designed to encourage a personal searching of the Scriptures to discover God's particular teaching and message for the reader from each portion of His Word. Third, explanatory notes are reduced to an absolute minimum on the principle that the truth which we dig out for ourselves is more likely to be remembered. There is real profit and enjoyment in wrestling with a difficult passage, as the many thousands who have already used the course can testify.

The right approach

The term 'Bible study' has been used to describe this course, but it is a phrase that needs some interpreting. We must not approach the Bible merely academically, as if it were some textbook we are required to read for an examination. We read and study our Bible because this is a means appointed by God by which we can encounter Him. It is vital that we seek the Lord, and desire to know His will as it applies to us. Otherwise, answering a question can become an end in itself and instead of a joyful meeting with our God our Bible study will become either a rather boring duty, or, at best, nothing more than an intellectually absorbing pastime.[1]

While it is true that in our study of the Bible we must use our minds, employing all the intellectual faculties which God has given us, our primary requirement is not intellectual but spiritual. The

[1] On this whole question of the right approach to personal Bible study and prayer see *The Quiet Time*, edited by J. D. C. Anderson (IVF, London; IVP, Chicago).

Bible itself declares: 'The unspiritual man does not receive the gifts of the Spirit of God, for they are folly to him, and he is not able to understand them because they are spiritually discerned' (1 Cor. 2: 14). Similarly, our Lord reveals in one of His prayers that the things of God are often hidden from those whom men reckon wise, and revealed to those He calls 'babes' (Mt. 11: 25, 26). Our approach to God's Word must be wholly without pride and self-confidence. We should begin with a humble acknowledgment of our dependence upon God, and a prayer that His Holy Spirit will open our blind eyes and give us spiritual discernment and understanding.

At the same time we must remember that God has been pleased to reveal His truth in documents written originally in ancient languages and in a particular historical environment. Consequently full discovery of all that God has to say to us through them demands diligent study involving patient and persistent enquiry and the use of all proper available aids to understanding. Bible study ought to be regarded, therefore, as demanding the serious and concentrated exercise of all one's intellectual powers. God rewards those who seek in order to find.

The time required

Those who originally planned *Search the Scriptures* had in mind people who would give at least twenty minutes a day to their personal Bible study. But experience over many years has shown that to get the maximum amount of help from the course rather longer than this may be required. Without it, prayerful meditation on the passage, which is a necessary preliminary to answering the questions, may well get curtailed. Those with little time to give would therefore be well advised to seek some slightly less demanding scheme as an aid to their Bible study.[1] But for those who can set aside, say, half an hour a day, experience has shown that this course can be of immense spiritual benefit. In addition, the question and answer method provides valuable practical training in how to study the Bible for oneself.

Arrangement

The full course can be completed in exactly three years by anyone who will keep at it and do the study each day without fail. This is the challenge it presents. But it is intended to act as a servant, not as a task master, to assist rather than to discourage. Obviously, illness

[1] For example, the introductory Bible study course, *Hold the Faith* (IVF, London; IVP, Chicago), which provides approximately six months' study.

or a change in circumstances may necessitate a change in routine. Others may find that they benefit by a move to another Bible study method for short periods. The important thing is to keep constantly before one's mind the aim of completing a personal study of the whole Bible, even though one finds it takes longer than the recommended three years.

The order in which it is suggested that the books of the Bible should be studied has been worked out with some care. There are both deliberate sequence and planned variety. Except where other considerations have demanded some different arrangement, Old Testament books are studied in their historical order. Since, however, 1 and 2 Kings are studied as part of this historical sequence, 1 and 2 Chronicles are inserted towards the end of the course as a final review of the history of the kingdoms of Israel and Judah.

Only where the study of a book occupies more than four weeks has its study been subdivided into sections to be taken with intervals in between. Studies which occupy the first year have been chosen to help the beginner. They contain, for instance, a much larger proportion of New Testament reading than is possible in the remainder of the course.

Those who are accustomed to reading only a short passage of Scripture each day may find the length of some of the Old Testament allocations rather forbidding. But there is much to be said for the practice of reading large sections (and even whole books) at a sitting. After all, this is what we usually do when reading for study or pleasure. With the time available, the detailed study of particular verses is less important than a broad, general acquaintance with the contents and main spiritual truths of the passage.

One big advantage of a course of this kind is that it can so easily be adapted to suit individual needs. For example, if the order of study recommended is not what the reader wants, it can very easily be altered. Again, the larger books of the Bible, which in this course are divided into sections, can, if preferred, be read without interruption in their entirety. Cross references are provided from the end of one section to the beginning of the next to make this simpler. If, on the other hand, it is preferred to break the books down into even smaller sections for the sake of variety, there is nothing to prevent the course being adapted in this way. Another suggestion is that readers may wish to increase the amount of New Testament study they do in the later stages of the course by turning again to some of the books studied in Part One. This will lengthen the time taken to complete the course but some may well decide that other considerations are more important.

To make this easier, the books are listed in their biblical order on pp. vi, vii and viii with the total number of studies allocated to each and the page where each section begins. But any deviation from the prescribed order ought not to be allowed to interfere with the ultimate aim of completing for oneself a study of the whole Bible.

A check-list on which each book or section can be ticked when completed appears at the beginning of each of the three Parts; and each individual study can also be ticked as it is done, in the small 'boxes' provided for the purpose.

Requirements

(a) *A Bible*

The course is based in general upon the Revised Standard Version of the Bible, and can naturally be used with this alone. There will be occasions when other translations may be helpful to the study of the passage; and there are, of course, numerous other versions of the Bible or New Testament available today. While care should be taken in their use (sometimes they are paraphrases rather than translations), they can often throw light on a passage that might otherwise be somewhat obscure.

(b) *A notebook*

This can be used both for rough notes made during the study each day and also for writing up more carefully those findings which are felt to be of more permanent value. Some have found it wise to leave the recording of these notes to a later time when the value of the daily discoveries can be seen in perspective. In the initial thrill of discovery all sorts of things may be thought to be of great and lasting worth which will not appear quite so relevant a week later. The majority, however, will probably not have time to come back to each study in this way. A good loose-leaf book can serve for both purposes.

(c) *Other aids to Bible study*

A Bible and a notebook are the only two *essential* requirements, but the following reference books can be recommended as useful aids to Bible study.

(i) *The New Bible Commentary.*[1] A popular one-volume commentary on the whole Bible. Some explanatory notes and a certain amount of background information are provided in the course, but to have a commentary available for reference can be very valuable. If time is limited, however, such helps should be used only sparingly.

[1] IVF, London; Eerdmans, Grand Rapids, Michigan. See also the Tyndale Commentaries on individual books (Tyndale Press, London; Eerdmans, Grand Rapids, Michigan).

What is discovered personally from a study of the Bible will mean far more than what is read hurriedly in a commentary.

(ii) *The New Bible Dictionary*.[1] This contains a great deal of useful information concerning places, customs and the meaning of words and ideas. Again, care must be taken to see that the time set apart for personal study is not replaced by reading some of the fascinating facts recorded in the Dictionary! On the other hand, such a reference work can be a very helpful supplement to the study of the Bible.

Procedure

What follows is put forward merely as a suggestion for those starting the course. After a while, each individual will naturally wish to make his own adaptations of this procedure as seem best to him in the light of his experience.

1 Begin with prayer along the lines previously suggested.

2 Read the portion of Scripture appointed for study. It is best not to read the questions before reading the Bible passage itself. Knowing what the questions are may mean that one's interest becomes limited too soon to those particular points.

3 Read the questions and any notes on the passage. Think about the passage in the light of the questions asked. Then try to work out the answer to these: they will be found a very useful aid to concentration.

4 Write answers to the questions in the notebook. The user of the course is strongly advised to discipline himself to do this, and not just to pass over the questions with a vague idea that they have been answered. Greatest profit will be derived from actually committing to paper what has been discovered from the passage. At the same time it is possible to be too dependent on the questions. Especially in the larger Old Testament sections the questions set obviously do not exhaust the meaning of the passage. The reader may even feel that at times they miss what is to him the main point of the passage or jump to application too quickly. Fair enough! If readers find themselves wanting to formulate their own lines of inquiry instead of being tied to the questions set, one of the aims of the course is being achieved.

Some users of the course may wonder at times whether their answer to a question is in fact the one intended! This does not really matter provided that scriptural teaching is being better understood. But where other Scripture references are provided for comparison these will often indicate the kind of answer expected. But it is better to concentrate first on getting an answer from the verses

[1] IVF, London; Eerdmans, Grand Rapids, Michigan.

set for study, and to leave the references to other Scriptures until that has been done. The temptation to study the cross references rather than the passage set must be avoided.

It can also be very helpful to have a weekly review of the ground covered, and of the outstanding truths which have been learnt or more fully appreciated.

Some people may find that all this gives them too much to do in the time they have allocated to Bible study. In that case an attempt could be made to adapt the course so that only one question is dealt with each day, concentrating on the one which seems likely to be the most profitable. Then move on to the next study. To do otherwise means that the course may well take six years or even longer to complete. When it is only occasionally that one finds there is not enough time to finish, it may well be possible to complete the study later in the day or at the weekend, while the reading is still comparatively fresh in the mind.

Where more than two questions are provided for the same study, the third (or fourth) question is to be regarded as an optional extra; or as an alternative to the first two; or for possible use when the same Bible passage is studied later. One of the advantages of a course of this kind is that it can be used repeatedly.

5 Use the passage as a basis for worship and praise. Pray over the lessons learnt. There will be some particular thought (or thoughts) which is God's word to you for the day. Seek to discover it, and then in prayer relate it practically to your own life. Remember that God's inspired Word has been given to us for an essentially practical purpose; to teach us, to reprove us, to correct us, to instruct us in righteousness, and to make us spiritually mature and equipped for every good work (2 Tim. 3: 16, 17).

ABBREVIATIONS

Books of the Old Testament: Gn., Ex., Lv., Nu., Dt., Jos., Jdg., Ru., 1, 2 Sa., 1, 2 Ki., 1, 2 Ch., Ezr., Ne., Est., Jb., Ps. (Pss.), Pr., Ec., Ct., Is., Je., La., Ezk., Dn., Ho., Joel, Am., Ob., Jon., Mi., Na., Hab., Zp., Hg., Zc., Mal.

Books of the New Testament: Mt., Mk., Lk., Jn., Acts, Rom., 1, 2 Cor., Gal., Eph., Phil., Col., 1, 2 Thes., 1, 2 Tim., Tit., Phm., Heb., Jas., 1, 2 Pet., 1, 2, 3 Jn., Jude, Rev.

AV	Authorized Version (1611)
ICC	*International Critical Commentary*
LXX	Septuagint Version (*i.e.*, translation of the Old Testament into Greek, *c.* 250 BC)
mg.	margin
Moffatt	*A New Translation of the Bible* by James Moffatt (1935)
NBC	*The New Bible Commentary* (2nd ed. 1954)
NBD	*The New Bible Dictionary* (1962)
NEB	The New English Bible: New Testament (1961)
RSV	Revised Standard Version (1946–52)
RV	Revised Version (1885)
TNTC	*Tyndale New Testament Commentaries*
TOTC	*Tyndale Old Testament Commentaries*
Way	*Letters of St. Paul and Hebrews* by Arthur S. Way (1921)
Weymouth	*The New Testament in Modern Speech* by R. F. Weymouth (1902

PART THREE

Check-list of material contained in this part (tick when completed):

MATTHEW 1 - 7

Introduction

It is customary to see in Matthew's Gospel the fact that Jesus is presented especially as the Messiah, the promised Son of David. This is true; but it also declares that He is the Saviour from sin (1: 21) and the Son of God (1: 23; 3: 17; 16: 16, 17); and although the writer was obviously a Jew to the core, and wrote primarily for Jewish Christians, yet he recognizes that Jesus is the Saviour, not of the Jews only, but of all nations (2: 1, 11; 28: 19, 20). Nevertheless, this is the most Jewish of the Gospels. It is significant that our Lord's genealogy is traced back, not to Adam, as in Luke's account, but to Abraham, the father of the Jewish race.

The story of the birth of Christ shows distinct signs of being derived from Joseph's side, as the story given by Luke would seem to come from Mary's.

The Gospel is characterized by the large place it gives to the teaching of our Lord, and in particular to His teaching in parables and about 'things to come'.

Analysis

1: 4 – 4: 11	Early days of the Messiah.	
	1 and 2	Genealogy, birth and childhood incidents.
	3: 1–12	The heralds proclaim His coming ministry.
	3: 13 – 4: 11	His baptism and temptation.
4: 12 – 16: 12	The ministry in Galilee.	
	4: 12–25	Preaching, and call of disciples.
	5 – 7	The Sermon on the Mount—the kingdom expounded.

	8 – 16: 12	Teaching, preaching and healing, mainly in Galilee. Commissioning and sending forth of the Twelve. Increasing opposition.
16: 13 – 18: 35	Peter's confession. Prediction of the cross. The transfiguration. Teaching of the Twelve.	
19: 1 – 21: 16	Journey to Jerusalem and entry into the city.	
21: 17 – 25: 46	Last days in Jerusalem.	
	21: 17 – 23: 39	Final words. Reciprocal rejection.
	24: 1 – 25: 46	Teaching the Twelve about 'things to come'.
26: 1 – 27: 66	The finished work.	
	26: 1–56	Last supper and betrayal.
	26: 57 – 27: 66	Trial, crucifixion and burial.
28: 1–20	The new beginning. The resurrection and the great commission.	

☐ STUDY 1 Matthew 1

1 Consider the names in the genealogy and note how sinful some of them were. How does this chapter indicate that the coming of Jesus was in God's plan from the beginning? In what ways does it demonstrate that in Jesus Old Testament prophecy is fulfilled? What truths are here indicated concerning His Person and work?

2 What do verses 18–25 teach us about the virgin birth? What is the importance of this truth for the Christian?

3 Examine the character of Joseph as revealed in these verses (*cf.* 2: 13–23). What may we learn from his courageous obedience?

Notes

1 Verse 17. This arrangement into three periods of fourteen generations each is not exact, some generations being omitted. Possibly this artificial arrangement is for easy memorizing.

2 Verse 19. According to Jewish law, Mary, being betrothed to Joseph, was already legally regarded as his wife.

☐ STUDY 2 Matthew 2

1 Consider the significance of the coming of the wise men from the East in the light of such passages as Is. 49: 6; Lk. 2: 32; Jn. 10: 16.

2 Note the different reactions to the birth of Jesus from the wise men, the chief priests and scribes, and Herod. How does this prove the truth of Jn. 9: 39; 18: 37?

3 Notice the accuracy of fulfilment of prophecy in our Lord's infancy (verses 15; 17, 18; 23). What does this teach us about the nature and authority of prophecy?

Notes

1 Verse 1. 'Wise men': the word 'Magi' (see RV mg.) refers to learned astrologers or those who practised magical arts. There is nothing but tradition to make them kings.

2 Verse 23. There is no Old Testament quotation about the Messiah as a Nazarene. Matthew may be making a play on the Hebrew word *netser* meaning 'branch' from Is. 11: 1 and Je. 23: 5. Or the phrase may refer to the contempt associated with Christ's home background. *Cf.* Jn. 1: 46; Is. 53: 2, 3.

☐ STUDY 3 Matthew 3

1 John the Baptist saw himself as preparing the way for Christ (verse 3). In what ways did he do this through (a) his preaching, and (b) his administration of baptism?

2 What do verses 13–15 tell us about the importance of His baptism to Jesus? How do you link this moment with the cross? *Cf.* Ps. 40: 7–8; Lk. 12: 50; 2 Cor. 5: 21. Can you see the Trinity clearly at work in these verses?

☐ STUDY 4 Matthew 4

1 Consider the temptations of Jesus as a testing of the kind of ministry He was going to exercise. What was the special point of appeal in each temptation? Can you link these three typical temptations with the threefold division of 1 Jn. 2: 16?

2 In what way do verses 1–11 help us to understand the meaning of temptation and the way in which Satan may be defeated?

3 What was Christ's first message? Try to define repentance. *Cf.* Acts 2: 38; 20: 21; Lk. 15: 18; Mt. 3: 8. What further demand did He make on those who became disciples, and why? Has your response to Christ been of this kind?

Note. The incidents recorded in Jn. 1: 29 – 4: 3 must have happened between verses 11 and 12 of this chapter.

☐ STUDY 5 Matthew 5: 1–16

1 Describe the qualities of the happy life as detailed in verses 1–12. What makes them such? To what rewards do they lead, and why?

2 Verses 13–16. What is the significance of the two metaphors with which our Lord describes the relation to the world of those who belong to the kingdom? And in what ways does He warn them that they may fail to exercise their proper function?

Note. Verse 3. 'Poor in spirit': *i.e.*, aware of their spiritual poverty and of their need of divine help. *Cf.* Is. 57: 15; Lk. 18: 13.

☐ STUDY 6 Matthew 5: 17–48

1 Our Lord demonstrates His respect for the law in verses 17–20. What does verse 20 mean? Does it leave us any hope? *Cf.* Rom. 3: 20–22; 8: 3, 4. In what way does our Lord make the law more demanding?

2 What is the relevance in our modern world of Christ's teaching in verses 33–48 on the subject of oaths and taking vengeance? Consider the application of the question in verse 47, 'What more are you doing than others?' to the whole subject of Christian love.

3 Comparing verses 31, 32 with 19: 3–9, what is our Lord's teaching on the sanctity of marriage and the possibility of divorce?

Notes

1 Verse 18. 'Not an iota, not a dot': a reference to the smallest letter or significant part of a letter in the Hebrew language.

2 Verse 48. 'Perfect' has more the meaning of 'mature' or full-grown than any concept of sinless perfection. *Cf.* Lk. 6: 36.

☐ STUDY 7 Matthew 6: 1–18

1 What was wrong with the religion of the scribes and Pharisees, here called 'hypocrites', and what kind of religion does our Lord commend in contrast? *Cf.* Je. 17: 10. How do you 'practise your piety' (verse 1)?

2 In the Lord's prayer, what may we learn (a) from the order of the petitions, and (b) from the kind of subjects which are particularly mentioned? What must be our relation (a) to God, and (b) to our fellow-men, if we are to make it our prayer?

Note. Verses 2, 5, 16. The word 'hypocrite' means an actor, *i.e.*, one who plays a part.

☐ STUDY 8 Matthew 6: 19–32

1 Verses 19–24 are a word to the rich. What should be a Christian' attitude to material possessions? In what way do these verses portray the character and danger of worldliness?

2 Verses 25–34 are a word to the not-so-rich. Note the recurrence of the phrase 'Do not be anxious', and list the reasons given why anxiety is wrong.

Note. Verse 23. An eye which is 'not sound' (RSV) or 'evil' (AV, RV) signifies a covetous or niggardly disposition. *Cf*. Dt. 15: 9; Pr. 28: 22; Mt. 20: 15 (mg.).

☐ STUDY 9 Matthew 7: 1–12

1 Compare verses 1–5 with verses 6, 16; and see Jn. 7: 24. If judging is not always wrong, what is our Lord here condemning?

2 What is the teaching of verses 7–12 on the practice of prayer? What place is there for persistency, and what place for trusting? Is there any conflict between these two ideas?

Note. Verse 6. This indicates that, while Christians must not be guilty of condemning anyone, they must learn to discriminate in their witness. *Cf*. Pr. 9: 8.

☐ STUDY 10 Matthew 7: 13–29

1 In verses 13–23 what threefold responsibility does our Lord lay upon those who would enter His kingdom (a) as to a right choice at the beginning (verses 13–14); (b) as to a right discrimination between false and true (verses 15–20); and (c) as to the condition of being acknowledged by Him at the last (verses 21–23)?

2 To what categories of men do verses 24–27 refer? In what way do the two houses differ? How is it possible to be building—yet building foolishly?

3 Verses 15–20. In what way may we tell the false prophet? *Cf*. Dt. 13: 1–5; 1 Jn. 4: 1–6. Can you think of any modern guise in which he appears?

For Studies 11–28 on the second section of Matthew's Gospel see p. 325.

JONAH

Introduction

Jonah is mentioned in 2 Ki. 14: 25 as having predicted the victories of Jeroboam II by which the borders of the kingdom of Israel were greatly enlarged. If Jonah prophesied at the beginning of Jeroboam's reign, he would precede Amos by about twenty years only. At that time Assyria was already a great power, and had begun to reach out westwards: in fact, Jeroboam's victories were partly due to Assyrian raids upon Damascus and neighbouring states, which weakened these kingdoms. It would seem that Jonah was afraid of Assyria, whose cruelties were well known, and whose power was dreaded.

To this man came the commission to go to Nineveh and cry against it. One might have thought that such a commission would not be unwelcome, but to Jonah it was so hateful that he resolved rather to resign his prophetic office than obey it. The book is the story of what happened. It is one of the most remarkable books in the Bible, and rich in spiritual teaching.

Analysis

1 Jonah's disobedience and its result.
2 His prayer of desolation and thanksgiving.
3 A recommissioned Jonah preaches in Nineveh with astonishing effect.
4 Jonah's anger, and God's reproof.

☐ STUDY 1 Jonah 1 and 2

The key to Jonah's flight is found in 4: 2. He feared the tenderness of God. If he went to Nineveh as commanded, Nineveh might repent, and be spared (*cf.* Je. 18: 8) to become later the destroyer of Israel. If he did not go, God's judgment would fall upon Nineveh, and Israel would be saved.

1 'But Jonah' (verse 3); 'But the Lord' (verse 4). *Cf.* Acts 11: 8, 9 (where the context also concerns Gentiles). Of what truth had Jonah lost sight? *Cf.* 1 Tim. 2: 4. How did the Lord retain control of the situation? With 1: 7b *cf.* Pr. 16: 33, and notice 'appointed' in 1: 17.

2 Jonah (like Adam and Eve, Gn. 3: 8–10) tried to escape from the presence of the Lord (1: 3, 10; *cf.* 2: 4). Why was this impossible? In the light of this passage, look up Ps. 139: 23, 24 and apply it to yourself.

3 Jonah's prayer, remarkable for its lack of direct petition, speaks of distress and passes into thanksgiving. What was the fundamental cause of his distress? What caused the transition?

Notes

1 1: 3. 'Flee . . . from the presence of the Lord': this amounted to renouncing his vocation, for the prophet stood in the presence of the Lord (*cf.* 1 Ki. 17: 1).
2 1: 17. 'Three days and three nights': *cf.* Mt. 12: 40. According to Jewish reckoning this may mean one full day with the night before and the night after.
3 2: 7. To the Hebrews, 'remembering' could be much more than a bare mental process; it could mean recreating to the imagination the historic deeds of the Lord; the use of the word repays detailed study. With this passage *cf.* Pss. 77: 11, 12; 105: 4–6; 143: 5.
4 2: 9. The vow was probably some sort of sacrificial thank-offering. Vowing is a biblical practice; but the Old Testament counsels against hasty (Pr. 20: 25) and empty (Ec. 5: 5) vows.

☐ STUDY 2 Jonah 3 and 4

1 God is unchangeably consistent in His attitude to men. What moral action is necessary to avoid judgment and find mercy? *Cf.* Joel 2: 12–14; Acts 10: 34, 35. How did Jesus commend the Ninevites' action? *Cf.* Mt. 12: 41.

2 Jonah the patriot almost hides Jonah the prophet. How do 4: 2b, 4, 10 and 11 rebuke his attitude? Contrast the attitude of Jonah with that of Jesus the Jew. *Cf.* Mt. 23: 37, 38; Mk. 10: 45.

3 What aspects of the character of God stand out in this short book?

Notes

1 3: 3. 'An exceedingly great city': the administrative district of Nineveh, which could be referred to here (as distinct from the city alone), was thirty to sixty miles across.
2 4: 2. 'Repentest of evil': the Hebrew root means 'to breathe heavily'. A change of mind is not so much meant; the thought is almost that the Lord takes a deep breath of relief that He does not have to act in judgment as the consistency of His character would otherwise demand.

3 4: 6. 'A plant': a fast-growing, trailing or climbing plant with broad leaves.
4 4: 9-11. 'Jonah (for selfish reasons) pities the insignificant plant for which he was not responsible. Should not God much more (and unselfishly) have pity on the poor ignorant inhabitants with their cattle in the evil city of Nineveh?'

JOEL

Introduction

Nothing is known of this prophet beyond what is stated in the first verse of his book, and the evident fact that he prophesied to Judah. It is generally agreed that he was either one of the earliest of the prophets, or one of the latest. The date is not important for the study of his message.

The occasion of his prophecy was an unprecedented plague of locusts, apparently accompanied by drought (1: 18–20). He summoned the people to national repentance and self-humbling, and on their doing this, he was authorized to declare the speedy departure of the locusts and the restoration of the land.

But the prophet was given also a more distant vision. The plague of locusts was a symbol of the approaching day of the Lord, and Joel foresees the outpouring of the Spirit, and the gathering of the nations to answer for their misdeeds towards Israel. The Lord will triumph, and Israel be blessed.

Analysis

1: 1 – 2: 17	The plague of locusts and a national summons to repentance.
2: 18–27	The locusts will be destroyed, and the land will recover its fertility.
2: 28–32	The outpouring of the Holy Spirit.
3: 1–21	The day of the Lord; the judgment of the nations, and blessings upon Judah and Jerusalem.

☐ STUDY 1 Joel 1: 1 – 2: 17

Two addresses on the plague of locusts, both describing in different ways its severity, and summoning the people to repent.

1 What teaching is given in this passage on the need for corporate repentance for national sin? What essentials of true repentance are given in 2: 12, 13?

2 Gather together the teaching on 'the day of the Lord' in this passage. What is its significance?

☐ STUDY 2 Joel 2: 18 – 3: 21

1 What is God's reaction to His people's repentance? What principle does this teach?

2 How has the prophecy of 2: 28, 29 been fulfilled far more wonderfully than Joel foresaw?

3 Chapter 3 is a vision of mercy upon Israel, and judgment on her enemies. In what ways had the nations angered God by their treatment of Israel, and what judgment would fall on them? What according to 3: 17 and 21 is the supreme blessedness of God's people?

ZEPHANIAH

Introduction

Zephaniah prophesied in the reign of Josiah, and probably in the early years of that reign, before Josiah began his religious reforms. For when Zephaniah delivered his message, idolatrous customs, which Josiah abolished, were still openly practised (*cf.*, *e.g.*, 1: 4, 5 with 2 Ki. 23: 4, 5). Zephaniah was therefore a contemporary of Jeremiah and possibly began his ministry somewhat earlier. If the

Hezekiah from whom his descent is traced (1: 1) was, as many think probable, the king of that name, then Zephaniah was related to the royal house.

The theme of his prophecy is the day of the Lord, which was about to break. It is pictured as a day of terrible judgment, under the imagery of war and invasion, in which Judah and Jerusalem would be thoroughly purged of those who practised wickedness. But the judgment would embrace all nations; it was to be a day of universal judgment.

When the judgment was completed there would be a remnant of Israel, a lowly but upright people who, trusting in the Lord, would rejoice in His favour. Zephaniah foresaw also that other nations would 'call on the name of the Lord and serve him with one accord' (3: 9). His message is marked by breadth of view and profound insight, and charged with an ardent vehemence of moral passion.

Zephaniah's words received a striking fulfilment in the fall of Nineveh, and a quarter of a century later in the fall of Jerusalem. But the fulfilment is not yet complete. The final day of God's judgment has yet to come.

Analysis

1: 1–18 The approaching day of the Lord, with special reference to Judah and Jerusalem.

2: 1 – 3: 7 A summons to repentance; prophecies of judgment against other nations; and the failure of Jerusalem to amend her ways.

3: 8–20 The remnant that will survive the judgment; their character and their felicity.

□ STUDY 1 Zephaniah 1

The effects of God's universal judgment (verses 2, 3) upon Judah and Jerusalem are described in detail (verses 4–13). The chapter ends with a terrifying picture of the day of the Lord (verses 14–18).

1 On whom particularly will God's judgment fall according to this chapter, and why? Can you think of any modern counterparts to the sinful actions described?

2 Having considered the reasons for judgment, now ponder the accompaniments of the day of the Lord in verses 14–18. What may we learn from these about God's view of sin? *Cf.* Pr. 11: 4; Ezk. 7: 19.

Notes
1 Verse 4. To 'cut off . . . the name of' mean to 'obliterate the memory of'.
2 Verse 5. 'Milcom': a foreign deity of this or a similar name was worshipped in several of the countries surrounding Judah.
3 Verse 12. 'Thickening upon their lees': *cf.* Je. 48: 11. This picture, taken from the wine-trade, refers to the sedimentation of wine. The idle, stagnant, muddy-minded men in Jerusalem, who thought they could settle down in their godless indifference, will be punished.

☐ STUDY 2 Zephaniah 2: 1 – 3: 7

1 What phrases are used to describe the nations over whom judgment is impending? See 2: 1, 10, 15. What was especially sinful about Nineveh's attitude (2: 15; *cf.* Is. 47: 6–11), and has it a modern counterpart? What qualities does God look for in those who desire his help (2: 3)?

2 'Hidden on the day of the wrath of the Lord' (2: 3). Is there such a hiding-place? *Cf.* Je. 23: 24; Am. 9: 3; Rev. 6: 15–17; Rom. 5: 9; 1 Thes. 1: 10.

3 The indictment against Jerusalem is the most grievous of all (3: 1–7). *Cf.* Lk. 12: 47, 48. List the evils found in her, and consider especially how they were sins against the Lord.

Notes
1 2: 1. 'Come together . . .': *i.e.*, in solemn assembly to seek the Lord.
2 2: 13–15. No man alive at the time had known anything but the greatness and glory of Assyria. So these words would have had an astonishing impact.
3 3: 5–7. The Lord's faithfulness in judgment on their enemies is matched by the shamelessness of His people. They were heedless of the lessons He was seeking to teach them.

☐ STUDY 3 Zephaniah 3: 8–20

1 Throughout this passage the Lord is seen acting. What is He pictured as doing? How many of these actions were, or can now be, fulfilled in Christ? Are there some which still await fulfilment, and, if so, why?

2 Consider the character of the remanant that the Lord leaves (verses 12, 13). Compare 2: 3; and contrast 2: 1; 3: 1, 2. Does 3: 17 suggest a reason for this change of character? How is it brought about? *Cf.* 2 Cor. 5: 17; Eph. 4: 24.

Note. Verses 9, 12. To 'seek refuge in the name of the Lord' is an expressive figure for trust in the Lord's revealed character. Truly to call Him Lord means to acknowledge Him as such, and to give Him the service that is His due. *Cf.* 1 Pet. 3: 6a.

NAHUM

Introduction

In the prophet Nahum God found a man who, with flaming conviction, proclaimed the astonishing message that great Nineveh, still at the height of her power and glory, must fall and disappear. Nahum concentrates on this seemingly incredible event to the exclusion of all else. With great poetic skill and vivid realism he portrays the attack upon the city and her final end. We can almost see the battle, the capture, the looting, and hear the noise of her fall and the silence of her desolation. Nahum's purpose in writing, however, is not to gloat over the downfall of the great enemy of his people. It is to magnify the God of Israel, to declaim that He is, on the one hand, faithful to His promises and strong to save those who put their trust in Him, and, on the other hand, the Holy One, who is the Adversary and Judge of the wicked. It is because the Assyrian Empire was built with ruthless cruelty upon the principle that might is right that God, as the moral Governor of the world, rises up to smite it to the dust.

Nahum prophesied between the overthrow of Thebes in Egypt, about 663 BC (to which he makes reference in 3: 8), and the fall of Nineveh in 612. There is no certain clue as to a more exact date, but the most likely period for his ministry seems to be in the early years of King Josiah. If so, he preceded Jeremiah by only a few years.

Analysis

1: 1	Title.
1: 2–15	The Lord, who is good to those who trust in Him, is terrible to His enemies, and will utterly destroy Assyria.
2	The attack upon the city, its capture and overthrow.
3	Nineveh's guilt and punishment. Her end is final, and all that hear of it shall clap their hands.

☐ STUDY 1 Nahum 1

1 What do we learn in this chapter about God (a) in relation to His own people, and (b) in relation to His enemies? *Cf.* Lk. 18: 7, 8; 2 Thes. 1: 8; Nu. 14: 17, 18; Ps. 46: 1.

2 Nineveh's boastful spirit is seen in Is. 36: 18–20; 37: 23–25; Zp. 2: 15. But how does Nahum regard her in relation to God's power? See verses 3b–6, 9–12a, 14; and *cf.* Ps. 37: 35, 36.

3 Consider how verse 7 is illustrated in the story of 2 Ki. 18 and 19, which happened less than a century before Nahum's time. Have you your own illustration to give out of your own experience?

Notes

1 Verse 1. 'An oracle concerning Nineveh', or 'The burden of Nineveh': see Note on Je. 23: 33–40. Where 'Elkosh' was is not known with certainty; it may be in Judah.

2 Verse 2. 'A jealous God': behind this description lies the figure of the marriage relation used in Scripture of Israel's relation to God. 'Just as jealousy in husband or wife is the energetic assertion of an exclusive right, so God asserts and vindicates His claim on those who belong to Him alone.' Or, in terms of kingship, it is His 'passionate determination' that His sovereignty be recognized among all men, 'to the benefit of the humble and loyal among his subjects and the confusion of the presumptuous'. *Cf.* Ex. 34: 14; 1 Cor. 10: 20–22.

3 Verse 7. 'Knows': *i.e.*, takes care of.

4 Verses 8–10. The translation here is often difficult: see mg. The RSV too readily follows alternative readings. In verse 8 read with mg. 'her place', *i.e.*, probably the sanctuary of Nineveh or its goddess Ishtar. Verse 10 has been rendered (*cf.* mg.): 'Though tangled as thorns, and drenched as their drink, they shall yet be consumed as stubble fully dry' (Eaton), *i.e.*, however tricky an enemy (for men) to deal with, God's flame will run through them like dry stubble.

5 Verse 11. Possibly a reference to Sennacherib. *Cf.* Is. 10: 7–11.

6 Verses 12, 13 and 15 are addressed to Judah, and verses 11 and 14 to Nineveh.

7 Verse 12b. RV mg. reads: 'So will I afflict thee, that I shall afflict thee no more' (*i.e.*, 'I shall not need to'). *Cf.* verse 9. Then the verse is addressed to Nineveh.

8 Verse 14. 'Vile' here does not mean depraved, but rather abject, reduced to the meanest condition.

9 Verse 15. The 'good tidings' is the news of Nineveh's downfall.

☐ STUDY 2 Nahum 2 and 3

These two chapters are two separate odes describing the fall of Nineveh. In chapter 2 the prophet depicts the approach of the enemy (verse 1a) and ironically summons the people to defend their city (verse 1b). Then follows a description of the attackers within and without the walls (verses 3–5). The river gates are forced, the palace is in panic, the queen captured, the people flee (verses 6–8), and looting follows (verse 9). The chapter ends with a picture of Nineveh overthrown, lying desolate in her ruins. Chapter 3 declares the city's guilt and her punishment (verses 1–7), and bids her take warning from the fate of Thebes (verses 8–10). Nineveh's strength fails (verses 11–15a). Though her people are without number, and her merchants are as numerous as locusts, yet, like locusts, they will fly away (verses 15b–17). Her rulers perish, her people are scattered. All who hear of her fall will rejoice (verses 18, 19).

1 Read each chapter aloud, if possible in Moffatt's translation. What were Nineveh's sins that brought upon her so terrible a retribution? See also 1: 11. What does this show of God's attitude even to non-Christian societies? Does He care whether they are righteous or corrupt? If God cares, should we?

2 How does Nahum show the converse of Rom. 8: 31; *i.e.*, if God be against us, who can be for us? *Cf.* Ps. 34: 16; Je. 37: 9, 10. Have you ever experienced this in your own life, with all circumstances going against you, that in fact God was against you?

Notes

1 2: 5. 'Officers': or '*elite* troops'. The same word is rendered 'nobles' in 3: 18. A 'mantlet' is a missile-proof screen under the shelter of which the attackers advance.

2 2: 7. 'Mistress': the word may refer to the queen (*cf.* verse 6), or to the Assyrian goddess Ishtar or her image.

3 2: 8. Nineveh is compared to a breached reservoir.

4 2: 11. 'Cave': 'pasture' (RSV mg., AV), or 'feeding place' (RV).

5 2: 13. 'Messengers': envoys; *cf.* 2 Ki. 19: 9, 23.

6 3: 4–6. The use of this figure to symbolize Nineveh was doubtless suggested by the sacred prostitution prominent in the cult of Ishtar.

7 3: 8. 'Sea': *i.e.*, the mighty waters of the Nile.

8 3: 9. 'Put': an African people, perhaps from Somalia or Libya.

HABAKKUK

Introduction

We know nothing about Habakkuk himself except that he was a prophet, and the only clear historical reference in the book is to the Chaldeans in 1:6, on the basis of which a date just after the Battle of Carchemish (605 BC) is suggested, when this 'bitter and hasty' nation was marching westwards to subjugate Jehoiakim, king of Judah. Habakkuk was thus a contemporary of Jeremiah, but the two men were very different. Jeremiah's problem was how God could destroy His people. Habakkuk's problem was how God could use so evil a nation as the Chaldeans as His instrument (*cf.* Isaiah and the Assyrians). The problem is set forth in chapter 1, and God's answer is given in chapters 2 and 3 in words of extraordinary depth and grandeur.

Analysis

1: 1–4	How long will lawlessness go unpunished?
1: 5–11	Incredibly, God points to the Chaldeans in reply.
1: 12–17	How can God allow the inhumanity and the idolatry of this wicked nation?
2: 1–5	The expectant prophet receives God's answer: Pride comes before a fall, but the truthfulness of the righteous will be his salvation.
2: 6–20	A series of woes directed against the Chaldeans.
3: 1–19	A psalm consisting of a prayer, a revelation of God coming in judgment and salvation, and a confession of faith.

☐ STUDY 1 Habakkuk 1: 1 – 2: 5

1 What is the prophet's first complaint, and what is to Habakkuk God's strange answer? See 1: 2–4, 5–11.

2 What further problem does this raise in the prophet's mind, and what answer is he given? See 1: 12–17 and 2: 2–5.

3 What course of action does 2: 1 suggest that the Christian should adopt when perplexed at God's dealings? *Cf.* Ps. 73: 16, 17; Mi. 7: 7. Are you faithful in this way?

Notes

1 1: 7b. The Chaldeans' so-called 'justice and dignity' are arbitrary and self-determined.

2 2: 2. God's answer is to be written down plainly so that it may be read at a glance.

3 2: 4, 5. God's answer is in two parts. (a) The arrogant Chaldean, whose soul is not upright, shall fail and pass away. *Cf.* Is. 2: 12–17. (b) The righteous man will endure. He will live by his faith, a faith inspired by God's faithfulness, which keeps him steadfast. The profound truth here expressed is seen in its full significance in the gospel of Christ. *Cf.* Rom. 1: 16, 17.

☐ STUDY 2 Habakkuk 2: 6–20

1 Sum up in one or two words each of the evils against which the five 'woes' of these verses are pronounced. Are these evils found in the world today? What may those who commit them expect?

2 In contrast to verses 18, 19, ponder the promise of verse 14 and the command of verse 20. How were these a warning to the plunderer, and a comfort to the plundered? What response should they inspire in us? *Cf.* Ps. 73: 16–26.

☐ STUDY 3 Habakkuk 3: 1–15

Habakkuk prays that God will show Himself once again as long ago (verses 1, 2), and then describes a vision of God coming to deliver His people. Past, present and future are intermingled. God's self-revelation in the past at Sinai, at the Red Sea and at the entrance into Canaan are pictured under the image of a thunderstorm rolling up from the south and breaking upon Palestine. The same 'Holy One' is at work also in the present, and the tumults of the nations are the tokens that He has come in judgment to work salvation for His people.

1 Habakkuk considered God's working in the past with longing and fear (verses 1, 2). Do we know such longing? *Cf.* Pss. 85: 6; 143: 5, 6; Is. 64: 1–3. Why was he afraid? *Cf.* Heb. 12: 21, 28, 29.

2 The poetry describes political upheavals. *Cf.* Is. 29: 5–8. Yet the poetry also is full of God's acts. How does this vision teach us to regard the world-happenings of our own day? What is God's purpose through them? *Cf.* Ps. 74: 12; Lk. 21: 25–28.

Notes

1 Verse 3. 'Teman', 'Mount Paran': *i.e.*, the region of Sinai.
2 Verse 4. Allusions to lightning and thick clouds.
3 Verse 8. The answer is found in verses 13–15.

□ STUDY 4 Habakkuk 3: 16–19

1 What two effects did the vision have upon Habakkuk? With verse 16, *cf.* Dn. 10: 8; Rev. 1: 17. With verses 17, 18, *cf.* Ps. 73: 25, 26; Phil. 4: 11–13. Are we as sensitive as Habakkuk was to the glory and the faithfulness of the God with whom, by grace, we have to do?

2 What three things did God—trusted and rejoiced in—do for the prophet? *Cf.* Ps. 18: 32, 39; Zc. 4: 6; Is. 40: 31. Which of these do you particularly need God to do for you?

Notes

1 Verse 16. 'Rottenness enters': a Hebrew idiom expressing complete loss of strength. *Cf.* Pr. 12: 4; 14: 30. With the last part of this verse, *cf.* 2 Thes. 1: 6–8.
2 Verse 19. To 'tread upon my high places': a picture of triumph and security. *Cf.* Dt. 33: 29c.

OBADIAH

Introduction

Obadiah's message is almost entirely a denunciation of Edom for unbrotherly conduct to Israel, and a prophecy of the destruction of that proud kingdom and people. But the prophet associates Edom's fall with the day of the Lord, and foresees Israel's recovery of their promised possessions, and the universal triumph of God's reign and kingdom.

The Edomites, as the descendants of Esau, and the Israelites, as the descendants of Jacob, were enemies from the time that Israel took possession of Canaan (see Nu. 20: 14–21), and there are many references in the historical and prophetic books to Edom, which show the antipathy between Edom and Israel, and the difference in their destinies. See, *e.g.*, 2 Sa. 8: 14; 2 Ki. 14: 7; Je. 49: 7–22; Ezk. 25: 12–17; Am. 1: 11, 12; Mal. 1: 1–5.

Analysis

1–9 The doom of Edom, despite his confidence in his impregnable strongholds.
10–14 The sin for which Edom is to be punished.
15–21 The day of the Lord is at hand when Edom shall be punished and Israel shall triumph.

☐ STUDY Obadiah

1 By act and attitude Edom had sinned against God and against His people. Trace the details of the sin; then look up 1 Cor. 10: 11, 12 and apply Obadiah's warnings to your own life.

2 The prophet claims divine inspiration (verses 1, 4, 8, 18). What do we learn of the Lord's character from this book? What wonderful truth had yet to be revealed which goes beyond verse 15? *Cf.* Rom. 8: 3, 4.

3 The prophet's words speak of searing (verse 18) and possession (verses 17, 19, 20). How do the words 'holy' (verse 17) and 'the kingdom shall be the Lord's' (verse 21) change the complexion of the situation? The Christian's expectation is the same: 'Thy kingdom come.' How and why does its spirit differ? *Cf.* Mk. 1: 14, 15; Mt. 12: 28; Acts 8: 12; Jn. 18: 36; Rev. 12: 10, 11; Mt. 5: 3; Rom. 14: 17.

Notes

1 Verse 1. The section 'We have heard . . . let us rise against her for battle!' is in parenthesis, suggesting the means by which Edom will be brought low.

2 Verse 3. RSV mg. draws attention to a possible pun here; *Sela* means 'rock', but it was also the name of the capital city of Edom, later called Petra.

3 Verses 5, 6. Thieves or grape-stealers leave something behind; but when God plunders, the pillage is complete.

4 Verse 7. The principle here is enunciated in verse 15b; this principle of strict justice is the basis of God's moral law. *Cf.* Gal. 6: 7.

5 Verses 10–14. *Cf.* Ps. 137: 7; La. 2: 15, 16.

6 Verse 16. The 'cup' of God's wrath was a vivid prophetic picture of divine punishment and consequent disaster. *Cf.* Je. 25: 27, 28; Is. 51: 17; Rev. 14: 10.

MATTHEW 8 - 18

☐ STUDY 11 Matthew 8: 1–22

1 Consider how different the people were who received healing, and how different our Lord's methods with them were. What does this teach us concerning (a) His power, and (b) our work for Him?

2 What was so remarkable in the centurion's faith as to elicit Christ's great commendation? Contrast Jn. 4: 48. Note how the statement of verses 11, 12 anticipates the revolutionary developments recorded in the Acts. See Acts 13: 45–48.

3 Verses 18–22. Why did our Lord leave the crowds, and why did He check two would-be disciples? *Cf.* Lk. 14: 25–27.

Note. In chapters 8 and 9 Matthew records nine miracles of our Lord, in three groups of three. Matthew has this habit of grouping in subject-matter rather than in strict chronological order.

☐ STUDY 12 Matthew 8: 23 – 9: 8

1 In 9: 6 and 8 the word 'authority' is used to characterize Christ's ministry. In what three realms is this seen in this passage?

2 9: 1–8 reveals Christ's power to deal with the deepest trouble of man. What is this? How do these verses illustrate the means whereby a man may find this healing? What follows from it as a visible proof of it?

3 Demon-possession was clearly treated seriously by our Lord. What may we understand by the demons' witness to Christ in 8: 29 (*cf.* Mk. 1: 24; 3: 11, 12; Acts 16: 16–18)? In what way does the incident of 8: 28–34 have any parallel in the ministry of the Spirit today?

☐ STUDY 13 Matthew 9: 9–34

1 In what ways do verses 9–17 disclose the revolutionary character of the ministry of Jesus? What do they teach us of the character of God (verse 13), and of the way a Christian ought to live amongst sinners?

2 Considering the miracles as signs, define the lessons we may learn from the incidents of verses 18–34 about the ability of our Lord to deal with the spiritual problems of weakness, deadness, blindness, dumbness. Have you such a problem which ought to be dealt with?

☐ STUDY 14 Matthew 9: 35 – 10: 23

1 Some of the instructions given to the twelve here are clearly temporary and would not apply to every situation. But what principles of Christian service can you find, which are always applicable?

2 Verses 16–23 offer the prospect of both persecution in, and power for, service. In this situation, what is to be the attitude of disciples?

Note. 10: 23 has probably no reference to the second advent, but rather to Christ's coming in triumph after the resurrection, or to His coming in judgment in the fall of Jerusalem.

☐ STUDY 15 Matthew 10: 24–42

1 With all the realism of the warning in verses 24, 25, Christ encourages His disciples not to fear. Consider the reasons given in verses 26–33 to encourage confidence.

2 In what way do verses 34–42 demand of the Christian both militancy and tenderness? How do you equate the statement of verse 34 with the thought of Christ as Prince of Peace?

☐ STUDY 16 Matthew 11: 1–24

1 What may we learn of the character of John the Baptist from his problems and doubts concerning Jesus, and from our Lord's commendation of him (verses 1–19)?

2 Verses 20–24. We may discern here some important principles behind God's judgment of mankind. What are they, and what relevance do they have in our situation?

Notes

1 There is a unity in chapters 11 and 12. Apparently disconnected incidents are linked together around the theme of the reality and nature of the Messiahship of Jesus.

2 Verse 12 may suggest either the dynamic of John's ministry or the cost of becoming a member of the kingdom.
3 Verse 19 may read 'deeds' or 'children' (mg.). In either case the verse means that God's ways are justified by their results.

☐ STUDY 17 Matthew 11: 25 – 12: 21

1 In 11: 25–30, there is an amazing combination of Christ's claims to unique authority and to humility. Can both be true? What do these verses teach concerning (a) His Person, and (b) the attitude He asks from us?

2 Summarize the main principles of sabbath observance outlined in 12: 1–14. In what way may we be guilty of the sin of the Pharisees? How are we to avoid a secularization of the Lord's day?

3 12: 15–21. These verses indicate the significance of the Suffering Servant passages in Isaiah for an understanding of Jesus and His ministry. *Cf.* 8: 17; Lk. 2: 29–32; 22: 37; Jn. 12: 37, 38. What are the outstanding features of this ministry?

☐ STUDY 18 Matthew 12: 22–50

1 Verses 22–32. What do you understand by the 'unforgivable sin' interpreted in the light of its context here? Consider the solemnity of these warnings; and note the connection with them of verses 43–45.

2 What is taught in verses 33–37 about the dangers of evil or foolish speaking? In what way may a Christian deal with failure at this level?

3 Why does Christ refuse to give a *special* sign to the Pharisees (verses 38, 39)? What is the significance of His references to the Old Testament in verses 40–42? What may we learn from verses 41, 42 and 50 concerning our right response to Christ?

☐ STUDY 19 Matthew 13: 1–23

1 The parable of the sower (or 'the soils') may be regarded as a parable to explain why our Lord taught in parables. How did this method serve to reveal truth to some and to hide it from others? What was the simple and searching condition of gaining benefit?

2 In the parable of the sower what were the reasons why the same seed produced such different results? What conditions are signified by the different kinds of soil? What is indispensable to fruitfulness?

☐ STUDY 20 Matthew 13: 24–52

1 What is the teaching of the parable of the wheat and the tares (verses 24–30)?

2 Verses 31–33 record two parables on the theme of growth. What is the main message of these verses? May these verses include warning against possible dangers?

3 Verses 44–50 illustrate different ways by which individuals may enter the kingdom. What are these? Why is there a mixture of good and bad? What is the condition of true enjoyment?

☐ STUDY 21 Matthew 13: 53 – 14: 12

1 What may we learn from the closing verses of chapter 13 about the nature of prejudice? Of what may it deprive us, and why?

2 In the story of 14: 1–12, identify the distinctive characteristics of both Herod and John the Baptist; what is the difference between John's faithfulness and Herod's keeping of his promise?

☐ STUDY 22 Matthew 14: 13–36

1 Consider the miracles of these verses as parables in action. What particularly do you learn from the response and failure of the disciples? For what qualities do we need to pray if we are to be found faithful?

2 From the same stories consider the light cast upon the Person of Christ. What characteristics are unmistakably revealed?

☐ STUDY 23 Matthew 15: 1–20

1 For what reasons does Christ condemn the religious outlook of the Pharisees? How may we be in danger of similar failure?

2 These verses emphasize the importance of man's heart. *Cf.* 5: 8, 28; 12: 34; 18: 35. What is meant here by the word 'heart'? *Cf.* Is. 10: 7, AV and RV. How then can a man's actions be put right?

3 What are the three groups of people to whom Christ speaks in these verses? Do you notice any difference in His manner of teaching them? Has this any implication for Christian teaching today?

☐ STUDY 24 Matthew 15: 21–39

1 Verses 21–28. Why did our Lord treat the Canaanite woman in this way? Do you see the purpose behind it? *Cf.* Lk. 11: 8; 18: 1; 1 Pet. 1: 7. Contrast Mt. 8: 23, 26; 15: 28, 30, 31.

2 In all the miracles in this passage Christ seems to be dealing with Gentiles. Note the phrase 'the God of Israel' in verse 31. This seems to be contrary to the principle of verse 24. What was our Lord thus beginning to reveal concerning the full purpose of His mission? *Cf.* Mt. 24: 14; 28: 19; Rom. 1: 16 (the last nine words).

Note. Verse 37. The word for 'basket' here is *sphuris*, the large Gentile basket, contrasted with the Jewish *kophinos* in 14: 20. The same accuracy of distinction is found in 16: 9, 10.

☐ STUDY 25 Matthew 16: 1–20

1 Christ condemns, in verses 1–4, the Jews' inability to read 'the signs of the times'. What does He mean by this? How were the disciples similarly guilty? See verses 5–12. What response should such signs produce?

2 Verses 13–20. This incident at Caesarea Philippi is clearly the 'hinge-point' of the Gospel narrative. From now on Christ withdraws from the crowds, and concentrates on teaching the disciples. Why is the question about His Person so crucial? *Cf.* 1 Jn. 4: 2, 3; 5: 1a, 5.

3 Note the three things which our Lord says to Peter in verses 17–19. With verse 17, *cf.* 1 Cor. 12: 3; with verse 18, *cf.* 1 Cor. 3: 11; 1 Pet. 2: 4–6; and with verse 19, *cf.* 18: 18; Jn. 20: 23.

Note. Verses 18, 19. There is a play on words in Greek in verse 18 (see mg.). '*Petros*' means 'stone'; '*petra*' means 'rock'. Note that Christ did not say, 'On *thee* I will build my church.' Peter had just made the classic confession of faith in Christ. Equally in verses 22, 23 he can be seen as an agent of Satan. The power of the keys, *i.e.*, of 'loosing' and 'binding', is one of great authority; but it is that of a steward rather than a door-keeper. The keys are the keys of knowledge (*cf.* Lk. 11: 52) which Christ entrusts to those who preach the gospel, and thus 'open the kingdom of heaven to all believers'.

☐ STUDY 26 Matthew 16: 21 – 17: 13

1 16: 21 indicates Christ's clear awareness of the cross ahead. The word 'must' expresses a sense of inward necessity. What does this reveal about the character of Christ's death?

2 What are the terms of discipleship (verse 24)? What incentives does Christ put forward in verses 25–28 to encourage His disciples to pay the cost? What did Peter particularly need to learn (verses 22, 23)?

3 In the story of the transfiguration (17: 1–13), can you see its purpose (a) for Christ Himself, and (b) for His disciples?

Note. 16: 28. The reference here to 'the Son of man coming in his kingdom' would seem to be not to His second advent but to His post-resurrection triumph and exaltation to the throne.

☐ STUDY 27 Matthew 17: 14–27

1 Verses 14–20. What were the reasons for the powerlessness of the disciples? What does Christ tell them is the one indispensable secret of success?

2 Verses 24–27. What practical lesson is enshrined in the story of the Temple tax? What does it teach about the Christian's responsibility towards his fellow-men? *Cf.* 1 Cor. 10: 31–33; Rom. 13: 6, 7.

☐ STUDY 28 Matthew 18: 1–35

1 Verses 1–14. Consider Christ's teaching on children (see also 19: 13–15). What are the qualities of the childlike spirit suggested in verses 3, 4? How should the Christian act towards children or those young in faith?

2 What do verses 15–20 teach us about the way of reconciliation? What do we also learn here concerning the nature and the ministry of the local church, and concerning the practical value of acting together with others?

3 How does the parable in verses 23–35 answer Peter's question in verse 21? What other lessons does it teach?

For Studies 29–48 concluding Matthew's Gospel see p. 341.

JEREMIAH 1-25

Introduction

Anathoth, the home of Jeremiah, was a small town some three miles north-east of Jerusalem. Jeremiah's father was a priest, possibly a descendant of Abiathar (*cf.* 1 Ki. 2: 26), and the family owned some property in Anathoth (32: 8). Jeremiah's fellow-townsmen were among those who turned against him and sought to slay him (11: 21).

Born probably towards the end of the reign of Manasseh, Jeremiah lived through the reigns of Josiah (thirty-one years), Jehoahaz (three months), Jehoiakim (eleven years), Jehoiachin (three months), and Zedekiah (eleven years). His prophetic ministry lasted for forty years, from his call in 626 BC, the thirteenth year of Josiah, to the fall of Jerusalem in 587 BC (1: 2, 3). Of the five kings Josiah alone was loyal to the Lord. Jehoiakim was hostile to Jeremiah, and Zedekiah, though personally friendly, was weak and unstable. Under these two kings Jeremiah endured much physical suffering at the hands of his enemies. His life, however, was preserved, and after the fall of Jerusalem he was permitted to stay with the remnant in the land, and was carried with them into Egypt (43: 4–7).

In the earlier years of his ministry, though his outward lot was easier, Jeremiah suffered great mental conflict, revealed in a series of soliloquies in which he struggles to accept the burden of his prophetic calling and message. He saw more and more clearly that the nation was thoroughly corrupt, and that judgment was at hand. The false prophets, who cried 'Peace, Peace', were misleading the people (14: 13, 14). The inevitability of disaster filled Jeremiah's heart with dismay and sorrow. It seemed as if God were annulling His covenant and casting off His people, and if that were to happen, what hope was left? God, however, revealed to Jeremiah that He still had a purpose of good beyond the judgment, and that He could and would make a new covenant of a different kind, in which He would give His people a new heart and put His fear in their inmost being: and the hope of this glorious future sustained him as he watched the dying agonies of his nation, and suffered with them. As a result of all this, 'Jeremiah's personality is the most sharply etched of any of the Old Testament prophets' (*NBD*, p. 608), and part of the distinctiveness of the book lies just here.

Jeremiah was appointed a prophet not only to Judah, but to the nations (1: 5, 10), and he kept an ever-watchful eye on the movements of neighbouring peoples. In Josiah's reign the power of Assyria was waning, and both Egypt and Babylon sought to take advantage of this for their own ends. Three events especially affected the kingdom of Judah, and had a profound influence upon Jeremiah's life and outlook. The first was the capture of Nineveh and of the Assyrian Empire by Babylon (612–609 BC), the second, the battle of Megiddo, when King Josiah was slain (608 BC), and the third, the battle of Carchemish, when Pharaoh-Necho of Egypt and Nebuchadrezzar of Babylon met face to face in a trial of strength and the Egyptian armies prevailed (605 BC). From that time Jeremiah was assured that Babylon was to reign supreme for many years, and that Judah would be wise to yield submission. In fearlessly proclaiming this he seemed in the eyes of many a traitor to his own nation, and aroused great opposition and enmity against himself; but his devotion to God and to his fellow-countrymen stands out clearly on every page, though from time to time he breaks out into passionate cries for vengeance upon his persecutors.

The prophecies are not all in chronological order. In some, mention is made of the king in whose reign they were uttered, but in others the date must be judged from the contents. The following may be taken as a rough guide:

The reign of Josiah: 1–6.
The reign of Jehoiakim: 7–20, 22, 25, 26, 30, 31, 35, 36, 45.
The reign of Zedekiah: 21, 23, 24, 27–29, 32–34, 37–39.

Analysis

1	Call of Jeremiah.
2–6	The sin of Israel. Call to repentance. The enemy from the north.
7–10	In the Temple gate. Prophecies of judgment. Jeremiah's sorrow.
11, 12	The broken covenant. Jeremiah's complaint and God's answer.
13	The linen waistcloth and other prophecies.
14, 15	The drought. Jeremiah's pleadings and God's reply.

16, 17 Jeremiah told not to marry as a sign of coming judgment; and other prophecies.
18–20 At the potter's house; and the breaking of the flask. Incident of Pashhur; Jeremiah's complaint.
21 Answer to Zedekiah at the beginning of the siege.
22 The doom of the royal house of David.
23 The faithless shepherds, and false prophets.
24 The two baskets of figs.
25 The seventy years' captivity.
26 In the court of the Temple. Jeremiah's life preserved.
27, 28 'Serve the king of Babylon and live.' Incident of Hananiah.
29 Jeremiah's letter to the exiles in Babylon.
30–33 The book of consolation. Prophecies of hope.
34 Zedekiah's captivity foretold.
35 The fidelity of the Rechabites.
36 Jehoiakim burns the scroll of Jeremiah's prophecies.
37, 38 Jeremiah's imprisonment and rescue.
39 Fall of Jerusalem.
40–43 Jeremiah left in the land; his final prophecies before being taken to Egypt.
44 Prophecy to Jews in Egypt.
45 Message to Baruch.
46–51 Prophecies against surrounding nations.
52 Historical appendix.

□ STUDY 1 Jeremiah 1

1 Verses 4–10 and 17–19. What did God require from Jeremiah, and what did He promise him? How can this apply to us?

2 What is the divine interpretation of the two visions which Jeremiah saw?

3 What aspects of God's character and activity are brought before us in this chapter? *Cf.* Eph. 1: 4.

Notes

1 Verse 5. 'Knew': in the sense of 'regarded', almost equivalent to 'chose'. 'I consecrated you': set you apart for Myself. For 'prophet', see verse 9.

2 Verse 11. 'A rod': probably meaning a straight shoot just beginning to blossom. The word for almond tree is from the same root as the word 'watching over' in verse 12 (see mg.). Moffatt translates 'wake-tree'. The almond was so called because it was the first to awake after the sleep of winter.

3 Verse 13. The boiling pot is ready to pour out its fiery contents southwards.

4 Verse 15. 'His throne': *i.e.*, of judgment.

☐ STUDY 2 Jeremiah 2: 1 – 3: 5

A review of Israel's backslidings from the beginning.

1 According to this section, what are the components of back-sliding? Compare Israel's beginnings with her later condition. Is any of this story true of you? *Cf.* Gal. 5: 7.

2 2: 12, 13. 'Living' water means fresh water from an ever-flowing spring. *Cf.* 6: 7; Jn. 4: 13, 14. What do the 'fountain of living waters' and the 'broken cisterns' stand for in spiritual experience? Do you take as serious a view of backsliding as God does?

3 What evil results does Jeremiah say have already followed from the nation's forgetfulness of God?

Notes

1 2: 10. 'Kedar' was a tribe east of Jordan. The verse means 'search from east to west . . .'

2 2: 16. 'Memphis' and 'Tahpanhes': cities of Egypt.

3 2: 25. 'Do not run thy foot bare, and thy throat dry in the eager pursuit of strange gods' (Driver).

4 3: 4. An allusion probably to the feigned penitence of many at the time of Josiah's reform. *Cf.* 3: 10; 2 Ch. 34: 33.

☐ STUDY 3 Jeremiah 3: 6 – 4: 31

1 3: 6–20. What is the offence of Judah? And what aggravated it in the eyes of God? What forms does this sin take today? *Cf.* Jas. 4: 4; 1 Jn. 5: 20, 21. What does God offer, and on what conditions?

2 Trace the process of restoration as outlined in 3: 21 – 4: 4. What is meant by such phrases as 'Break up your fallow ground' and 'Circumcise yourselves to the Lord'? *Cf.* 9: 26; Dt. 10: 16; Rom. 2: 28, 29.

3 4: 5–31. A vivid picture of the approach of an invader from the north. What place does he have in the purposes of God?

Notes

1 3: 8. An allusion to the conquest of northern Israel in 721 BC by the Assyrians.

2 3: 10. See Note on 3: 4.

3 3: 14. 'Master': in the sense of 'husband'. *Cf.* verses 19, 20 for similar mixing of metaphors from the family.

☐ STUDY 4 Jeremiah 5 and 6

Further indictments of Judah (5: 1–5—all classes are alike corrupt), warnings of coming judgment, and depictions of the invasion and its effects.

1 Make a list of the main sins charged against the people. Are we in danger of any of these sins? Note especially Judah's response to God's word and messengers.

2 Was judgment inevitable? Was God not willing to pardon? What are we taught here about the 'kindness and severity of God' (Rom. 11: 22)? *Cf.* Rom. 4: 4, 5.

Notes

1 6: 1. Tekoa and Beth-Haccheram were a few miles south of Jerusalem. The 'signal' (*i.e.*, a beacon; *cf.* Jdg. 20: 38) would alert the south, or perhaps guide the refugees from Jerusalem.

2 6: 3. 'Shepherds with their flocks' here means kings and their armies.

3 6: 16. 'By the roads': *i.e.*, Judah must return to the cross-roads to regain the right path. *Cf.* 18: 15.

4 6: 27–30. Jeremiah's work is described as that of a tester of silver. But no pure silver results from the process of refining. *Cf.* 9: 7.

☐ STUDY 5 Jeremiah 7: 1 – 8: 3

It is thought by many that this is the address given by Jeremiah in the fourth year of Jehoiakim, as described in 26: 1–9.

1 How does this passage show the uselessness of outward worship when separated from the daily practice of godliness? What was lacking in the people of Jerusalem? Are your worship and your life all of a piece? *Cf.* Mt. 5: 23, 24.

2 In what ways may we in our day act in a spirit similar to that rebuked in 7: 10? What is involved in a Christian's being 'delivered' or 'saved'? *Cf.* Col. 1: 13; Tit. 2: 14; Mt. 7: 21–23.

3 How does this section illustrate our Lord's warning in Lk. 8: 18?

Notes

1 7: 4, 8. Confidence in the Temple itself as a protection was a delusion. *Cf.* 1 Sa. 4: 3–11.

2 7: 10b. 'Thinking you are now quite safe—safe to go on with all these abominable practices' (Moffatt).

3 7: 12. Shiloh was probably destroyed around the time of the disaster recorded in 1 Sa. 4.

4 7: 18. 'The queen of heaven': probably Ashtoreth, a goddess widely worshipped in the Semitic world.

5 7: 22, 23. Such a categorical statement ('not this . . . but that . . .') is a Hebrew idiom to express where the real emphasis falls. The essence of the covenant made at the exodus was, on Israel's side, obedience (11: 6, 7). God did not commission sacrifice for its own sake—or for *His* own sake—but to be the expression and embodiment of heart-devotion and ethical obedience. *Cf.* 6: 19, 20; 11: 15; 1 Sa. 15: 22; Is. 1: 10–17. Where these were absent, mere external ritual was worse than nothing. Hence in 7: 21 the people are bidden to eat the meat of the burnt offerings, which were wholly offered to God, as well as their proper portions of the other sacrifices. Emptied of all spiritual significance, it was now merely meat, and might as well be eaten.

But in the worship of a purified people, sacrifices would again have their rightful place. See 17: 24–26; 33: 18.
6 7: 32. 'The valley of the son of Hinnom': a valley on the south side of Jerusalem, where the city refuse was cast. The day will come, says the prophet, when the slain will be so many that they will have to be buried even in this unclean spot.

☐ STUDY 6 Jeremiah 8: 4 – 9: 22

Further exposure of the moral and spiritual plight of the people, and descriptions of the coming judgment. Jeremiah's heart is almost broken.

1 What specific charges does God level against His people in these chapters? Are there any traces of these faults in your own life?

2 Consider the evidence this passage gives of the effects of sin upon a nation's morale and prosperity. See, *e.g.*, 8: 14, 15, 20; 9: 5, 6.

3 Compare 8: 11 with Jeremiah's anguish. What modern counterparts to the former must we beware of? Are we ready to sorrow for others like Jeremiah, and to keep on pleading with them as he did? See 25: 3.

Notes
1 8: 4–7. The sin of Judah runs counter to the pattern of nature. *Cf.* Is. 1: 3.
2 8: 20. Probably a proverbial saying expressing the thought that it is too late.

☐ STUDY 7 Jeremiah 9: 23 – 10: 25

1 9: 23, 24. What is better than wisdom, power and wealth? *Cf.* also 1 Cor. 1: 26–31; Phil. 3: 8–11. What do you set most store by in the normal course of life?

2 Set down, on the one hand, the characteristics here mentioned of the idols of the heathen, and on the other, the character of the living God.

3 What are the implications of 10: 23, 24? Have you learnt to live by them? See 30: 11 and *cf.* Pr. 3: 5–7, 11, 12.

Notes
1 9: 25, 26. All these nations practised circumcision, and Judah, despite the fact that her circumcision was ordained to mark a unique relationship with God, takes her place here between Egypt and Edom because her spiritually uncircumcised state (*cf.* 4: 4; Rom. 2: 28, 29) has rendered her physical circumcision no more meaningful than theirs.
2 10: 11. See mg. Probably originally a reader's marginal comment, in response to the denunciation of idols.
3 10: 17. 'Bundle': a few hastily gathered possessions for immediate flight.
4 10: 21. 'Shepherds': see 2: 8 and mg.; 3: 15.

☐ STUDY 8 Jeremiah 11 and 12

These chapters fall into three sections: 11: 1–17, Judah's stubborn idolatry and breaking of the covenant; 11: 18 – 12: 6, a complaint of the prophet because of plots against his life, and God's answer to his questionings; and 12: 7–17, which seems to refer to the attacks of surrounding peoples (see 2 Ki. 24: 1, 2), and closes with a remarkable promise to these nations on condition of their turning from idols to worship the Lord.

1 What were the constituent elements of 'this covenant' (11: 2)? What was God's part and what the people's? *Cf.* 2 Cor. 6: 14 – 7: 1.

2 What did Jeremiah do with his perplexities, and what answer did he receive? Can we come with his confidence? Note 12: 5 and 6 in particular. What does this answer of God imply? *Cf.* Heb. 12: 3, 4.

3 Jeremiah is often described as a Christ-like figure. As you read the book chapter by chapter, note the similarities. With 11: 21 and 12: 6, *cf.* Mk. 3: 21; Lk. 4: 24, 29; 21: 16.

Notes

1 11: 15. See Note on 7: 22, 23.
2 12: 13. 'They': *i.e.*, the people of Judah.

☐ STUDY 9 Jeremiah 13

1 What is the purpose of the incident of the waistcloth? Which is a truer description of you, verse 10 or verse 11?

2 Consider the images used to describe the coming judgment, and their usefulness for preaching today. See Notes below; and *cf.* Pss. 1: 4; 60: 3; Is. 8: 22; 51: 17; Mi. 3: 6, 7; Jn. 12: 35; 2 Thes. 2: 11, 12.

3 Verse 23. What answer does the New Testament give to this question? See Rom. 5: 6; 2 Cor. 5: 17.

Notes

1 Verses 13, 14. 'Drunkenness' is used in a figurative sense to describe mental fear and bewilderment, when men in their panic turn against each other.
2 Verse 16. 'Give glory to the Lord': a Hebrew expression for confession of sin, recognizing God's holiness, and turning from sin to obedience. *Cf.* Jos. 7: 19; Mal. 2: 2; Jn. 9: 24.
3 Verse 18: *i.e.*, Jehoiachin and his mother Nehushta (2 Ki. 24: 8, 9). Queen mothers regularly wielded great influence at court.
4 Verse 19. 'The Negeb' is the area of Palestine south of Beersheba.
5 Verse 21. Another translation reads 'he', *i.e.*, God, instead of 'they' (Driver). *Cf.* Dt. 28: 13, 44; La. 1: 5.

☐ STUDY 10 Jeremiah 14 and 15

These two chapters consist of a kind of colloquy between Jeremiah and God. The prophet is driven to prayer by a time of drought (14: 1–6).

1 What pleas of the people does the prophet present before God in 14: 7–9, and what does God's answer (14: 10–12) tell us of the people's confession? *Cf.* 3: 10; 15: 6, 7; Is. 59: 1, 2. What further pleas does Jeremiah urge in his second and third prayers (14: 13 and 19–22)? What are God's answers in each case?

2 The prophet, ceasing to pray for the people, breaks into a lament (15: 10) and prays for himself (15: 15–18). Observe carefully God's answer, especially in verses 19–21. How well did Jeremiah know himself? What new element is added in verse 19? Have you ever had a comparable answer to prayer? *Cf.* 2 Tim. 2: 19–21.

Notes

1 14: 2; 15: 7. 'Gates': *i.e.*, cities.
2 14: 7, 21. 'For thy name's sake': God's Name is 'His nature as revealed in the covenant, which is the ultimate ground of prayer' (Cunliffe-Jones). *Cf.* Ex. 33: 19; 34: 5–7.
3 15: 1. *Cf.* Ps. 99: 6–8. Moses (*e.g.*, Ex. 32: 11–14, 30–32) and Samuel (*e.g.*, 1 Sa. 7: 8, 9) were outstanding in intercession for their people.
4 15: 4. See 2 Ki. 21: 1–5, 16.
5 15: 11. The Hebrew is very difficult, and RSV, AV, and RV all differ considerably from each other.
6 15: 12. A reference to the Chaldeans. There is no hope of breaking their power.
7 15: 19. The tone is severe. Jeremiah must return to a more undivided allegiance. For 'stand before', *cf.* verse 1 and Note 3 above, and 18: 20.

☐ STUDY 11 Jeremiah 16: 1 – 17: 18

1 Consider how hard it must have been for a man of Jeremiah's affectionate and sympathetic nature to obey the commands of 16: 2, 5 and 8. Why did God lay this burden upon him? What other trials that Jeremiah had to bear are referred to in 17: 14–18?

2 How does the passage illustrate Jeremiah's oft-repeated statement concerning God's dealings with His people: 'I will not make a full end of you'? See 4: 27; 5: 10, 18; 30: 11; 46: 28. *Cf.* Ps. 94: 14; Rom. 11: 1–5.

3 Contrast, clause by clause, 17: 5 and 6 with 17: 7 and 8. How do verses 9–13 reinforce the certainty of curse or blessing? Examine yourself in the light of this contrast. *Cf.* Ps. 146.

Notes

1 16: 6, 7. Mourning customs. *Cf.* Am. 8: 10; 2 Sa. 12: 17; Pr. 31: 6b.
2 17: 1, 2. 'The tablet of their heart': *i.e.*, their inmost being. 'The horns of

their altars': an allusion to their polluted idolatrous sacrifices (*cf.* Lv. 4: 7, 30; and with verse 2, *cf.* 2: 20). 'Asherim': probably wooden images of the Canaanite goddess, Asherah.
3 17: 15. *Cf.* 2 Pet. 3: 3, 4.

□ STUDY 12 Jeremiah 17: 19 – 18: 23

1 The issue between God and His people turned on the question of obedience. How was it brought in 17: 19–27 to a single test? In your Christian obedience are there test issues of this kind, which, although possibly not themselves the most important subject, are the heart of the question of obedience at the time?

2 To Jeremiah the condition of the people made the destruction of the kingdom inevitable; yet the destruction seemed to involve the failure of God's purposes. How does the illustration of the potter throw light upon this problem (18: 1–12)? What other lessons about God does it teach? *Cf.* Rom. 9: 20, 21.

3 How does 18: 13–23 reveal the costliness for Jeremiah of being a more faithful spokesman of the Lord? *Cf.* Mt. 10: 24, 25, 28–33.

Notes
1 17: 26. 'The Shephelah': *i.e.*, the lowlands of Palestine between the coastal plain and the higher central hills.
2 18: 14. The Hebrew is uncertain, but the meaning is clear. The snows of Lebanon remain, and its streams do not run dry; but God's people have failed.
3 18: 18. 'The law shall not perish . . .': the people refused to believe that the present order of things would be destroyed.

□ STUDY 13 Jeremiah 19 and 20

1 Reflect on Jeremiah's courage, and what it must have cost him to deliver the message of 19: 1–13. What was his immediate reward? See 19: 14 – 20: 6.

2 The strain and tension caused the prophet to break out into a more bitter lament than he had yet uttered (20: 7–18). In the midst of it his faith triumphed in the assurance of God's protection, and he was able even to sing His praise (20: 11–13). Then once more waves of sorrow swept over him. In the light of this passage, try to enter into the loneliness, hardship and suffering of Jeremiah's life. Note especially verse 9. Do we know anything of this almost irresistible constraint to speak God's word, even when we are daunted by the costliness of speaking? *Cf.* Acts 5: 27–29.

Notes
1 19: 5, 6, 11b. See 7: 31–33 and Note on 7: 32.
2 19: 13. 'Defiled': *i.e.*, by dead bodies.
3 20: 16. 'The cities': *i.e.*, Sodom and Gomorrah; see Gn. 19: 24, 25.

☐ STUDY 14 Jeremiah 21 and 22

These chapters refer in turn to the last five kings of Judah: Josiah (22: 15, 16), Jehoahaz or Shallum (22: 10–12), Jehoiakim (22: 13–19), Jehoiachin or Coniah (22: 24–30), and Zedekiah (21).

1 Zedekiah's hope was that God would work a miracle, as He had done in the days of Hezekiah, a little over a century before (21: 2; 2 Ch. 32: 20–22). What was Jeremiah's answer, and what light does this throw on 'unanswered prayer'? *Cf.* 7: 16; 11: 14; 14: 11, 12; Is. 59: 1, 2.

2 Chapter 22. Why did Jeremiah condemn injustice and outrage? Consider the contemporary application of this word from the Lord. Are we guilty of conforming to any current social iniquities or sharp practices?

3 22: 21. (The northern kingdom behaved in the same way—see 3: 25.) Reflect upon this verse as depicting the pattern of Judah's history.

Notes

1 22: 6. Gilead and Lebanon typify prosperity.
2 22: 20. 'Abarim': a mountain range to the south-east of Palestine.
3 22: 22. 'Shepherds': see 2: 8 and mg.

☐ STUDY 15 Jeremiah 23

1 Verses 1–8. To meet the situation created by the failure of Judah's rulers, what does God say He will do? *Cf.* Ezk. 34: 1–16. How much of what is promised here has been fulfilled? *Cf.* Jn. 10: 1–18; Lk. 1: 32, 68–70; 1 Cor. 1: 30.

2 What does Jeremiah say concerning (a) the religious life, worship and ministry of the prophets of his day; (b) their moral character and conduct; and (c) their influence? What qualifications are essential in those who are called to speak in the name of the Lord?

Notes

1 Verse 1. 'Shepherds': see 2: 8 and mg.
2 Verse 5. 'Branch': better, 'shoot' or 'sprout', *i.e.*, a growth of new life. *Cf.* 33: 15; Is. 11: 1.
3 Verses 7, 8. 'The new and more wonderful Exodus' (C. R. North).
4 Verse 9 describes the effect of God's words upon Jeremiah himself.
5 Verses 33–40. The Hebrew word translated 'burden' could also mean, figuratively, a solemn utterance, an oracle, normally of ominous import (*cf.* Is. 13: 1; 15: 1; 17: 1). The people had evidently been speaking mockingly of the prophet's utterances as 'burdens'. Jeremiah uses it to rebuke its users (verses 33, 39), and forbids its employment in such an irreverent context.

☐ STUDY 16 Jeremiah 24 and 25

Chapter 24 dates from the reign of Zedekiah. Chapter 25 declares to Judah and the surrounding nations that they shall all be brought under the power of Babylon with great slaughter.

1 Who are the good figs and who the bad, and what will happen to them respectively? *Cf.* Ezk. 11: 14–20.

2 25: 1–11. The fulfilment of the vision of the boiling pot (1: 13–15). Much of what is said in these verses is found in preceding chapters. See, *e.g.*, 7: 6, 7, 13; 16: 9; 18: 11, 16. What, however, do you find here that is new?

3 'The supreme factor in history for the Hebrew is the activity of the eternal God.' Illustrate this statement from today's portion. Note especially 25: 29. *Cf.* Am. 3: 2; 1 Pet. 4: 17, 18. What is the correlative of special privilege?

Notes

1 25: 12–14. These verses break the sequence of thought, and were possibly introduced at a later date; so also the words 'as at this day' in verse 18 (they are not in the LXX) and the last clause of verse 26.

2 25: 23. Dedan, Tema and Buz were tribes of northern Arabia. Unlike the Jews (Lv. 19: 27), they shaved the hair from the sides of their forehead. *Cf.* 9: 26.

For Studies 17–35 on Jeremiah see p. 348.

MATTHEW 19–28

☐ STUDY 29 Matthew 19: 1–22

1 In Christ's answers to the Pharisees and the disciples on the subject of marriage (19: 1–12), what does He teach about the place and character of marriage, and what does He say about the celibate life?

2 Verses 16–22. What do you find commendable in the young man in this incident? What were the factors which nevertheless made him turn away from Christ?

☐ STUDY 30 Matthew 19: 23 – 20: 28

1 Consider the teaching of Jesus on riches and possessions. With verses 23–26, *cf.* Lk. 6: 24; 8: 14; 12: 13–21. Compare Paul's teaching in 1 Tim. 6: 7, 10, 17. But note that Christ gladly received help from the rich (*cf.* Lk. 8: 2, 3).

2 Is there a place for the concept of reward in Christian service? What do verses 27–30 teach about this?

3 Verses 1–16. What is the main teaching of the parable of the labourers in the vineyard? What does it have to say about the legalistic spirit in Christian service?

4 Verses 17–19 are the third prediction by Christ of His own passion. *Cf.* 16: 21; 17: 22, 23. What new details are added here? What do verses 22 and 25–28 reveal of the mind of Christ with regard to what was ahead?

5 In what ways do verses 20–28 prove the disciples to be out of sympathy with Christ at this moment? What do both Christ's teaching and His example demand of us?

☐ STUDY 31 Matthew 20: 29 – 21: 22

1 What claims concerning the Person and work of Jesus are here (a) publicly made by Jesus Himself, and (b) openly acknowledged by others? What particularly provoked either rebuke and indignation, or prayer and acclamation? Can you keep silent?

2 What was Christ condemning in His cleansing of the Temple (21: 12, 13), and in His cursing of the fig tree (21: 18, 19)? If He similarly came into our church or examined our lives, what would He see and say?

☐ STUDY 32 Matthew 21: 23–46

1 Verses 23–27. People often ask for more understanding or for more proof before they respond to Christ. How did Christ Himself answer such a demand? What are the conditions of receiving more light? *Cf.* Jn. 7: 17. In what way does the brief parable of verses 28–32 underline the same teaching?

2 Verses 33–44. What is taught by this parable concerning the character of God, the Person of Christ, the responsibility of men, and the reality of judgment? Do you find anything significant in the reaction of the Pharisees in verses 45, 46?

Note. Verse 44 (see mg.) is omitted in many manuscripts. But it teaches that there will be brokenness either in repentance or in final judgment.

□ STUDY 33 Matthew 22: 1–14

1 In this parable what are we taught about the pattern of Christ's ministry, and what challenge do you find to evangelistic outreach?

2 In verses 11–13 what do you understand to be the significance of the wedding garment? *Cf.* Zc. 3: 1–5. Consider the balance in these verses of the free invitation of the gospel and the demand for holiness, 'without which no one will see the Lord' (Heb. 12: 14).

□ STUDY 34 Matthew 22: 15–46

1 Comparing the teaching of Jesus in verses 15–22 with Paul's teaching in Rom. 13: 1–7, outline the duty of the Christian to the state.

2 Verses 23–33. On what does Christ base His teaching about the fact of resurrection? What features of the life of the world to come emerge from this teaching?

3 Verses 41–46. Christ's counter-question here makes some clear claims. What are these? Ps. 110: 1 is cited in verse 44. Consider the use made of this elsewhere in the New Testament. *Cf.* Acts 2: 33–36; Heb. 1: 13; 10: 11–13. Of what truths and hopes are we thereby assured?

□ STUDY 35 Matthew 23: 1–22

1 Verses 1–12 are an indictment of the Pharisees because of their concern for personal prestige and outward show. Do you see how this may happen within the Christian church? In what ways may this temptation come?

2 Note the repetition of the word 'hypocrite' or 'play-actor'. How is this seen in the attitude of the Pharisees to others (verses 13–15), and in their vows and promises (verses 16–22)? What do we need to do to avoid becoming like them?

Notes

1 Verse 5. The phylactery was a small box of leather containing portions of the law and strapped to forehead and to left arm. The fringes of the garments were four in number, attached to the dress as a symbol of the law.

2 Verse 15. 'A child of hell': Greek *Gehenna*, meaning 'worthy of suffering punishment in the after-life'.

□ STUDY 36 Matthew 23: 23–39

1 The Lord accuses Pharisees in verses 23–26 of a serious lack of proportion in their practice of religion. Can you find modern examples of this dangerous tendency?

2 The chapter comes to a climax with our Lord's teaching on the inevitability of judgment (verses 29–39). Yet consider the love of Christ for Jerusalem which is clearly shown. What was it that made judgment inevitable?

□ STUDY 37 Matthew 24: 1–31

1 What is the pattern of future history as predicted by Christ in verses 1–14? Make a list of the prominent features and see how they apply to our present age.

2 According to the teaching of these verses how should a Christian react in days of political upheaval and world-wide distress? On what can he count?

Notes

1 The teaching of this chapter is in answer to the two questions of verse 3. The disciples seemed to think of these events as contemporaneous. Christ sees the fall of Jerusalem as a foreshadowing of the day of His return. It is impossible to be dogmatic about the division of the chapter, since references to the two events are so interwoven, but the following is suggested. Verses 4–14: general principles. Verses 15–28: the siege and destruction of Jerusalem. Verses 29–31: the day of Christ's coming. Verses 32–51: preparation for both events.

2 Verse 15 refers back to Dn. 11: 31 and in this context seems to point to the setting up of the Roman ensign within the sacred precincts of the Temple.

3 Verse 27. 'Coming' is in Greek *parousia*, meaning the official visit of a king. *Cf.* verses 3, 37, 39.

□ STUDY 38 Matthew 24: 32 – 25: 13

1 What truths concerning our Lord's return are unmistakably certain, and what matters are left uncertain? What, in consequence, ought the Christian's attitude to be?

2 The parable of the ten virgins (25: 1–13) teaches a final division. What is the basis of that division? How can we join the company of the wise? *Cf.* Mt. 7: 21–27.

☐ STUDY 39 Matthew 25: 14–46

1 Verses 14–30. Compare this parable with that in Lk. 19: 11–27. What is the message underlying both parables? Can you distinguish the particular emphasis of each parable?

2 Verses 31–46. What claims does Christ here make concerning Himself? How is men's final destiny determined?

3 What does this passage teach about the gravity of the sin of omission? What does the absence of good works prove?

Notes

1 Verse 34. This is the only place in the Gospels where Christ speaks of the Son of man as King. No doubt there was too great a danger of the popular misunderstanding of that title for its frequent use to be possible.

2 Verse 46. 'Eternal': this speaks primarily not of endless duration but of that which in quality is characteristic of the age to come.

☐ STUDY 40 Matthew 26: 1–16

1 Note the difference between the prophecy of Christ in verses 1, 2, and the plans of the Jewish religious leaders in verses 3–5. Whose word, in fact, prevailed, and why? *Cf.* Acts 2: 23; Ps. 33: 10, 11.

2 In verses 6–16 consider the contrast between the action of Mary, anointing Christ, and Judas selling Him. How does this demonstrate the truth of Lk. 2: 35b? What were the motives behind these different actions?

☐ STUDY 41 Matthew 26: 17–29

1 What does the phrase in verse 18, 'My time is at hand', teach us of Christ's understanding and control of the situation even at this moment? Notice the repetition of this reference to 'the hour' (verse 45). *Cf.* Jn. 12: 23, 27; 13: 1. Note also in verse 24 the combined recognition of God's foreordained purpose and man's personal responsibility.

2 In the institution of the Lord's Supper, Matthew notes the idea of a covenant in verse 28. In what way does this link with Ex. 24: 6–8 and with Je. 31: 31–34? What ought drinking from such a cup to mean to us?

☐ STUDY 42 Matthew 26: 30–56

1 How do these verses indicate the strength to do God's will that Christ found through His knowledge of Scripture? Consider how frequently during these last hours our Lord quoted the Old Testament. What ought we to learn from this concerning the way to face the demands of Christ's service?

2 Wherein lay the particular agony to Jesus of the experience in the garden? Why did He shrink so much from the cross? Consider this section in the light of Heb. 5: 7–9; 10: 4–10; 1 Pet. 2: 24.

3 What does our Lord pinpoint as the reason for the disciples' failure in the garden? Consider in how many ways they did fail that night, and how relevant this is to our situation. *Cf.* what Peter wrote in 1 Pet. 5: 8, 9.

☐ STUDY 43 Matthew 26: 57–75

1 The trials of Jesus and Peter were running concurrently, but with such different results. What was Peter's failure, and what was the reason for it? Do you see any difference between this and the failure of Judas?

2 Verses 59–68. In what ways was the trial of Jesus unworthy of the name of justice? In contrast note the majesty of Jesus at this point. What would you consider the salient characteristics of His witness here?

Note. Verse 64. 'You have said so' is more than the equivalent of 'Yes'. It indicates that Christ's Kingship was real, but different from the concept in Caiaphas' mind.

☐ STUDY 44 Matthew 27: 1–14

1 What lessons concerning the inevitable judgment upon sin are to be found in the account of the death of Judas? Can you see any sense in which we may be tempted to act like Judas in our situation, or is he unique?

2 Consider the silence of Jesus in these last hours of His life. *Cf.* Lk. 23:9. In the light of this, read 1 Pet. 2:21–23 and note the lessons for our own life and witness.

☐ STUDY 45 Matthew 27: 15–31

1 In these verses the Jewish people made a fateful choice. Note especially verses 20 and 25. It was the choice of what kind of saviour they wanted (see Note below). What was the result of this choice in the life of the nation?

2 In how many ways did Pilate seek to avoid a decision about Christ? *Cf.* Lk. 23: 7. Read again the question in verse 22. Is this not a question which I, too, must ask and answer?

Note. Verses 16, 17. There is good textual evidence in favour of reading 'Jesus Barabbas'. This makes the question of verse 17 even more telling. This was a choice between a false claimant and the true Saviour.

☐ STUDY 46 Matthew 27: 32–50

1 What were the real sufferings of Christ? In what way are physical, mental and spiritual sufferings here indicated?

2 What, if any, truth is there in the taunt of verses 41–43? Why did God not intervene? What is the meaning behind Christ's own sense of desertion in verse 46? Can you hold this truth with that contained in 2 Cor. 5: 19, 'God was in Christ reconciling the world to himself'? See also 2 Cor. 5: 21.

☐ STUDY 47 Matthew 27: 51–66

1 What is the significance of the torn curtain of the Temple (verse 51)? *Cf.* Heb. 9: 8; 10: 19–23. How are the manifestations recorded in verses 52, 53 linked with these truths?

2 What made Joseph of Arimathea (and Nicodemus, Jn. 19: 39) come out into the open at this late stage? Is it not at first sight strange that they should now publicly associate themselves with Christ? What, in the purposes of God, did such a burial demonstrate and make possible?

Note. Verse 62. 'Next day, that is, after the day of Preparation': it looks as if, in their concern to safeguard the tomb, the Jewish leaders even broke their own sacred sabbath laws.

□ STUDY 48 Matthew 28: 1–20

1 Note the foremost place taken by women disciples in the story of the resurrection appearances. Why should this be (*cf.* Jn. 14: 21)? Contrast the effect of the news of the resurrection on the disciples with the response of Christ's enemies recorded in verses 11–15. How does this prove the truth of Lk. 16: 30, 31?

2 Verses 18–20. Note the fourfold repetition of the word 'all' in Christ's final commission. What is the threefold task given to the Christian church? Are we obeying, as we ought to do, in the light of (a) Christ's authority, and (b) the promise of His presence?

JEREMIAH 26 – 52

□ STUDY 17 Jeremiah 26

Jehoiakim was a very different king from Josiah. At the beginning of his reign, therefore, God sent Jeremiah to warn the people against being led astray into further disobedience to Him.

1 What reason does God give for sending His servant on this dangerous mission? See verse 3 and *cf.* 2 Ch. 36: 15; 2 Pet. 3: 9; Lk. 13: 34, 35.

2 Note the points of resemblance between Jeremiah and Jesus (see Study 8, Question 3; and Mt. 16: 14); *e.g.*, *cf.* Mt. 24: 1, 2; 26: 61; 27: 4, 24, 25. Consider also the experiences of Jeremiah and Uriah in the light of what Jesus foretold for His disciples. *Cf.* Jn. 15: 18–20; 16: 33; 1 Pet. 4: 12, 13.

Notes

1 Verses 4–6. It seems probable that this brief summary of Jeremiah's words is given more fully in chapter 7.

2 Verse 18. 'Micah of Moresheth': see Mi. 1: 1, 14.

3 Verse 24. 'Ahikam the son of Shaphan': one of those sent by King Josiah to consult the prophetess Huldah (2 Ki. 22: 12, 13), and the father of Gedaliah, who was made governor after the fall of Jerusalem (40: 5, 6).

☐ STUDY 18 Jeremiah 27 and 28

Five kings of surrounding nations seek Zedekiah's co-operation in an attempt to throw off the yoke of Babylon. Jeremiah opposes the plan.

1 What means did Jeremiah use to impress upon the five kings the futility of resistance to Babylon? Notice the claim which God made for Himself in His message to these heathen rulers (27: 4–7).

2 What did Jeremiah condemn in the propaganda of the prophets?

3 In chapter 28 we have a leading prophet of the time attacking Jeremiah, and we can consider the two men at close range. In what respects did they resemble each other, and in what respects did they differ? Ponder Jeremiah's now unwavering courage in predicting passive acceptance of Babylonian control in the face of prominent *religious* opposition. What ought we to learn from this?

Note. 27: 16–22. Only a part of the vessels of the Temple had at this time been carried off to Babylon.

☐ STUDY 19 Jeremiah 29

Those who had been carried into exile in the first captivity under Jehoiachin (2 Ki. 24: 14–16) were being made restless by prophets who prophesied falsely that they would soon be set free. Jeremiah therefore wrote a letter to them declaring that the exile would last seventy years.

1 What, as revealed to Jeremiah, were the Lord's thoughts (a) towards the exiles in Babylon, and (b) towards Zedekiah and those who remained in Jerusalem? With verse 17, *cf.* chapter 24.

2 Verses 10–14. What is God's doing and what man's in the promised restoration? Note the divine initiative and sovereignty throughout this chapter, and indeed throughout the book. Note also how its benefits are to be enjoyed.

3 What three prophets are mentioned by name by Jeremiah? What accusations did he bring against them, and what judgment did he pronounce upon them?

Notes

1 Verse 24. 'Shemaiah': that he, too, was a prophet is seen from verse 31.

2 Verse 25. 'Zephaniah': probably the same as the Zephaniah who in 52: 24 is called 'the second priest', *i.e.*, second to the high priest. *Cf.* 21: 1.

☐ STUDY 20 Jeremiah 30: 1 – 31: 26

See Analysis. This passage forms part of a group of prophecies. It was a time of darkness and despair, and Jeremiah himself apparently derived much comfort from the message (31: 26).

1 This passage falls into sections which are all variants of the one theme, that after judgment will come restoration. See 30: 1–3, 4–11, 12–22, 23, 24; 31: 1–9, 10–14, 15–20, 21–22, 23–25. What are the blessings promised?

2 To what extent have these blessings been fulfilled? Observe that they are spoken of northern Israel as well as of Judah (30: 4; 31: 1). *Cf.* Rom. 2: 25–27.

3 Meditate on the greatness of the blessings here promised as fully realized only in Christ. *Cf.* Jn. 7: 37, 38; 15: 9–11; 16: 27.

Notes

1 30: 14. 'All your lovers': *i.e.*, the nations with whom Israel had sought alliance. *Cf.* verse 17b.
2 31: 2. 'The wilderness': here denoting the place of exile.
3 31: 15. 'Rachel is weeping for her children': a graphic picture of the sorrows of the exile. Rachel, the mother of Joseph and Benjamin, is depicted weeping in her grave, which was near Ramah, as the exiles pass by. *Cf.* 40: 1; also Mt. 2: 17, 18.

☐ STUDY 21 Jeremiah 31: 27–40

1 Verses 31–34. If Israel has broken the covenant between herself and the Lord, how can there be any future blessing for her? What is God's answer to this question? Note the four occurrences of 'says the Lord', and the repeated use of 'I'. *Cf.* Jn. 15: 5c.

2 What four features of the new covenant are set forth in 31: 33, 34? With verse 33, *cf.* Ex. 31: 18; 2 Cor. 3: 6; and with verse 34 contrast Ex. 20: 19. See Heb. 8: 3–13 and 10: 14–22 for the fulfilment in Christ.

3 Verses 35–40. How do these verses show the certainty and completeness of the restoration? See Note on verses 39, 40. *Cf.* 33: 20–22.

Notes

1 Verse 28. *Cf.* 1: 10–12.
2 Verses 29, 30. It appears likely that among the exiles, the proverb of verse 29 was being quoted as if they, the innocent, were suffering for their parents' sins. Part of the new order will be the certain accountability of every individual to God personally.
3 Verse 32. The writer to the Hebrews, in quoting this passage, follows the LXX. See Heb. 8: 9.
4 Verse 34. The word 'know' is used here not of intellectual knowledge, but of personal intimacy.
5 Verses 39, 40. The localities Gareb and Goah are not now known. The 'valley of the dead bodies' is the valley of Hinnom. The meaning is that in the new city all shall be holy.

☐ STUDY 22 Jeremiah 32 and 33

1 What was Jeremiah's response to God's command to purchase land (a) immediately (32: 9–12), and (b) subsequently (32: 16–25)? What has this to teach us when faced by perplexities of Christian obedience? What was God's answer to Jeremiah's prayer? What was the significance of his being commanded to buy land at such a time?

2 What blessings are promised in chapter 33? Which of them are for us also under the new covenant? *E.g.*, with 33: 3, *cf.* Eph. 1: 17–19a; 1 Cor. 2: 9, 10.

Note. 33: 1. 'The court of the guard': Jeremiah's friends would be able to visit him, but he would not go outside the court.

☐ STUDY 23 Jeremiah 34

Two incidents that occurred during the siege of Jerusalem at the end of Zedekiah's reign.

1 Nebuchadrezzar doubtless thought that he, with his numerous and powerful forces (verse 1), was master of the situation. But who is revealed here as the controlling power, deciding the fate of cities and kings? *Cf.* Is. 40: 15, 17, 21–24; Lk. 3: 1, 2.

2 Why was the failure to go through with the freeing of the slaves so severely condemned? *Cf.* Ec. 5: 4, 5; Mt. 7: 21; 21: 28–31a; Lk. 9: 62. With verse 17, *cf.* 22: 16. Do I owe some promised obedience which has not yet been performed?

Notes

1 Verses 2–5. *Cf.* 32: 3–5; 52: 11.
2 Verse 14. *Cf.* Dt. 15: 12–15.
3 Verse 17. 'Liberty to the sword': *i.e.*, freedom to be destroyed by conquest.
4 Verses 18, 19. The ceremony of the covenant of repentance (verse 15) included the participants' passing between the parts of a calf which had been cut in two (*cf.* Gn. 15: 7–18). By such ritual they asked to be put to death in a similar violent manner, if they failed to keep their promise. See verse 20.

☐ STUDY 24 Jeremiah 35

The Rechabites were a small class or sect who regarded Jonadab (*cf.* 2 Ki. 10: 15) as their father or founder, and had received a charge from him to abstain from wine, from settled dwellings and from agriculture, *i.e.*, the marks of a settled civilization. They normally lived a nomad life, but, in fear of the advance of the armies of the north, they had taken refuge in Jerusalem.

1 What test did Jeremiah, at God's command, apply to the Rechabites? And what message did God then give him to take to the people of Jerusalem?

2 Verses 13–17. Consider the frequency of this complaint: see 7: 13, 25, 26; 25: 3, 4, 7; 26: 4, 5; 29: 19; 44: 4. Are you careful to heed God's word to you, *e.g.*, through teachers and preachers?

3 What traits of the Rechabites should be the distinguishing features of Christians today? *Cf.* Mt. 24: 12, 13; Heb. 10: 36, 38, 39.

☐ STUDY 25 Jeremiah 36

1 The events of this chapter cannot have been very long after those of chapter 26 (compare the dating in verse 1 with 26: 1). God in His compassion bids Jeremiah make one more appeal. In what respects does it differ from that of chapter 26 (a) in its content, (b) in the manner of its delivery, and (c) in its outcome?

2 Why do you think the princes felt they must tell the king (verse 16)? Was it to get Jeremiah silenced (*cf.* Am. 7: 10–13), or in the hope that the king might hearken to God's word, as Josiah had done (2 Ki. 22: 10, 11)? With verse 24, *cf.* Is. 66: 2. Do you have the impression that this was a fateful moment for the nation, and that very much depended on the king's action? Are there comparable decisions in your life?

3 Compare verses 19 and 26. How do I describe a successful action or activity of my own?

Notes

1 Verse 5. 'I am debarred': perhaps because of the fear of his causing a disturbance (*cf.* the impact of his Temple sermon in chapter 26), or perhaps because of some ceremonial defilement.

2 Verse 8. This verse sums up in brief the story of the following verses. Note from verses 1 and 9 the time taken to complete the scroll. The incident of chapter 45 falls between verses 8 and 9.

☐ STUDY 26 Jeremiah 37 and 38

Although Egypt had been decisively defeated by the armies of Babylon at Carchemish twenty years before (46: 2), now a new king had arisen in Egypt who sought to oppose Nebuchadrezzar's southward advance. He sent an army, while Nebuchadrezzar was besieging Jerusalem, whose approach forced the Chaldeans to raise the siege. This excited great hopes, but Jeremiah was not deceived. The Chaldeans, he said, would come back and burn the city with fire.

1 How do these two arrests of Jeremiah illustrate 1: 18, 19? His arrest seems to have contributed to his safety (37: 21). Should we expect to find God's goodness in our hardest experiences? *Cf.* Ps. 23: 4; Acts 27: 21–25.

2 Which do you think were harder to bear—the physical sufferings or the reproaches hurled at him? Why did he not keep silent and so escape censure? See 20: 7–11; Acts 4: 18–20; 5: 29.

3 What can we learn from the character of Zedekiah as revealed in these chapters? *Cf.* Pr. 29: 25a; Jas. 1: 8.

Note. 37: 12. 'To take over some property among his own people' (Moffatt).

□ STUDY 27 Jeremiah 39–41

The fall of Jerusalem and the events immediately following.

1 What message did Jeremiah give to Ebed-melech, and why? *Cf.* Mt. 10: 40–42. Is your faith equally practical? *Cf.* Jas. 2: 21–24.

2 Note carefully 40: 2, 3. Could the matter be better summed up than in these words of a heathen officer? *Cf.* Pr. 29: 1; Is. 30: 9–14.

3 Most Christians are too ready to believe evil of others. Gedaliah was the opposite. What can we learn from this example? Note that as a public leader he had responsibility for others (40: 10; 41: 10) as well as for himself.

Notes

1 39: 3. 'Rabsaris' means chief of the princes; and 'Rabmag', chief of the magi.

2 39: 4. 'Between the two walls': *i.e.*, of the city, probably 'the wall along the west side of the east hill, and along the east side of the west hill' (Driver).

3 39: 5. 'Riblah': in the far north, fifty miles south of Hamath.

4 41: 1. Ishmael was probably jealous that Gedaliah had been appointed governor, and sought to get the remnant of the Jews under his control (41: 10).

□ STUDY 28 Jeremiah 42 and 43

1 It is clear that the remnant of the people left in the land were obsessed by fear—fear of the Chaldeans (42: 11) and fear of famine (42: 16). From both these evils Egypt appeared to offer a secure place of refuge (42: 14). But what did God say they ought to do? And what did He say would happen to them if they went to Egypt?

2 Why did the people, in spite of their promise to obey God, take a wrong course? What did they lack spiritually that they failed so badly? Read carefully 42: 20, 21 (see Note 1 below), and *cf.* Mt.

15: 7, 8; Heb. 3: 18, 19. What does this teach us about our attitude in seeking to know the will of God? Note 42: 6. Are we guilty of making up *our* minds in advance? *Cf.* 43: 2.

3 Over against the people and their failure contrast the character of Jeremiah. God had made the same promise to him that He now made to these Hebrews (see 1: 18, 19); but how different was the response in Jeremiah's case? What are the outstanding features that you observe in Jeremiah in these chapters?

Notes

1 42: 21. Jeremiah anticipates the reply they were about to make in their fixed resolve to seek refuge in Egypt. Perhaps during the interval (verse 7) preparations for flight had been in hand.

2 43: 7. 'Tahpanhes' was on the eastern branch of the Nile not far from the Mediterranean.

3 43: 10–13. Nebuchadrezzar did invade Egypt before two decades were out.

☐ STUDY 29 Jeremiah 44 and 45

This is the last recorded scene of Jeremiah's life. The now aged prophet, exiled in Egypt, visits some place where his fellow-countrymen are gathered and delivers a last message from their God, a message which they resolutely reject, thus drawing upon themselves their own destruction. Chapter 45 is a much earlier fragment, belonging to the fourth year of Jehoiakim (see Note on 36: 8).

1 How would you sum up Jeremiah's message in 44: 2–14? What was the spiritual condition of the people as revealed in their reply (*cf.* 17: 9; Is. 44: 20)? And what was God's final word to them through His servant? *Cf.* 1 Jn. 5: 21.

2 44: 17, 18, 21–23. Here are two divergent interpretations of Judah's recent past. Outwardly, at least, there seems much to support the idolaters' standpoint. Since Josiah's reformation Judah had experienced nothing but trouble and calamity. Could outward events *alone* adjudicate between these two interpretations? Is there always an immediate correspondence between godliness and prosperity? *Cf.* Ps. 73.

3 Chapter 45. Baruch was the son of a princely house. His brother Seraiah held an important office under the king (see 51: 59), and he himself probably had ambitions (45: 5). His work for Jeremiah would reveal to him the doom of the city and the kingdom. What were his natural reactions? What was God's message to him, and what may we learn from it for ourselves? Was Baruch's distress greater than the Lord's in having so to deal with His people (verse 4)? *Cf.* Mk. 10: 42–45; Mt. 10: 24, 25a.

Notes
1 44: 1. The three cities represent Jewish settlements in northern Egypt, and Pathros was the name given to Upper (*i.e.*, southern) Egypt.
2 44: 17. 'The queen of heaven': see Note on 7: 18 (p. 335).

☐ STUDY 30 Jeremiah 46 and 47

46: 1 introduces chapters 46–51 (see Analysis). Chapter 46 falls into three sections: verses 2–12 (description of Egypt's bid for power and defeat by the Chaldeans at Carchemish); verses 13–26 (prophecy of Nebuchadrezzar's invasion of Egypt); and verses 27, 28 (a message of comfort for Israel: see these verses in their original setting at 30: 10, 11). Chapter 47 prophesies the Chaldean conquest of Philistia.

1 Read each section aloud, perhaps in Moffatt's translation, to catch the rhythm and force of these utterances. What is the relation of the God of Israel to the clash of these mighty powers? *Cf.* 46: 10, 15, 25–26; 47: 4, 6, 7. Note that God's chosen people is not directly involved. *Cf.* Am. 9: 7; Is. 40: 15, 17, 23; 41: 2. What does this tell of God's control of the history of *all* the nations of the world, even if that control is hidden from our sight? *Cf.* Ps. 22: 28.

2 How is Egypt described (a) before the battle, (b) after it, and (c) during the invasion? Compare all this with her boast in 46: 8, and read again 9: 23–26.

Notes
1 46: 9. 'Put' and 'Lud' were African tribes of uncertain location.
2 46: 15. 'Apis': *i.e.*, the sacred bull of Egypt, the supposed incarnation of Osiris.
3 46: 16. 'And they said': the reference must be to foreign settlers or traders in Egypt, or to foreign mercenaries (verse 21).
4 46: 18. 'Like Tabor . . . like Carmel': *i.e.*, 'towering above' the nations.
5 46: 22. The fleeing Egyptians are likened to a snake gliding away before the woodcutters, *i.e.*, the invading armies from the north.
6 46: 25. Thebes was the famous capital of Upper Egypt, and Amon its local god.
7 47: 1. 'Before Pharaoh smote Gaza': it is uncertain when Necho smote Gaza. The LXX omits the phrase.
8 47: 4. 'Caphtor' is the name used of Crete, the original home of the Philistines, and also of the neighbouring coastal regions which came under its control.
9 47: 5. 'Baldness' and 'gash yourselves' are tokens of mourning. *Cf.* 16: 6 (and see Note, p. 338); 48: 37. The 'Anakim' were among the pre-Israelite inhabitants of Palestine.

☐ STUDY 31 Jeremiah 48

Within Jeremiah's lifetime, Moab was in league with the Chaldeans against Judah during Jehoiakim's reign (2 Ki. 24: 2; *cf.* Je. 12); and later, in Zedekiah's reign, discussed with other nations a possible revolt against Babylon (27: 1–11).

1 The chapter may be divided into five sections: verses 1–10, verses 11–20, verses 21–27, verses 28–39, verses 40–47. What heading would you give to each of these sections to sum up its contents?

2 What reason for the judgment is given in verse 11? What warning should we take for ourselves? *Cf.* Dt. 8: 11–18; Is. 47: 8–11; Am. 6: 1–7; Zp. 1: 12. What other reasons for the judgment are set forth in this chapter?

Notes

1 All the numerous place-names refer to Moabite territory. Some have not been identified, including 'Madmen' (verse 2; the LXX reads 'Yet you, *i.e.*, Moab, shall be brought to silence').

2 Verses 7, 13. 'Chemosh': the god of Moab. 'Bethel, their confidence': see Am. 5: 5; 7: 10–13 for false worship at Bethel. Bethel means 'house of God', and there may be present also an allusion to false trust in the Temple; see Je. 7: 1–15.

3 Verses 11, 12. An illustration from the treatment of the juice of grapes. It is left in a vessel until a sediment called 'lees' has formed at the bottom; then the liquid is poured into another vessel, and so repeatedly, until the liquid is clear. Moab had experienced no such purifying process, and so retained its original unrefined character.

4 Verse 26. 'Make him drunk': *i.e.*, stagger with shock and despairing grief. *Cf.* 13: 13 (and see Note, p. 337); 25: 16.

☐ STUDY 32 Jeremiah 49: 1–33

This chapter contains prophecies on four neighbouring nations, namely Ammon (verses 1–6), Edom (verses 7–22), Damascus (verses 23–27), and Kedar and the kingdoms of Hazor (verses 28–33). Ammon was concerned along with Moab in the two incidents mentioned in the introduction to chapter 48. Antagonism between Israel and Edom was long standing, and Edom had recently taken advantage of the fall of Jerusalem in 587 BC to occupy cities in southern Judah (Ob. 10–14). Edom had also considered revolt against Babylon (27: 3). Kedar was a nomadic Arabian tribe, and Hazor is probably used collectively of the region occupied by semi-nomadic Arabs (*cf.* 25: 23, 24).

1 What was Ammon's sin against Israel? *Cf.* Am. 1: 13; Ex. 20: 17; Lk. 12: 15. In what was her trust placed? *Cf.* 48: 7; Pr. 10: 28; Mk. 10: 23, 24. What was to be her punishment?

2 Notice the vivid metaphors describing the severity of Edom's fate, as, *e.g.*, in verses 9, 10, 19, 20. Note, too, its comprehensiveness, from Teman and Bozrah in the north, to Dedan, south of Edom in Arabia. Why is the judgment against Edom (Esau's descendants) so severe? *Cf.* verse 16; Mal. 1: 2–4; Heb. 12: 16, 17.

3 The sins that brought judgment upon Damascus and Kedar are not specified. Read again 25: 15–38, and note the reasons given there for judgment upon nations mentioned in this chapter.

Notes

1 Verses 1, 3. 'Milcom' was the national deity of the Ammonites. The Ammonites took advantage of the deportation of the Gadites by the Assyrians in 733–732 BC (2 Ki. 15: 29).

2 Verse 3. The word 'daughters' here refers to towns and villages which looked to Rabbah as their head. In verse 4 'daughter' refers to the whole people.

3 Verse 8. 'Dwell in the depths': *i.e.*, hidden away from observation. *Cf.* verse 30.

4 Verse 17. 'Hiss': *i.e.*, draw in the breath with astonishment, gasp.

5 Verses 19, 20. The picture of a lion coming up out of the jungle on the fringe of Jordan and doing what it pleases with the flock, no shepherd being able to challenge him.

☐ STUDY 33 Jeremiah 49: 34 – 50: 46

Elam was a country north of the Persian Gulf and east of Babylon. This prophecy, delivered soon after the first deportation from Judah in 597, no doubt warns the exiles against expecting relief from this direction. Jeremiah looked ahead, beyond the judgment of which Babylon was to be the instrument, to the time when Babylon herself would be judged. Chapter 50 may be divided as follows: Babylon's fall (verses 1–3); a message of comfort to Israel (verses 4–7); renewed declaration of Babylon's doom (verses 8–13); summons to the attackers to begin their work (verses 14–16); Israel's return to her land and to her God (verses 17–20); the attackers bidden to press on (verses 21–28, 29–34, 35–40); description of the attackers (verses 41–46).

1 Why is God's people to be restored?

2 Consider the solemn truth that, while God may use a nation as His instrument, this does not absolve that nation from responsibility before God. Why would Babylon receive no mercy? See especially verses 7, 11–15, 24–25, 27–29, 31; Is. 14: 5, 6, 17; 47: 6, 7; 51: 22, 23; La. 1: 7.

Notes

1 50: 2. 'Bel' and 'Merodach' are names of the supreme god of Babylon.

2 50: 7. *Cf.* 40: 3.

3 50: 16. A reference to foreigners in Babylon. *Cf.* 46: 16 and Note.

4 50: 21. 'Merathaim' (perhaps a name for southern Babylonia) and 'Pekod' (a people of eastern Babylonia) are probably used here because they are very close to the Hebrew words for 'double rebellion' (or 'bitterness') and 'punishment' (or 'visitation') respectively.

5 50: 36a. *Cf.* Is. 44: 25.

☐ STUDY 34 Jeremiah 51: 1–58

This chapter may be divided as follows: Babylon's doom and Israel's vindication (verses 1–10); summons to the attackers to press home their assault (verses 11–14); the Lord in contrast to idols (verses 15–19); the Lord's fierce anger against Babylon (verses 20–26); capture of the city (verses 27–33); Israel's wrongs avenged: let her hasten her escape (verses 34–57); summing up God's judgment upon Babylon (verse 58).

1 In the time of her prosperity the idols of Babylon seemed powerful and mighty; but now in the hour of her fall how do they appear? See verses 15–19, and *cf.* 1, 2; Ps. 146: 5–10.

2 What, according to chapters 50 and 51, were the sins of Babylon which called down upon her such terrible vengeance? How far are these sins prevalent in the world today?

Notes

1 Verse 1. Note mg. The Hebrew means literally 'the heart of those who rise up against me'.

2 Verse 3a. The Hebrew is difficult. Either it means that the defenders of Babylon need not trouble to fight, for it will be of no avail (*cf.* verse 30; 31: 4; 32: 5b); or the text is to be amended, *e.g.*, by omission of the negatives.

3 Verse 20. A reference to Cyrus, the conqueror of Babylon.

4 Verse 27. 'Ararat, Minni and Ashkenaz' were three peoples north of Babylonia earlier conquered by the Medes.

5 Verse 36. 'Her sea': perhaps a reference to the great lake Nebuchadrezzar constructed for the defence of the city, or perhaps to the Euphrates.

6 Verse 55a. 'Her mighty voice': *i.e.*, the noise of the great city. Verse 55b refers to the roar of the attackers.

7 Verse 58c. 'So ends the toil of nations, ends in smoke, and pagans waste their pains' (Moffatt).

☐ STUDY 35 Jeremiah 51: 59 – 52: 34

1 51: 59–64. Note the date of this incident. At the time, Babylon was rising to the height of her power and glory, and Jeremiah was convinced that she would enjoy complete supremacy over the nations. See chapter 28 which belongs to the same year. How, then, does this commission which Jeremiah gives to Seriah illustrate the truth of Heb. 11: 1, that 'faith is . . . the conviction of things not seen'?

2 Chapter 52 is very similar to 2 Ki. 24: 18 – 25: 30. It tells once more the story of the fall of Jerusalem, the destruction of the Temple and the captivity of the people, perhaps to emphasize how complete was the fulfilment of Jeremiah's words. For example, compare verse 3 with 7: 15; verse 6 with 14: 15–18; verses 8–11 with 34: 3; verse 13 with 7: 14; 9: 11; 19: 13; 32: 28, 29; verse 15 with 16: 9–13; 21: 9; verses 18, 19 with 27: 19–22. See 1: 12. Do you believe this, and live by it?

Note. 52: 24. 'The three keepers of the threshold': denoting three high officials of the Temple who had charge of the three gates.

LAMENTATIONS

Introduction

The book of Lamentations consists of five songs or elegies, the theme of which is the sorrows of Judah and Jerusalem in the siege and destruction of the city. The cause of these calamities is traced to the sin of the people bringing God's judgment upon them, and the songs contain confessions of sin, statements of faith and hope, and prayer for the restoration of God's favour.

Tradition from the time of the LXX has assigned the authorship of the songs to the prophet Jeremiah. In the Hebrew Bible, however, the book is anonymous, and is placed not among 'The Prophets', but in the section known as 'The Writings'. The book certainly has close affinities with Jeremiah. Chapters 1–4 seem to be the work of an eye-witness of Jerusalem's fall; and if not by Jeremiah himself, may well be the work of one or more of his associates, such as Baruch. Chapter 5 probably dates from a slightly later period.

The songs are written in acrostic form. In chapters 1, 2 and 4 each verse begins with a fresh letter of the Hebrew alphabet from beginning to end. In the poem of chapter 3 there are twenty-two groups of three verses each, and each verse of each group begins with the same letter of the alphabet in order. In chapter 5 the acrostic form is not followed. This acrostic arrangement is partly an aid to memorization, but also seems intended to give a sense of completeness in confession of sin and grief.

Analysis

1 The deep sorrows of Jerusalem with contrite confession of sin.
2 It is God who has acted according to His word. Seek Him in prayer.
3 Speaking on behalf of the nation, the writer pours out his grief before God, and, staying himself upon the Lord, pleads earnestly for help.

4 The miseries of the siege. The guilt of prophets and priests. The capture of the city.
5 A prayer describing the nation's suffering, confessing sin, and pleading for salvation.

☐ STUDY 1 Lamentations 1

Verses 1–11 depict the covenant people in the guise of a widow. The second half of the chapter is a lament by the desolate widow herself.

1 What ingredients make up Jerusalem's cup of sorrow, *e.g.*, loneliness, bereavement, reversal of fortune, *etc.*? Make a list of them. How and why had Jerusalem come to such a pass? See especially verses 5, 8, 9, 12, 14, 17, 18, 20; and *cf.* Heb. 10: 29–31; Lv. 26: 27–33.

2 Do you find any note of resentment in this complaint? 'The sense of tragedy is heightened by the recognition that it was avoidable.' What is commendable in the attitude of this chapter? Note verse 18, and *cf.* Ps. 51: 3, 4; Dn. 9: 6–8; Rom. 3: 4–6.

Notes
1 Verse 2. 'Lovers . . . friends': *i.e.*, neighbouring peoples with whom she had sought alliance. *Cf.* Je. 30: 14.
2 Verse 6. 'Her princes . . .': *cf.* Je. 39: 4, 5.

☐ STUDY 2 Lamentations 2

Verses 1–9 deal particularly with the devastation of buildings in Judah and Jerusalem, and the rest of the chapter with the sufferings of various classes of the inhabitants.

1 Try to imagine the desolation here portrayed and the intensity of the people's sorrow. *Cf.* 1: 12. What is said of God's 'right hand' in verses 3, 4? Contrast with this such passages as Ex. 15: 6, 12; Pss. 63: 8; 139: 10.

2 What evidence in this chapter suggests that already the disaster of the judgment is having one of its intended effects? *Cf.* 2 Ch. 7: 13, 14. Are we, as God's children, as sensitive as we ought to be to His disciplinary dealings?

Notes
1 Verse 2. 'Habitations': *i.e.*, country dwellings, as opposed to 'strongholds'.
2 Verse 4. 'Tent' here denotes the city.
3 Verse 6a refers to the Temple. 'He has broken down his tabernacle like a garden hut' (Gottwald).
4 Verse 22a. Instead of summoning worshippers to a festival, God has called together 'terrors on every side', so that none of His people escaped. *Cf.* Is. 28: 21.

☐ STUDY 3 Lamentations 3

1 In verses 1–20 the poet, speaking in the name of the community, pours out his heart 'like water before the presence of the Lord' (2: 19). Notice the change from the minor to the major key at verse 21. What causes it? Do the psalmists' experiences in Pss. 42: 1–5 and 73: 16, 17a provide a clue?

2 Consider how remarkable is the appearance here, in verses 22–42, of such a noble expression of assurance concerning God's mercies. What aspects of God's character are most emphasized in these verses, and what should be our attitude of mind and spirit in time of affliction or chastisement? *Cf.* Joel 2: 12–14. Why is it both foolish and wrong for a man to complain and murmur in time of chastisement (verses 37–39)? *Cf.* Je. 5: 19–24; Pr. 19: 3.

3 In verses 43–54 the poet, in the name of the people, again pours out his heart before the Lord and, having done so, is strengthened to pray again, and receives comfort. What is his prayer (verses 55–66)? What factors in the poet's situation might lead us not to judge this prayer for requital too harshly?

Notes

1 Verse 20. An alternative reading is, 'Thou wilt surely remember and bow down to me' (Gottwald).

2 Verse 38. The word 'evil' is used here in the sense of misfortune or calamity. *Cf.* Am. 3: 6; Is. 45: 7.

3 Verse 63. *Cf.* Jb. 30: 9.

☐ STUDY 4 Lamentations 4

1 Make a list of the statements in this chapter which emphasize the extraordinary severity of the divine judgment. Notice how all the classes of the community are affected. What is the particular cause here assigned for so great a calamity? *Cf.* Je. 23: 9–14.

2 With verse 17, *cf.* Je. 2: 36, 37; 37: 7, 8; and with verse 20, *cf.* Ps. 146: 3, 4; Je. 17: 5, 6.

Notes

1 Verse 6a. Note the variants in mg.

2 Verse 20. A reference to King Zedekiah; *cf.* Je. 39: 4–7.

☐ STUDY 5 Lamentations 5

1 How would you infer from this chapter that it was written some time after Jerusalem had fallen? How would you sum up the conditions in the land? How does this chapter illustrate what is said in

Heb. 12: 11? Contrast the present disposition of the people with what they formerly said (Je. 5: 11, 12; 18: 18). What did they still lack?

2 With verse 16, *cf.* Je. 13: 18, and with verse 21, Je. 31: 18. Consider how much God's word spoken before through Jeremiah meant to the people at such a time. *Cf.* Jn. 13: 19; 14: 29; 16: 4.

Note. Verse 9. A reference to the danger of attack from desert robbers when the people ventured out to reap the harvest.

PHILIPPIANS

Introduction

Paul had a special love for the Christians in the church at Philippi (see 1: 8; 4: 1). From the beginning they had entered into his labours and sufferings with financial support and prayerful personal interest (1: 5, 19; 4: 15, 16). Shortly before this letter was written they had greatly encouraged him by sending a gift to Rome, where he was a prisoner (4: 10, 14, 18). His letter is marked to an unusual degree by personal affection for his readers, and consists largely of an account of his personal experience of Christ, with special reference to his circumstances as a prisoner.

The church in Philippi seems to have been singularly free from both serious error in doctrine and moral lapses. At the same time there were threatening dangers. A measure of friction had arisen between certain members, and in the earlier part of the letter Paul urges the importance of being of one mind in the Lord. He also warns them against other dangers, and urges them to stand fast in the Lord. It is in this connection that the main doctrinal passages of the letter occur, namely in 2: 5–11 and 3: 1–21.

The letter is dominated by a spirit of joy and peace, and is an outstanding witness to the power of Christ to lift the person weighed down with the sorrow and suffering of earth to rejoicing and gladness in the Lord.

Analysis

1: 1, 2	Greeting.
1: 3–7	Thanksgiving.
1: 8–11	Prayer.
1: 12–26	Paul's present circumstances and outlook.
1: 27 – 2: 18	Encouragement to the Philippians to lead godly lives.
2: 19–30	Future plans.
3: 1–21	Warning against threatening dangers. The faith and aim of a Christian illustrated by Paul's own life.
4: 1–9	Further marks of a Christian.
4: 10–20	An appreciation of the Philippians' gift.
4: 21–23	Greetings and benediction.

☐ STUDY 1 Philippians 1: 1–11

1 Verses 3–7. Why is the joy with which Paul remembers the Philippians remarkable? *Cf.* Acts 16: 22; 1 Thes. 2: 2. How had they made up for the treatment given to Paul at the start? What made him sure that they were now permanently on the right road?

2 Verses 8–11. What twofold preparations for the return of Christ does Paul pray that the Philippians will make? Is it really they who are to make it? *Cf.* 2: 12, 13. How will this preparation be reflected in their character and behaviour? Express Paul's petitions for them in your own words, and then use them in your own praying.

3 Make a list of the places in the Epistle where Paul stresses that he is writing to *all* the Philippian Christians. (See especially verses 1, 3, 7, 8.) Does any part of the letter suggest a reason for this?

Notes

1 Verse 1. 'Saints': a name for the people of Christ as 'holy' or set apart for God's possession and service.

2 Verse 5. See 4: 15, 16.

3 Verse 6. 'The day of Jesus Christ': *i.e.*, the coming day of His manifestation in glory, in the light of which the truth about men's lives will be revealed. *Cf.* 2: 16; 1 Cor. 1: 7, 8; 3: 13; 2 Thes. 1: 9, 10.

☐ STUDY 2 Philippians 1: 12–26

1 The things that had happened to Paul must have seemed calamitous to those who loved him. Why did he himself view the situation

differently? What lesson about suffering may a Christian draw from Paul's attitude?

2 What was Paul's attitude as a Christian (a) to life, and (b) to death? What were his reasons for choosing one rather than the other? What were his overriding concerns? Have you faced every possibility that lies before you in the same way?

3 What temptation in Christian service is it clear from this passage that Paul steadfastly resisted? How had others succumbed? What kind of slant might their preaching have had in relation to Paul? In what shape does the same temptation come to us? What should be our chief reason for joy? *Cf.* Jn. 3: 25–30.

☐ STUDY 3 Philippians 1: 27 – 2: 18

1 Make a list of the things (a) to be coveted, and (b) to be avoided in one's life as a member of a company of Christians. Then pray, and by God's grace determine, that these things shall be (a) realized and (b) avoided in your own Christian fellowship. Note especially the direct connection between these things and witness to those who are not Christians.

2 What two qualities of personal character and conduct are here shown to be supremely exemplified in the incarnation and the redemptive work of the Son of God? What ground have we for hoping to be able to have and to express the same qualities? How ought we to act in consequence?

3 Why does disunity amongst Christians discredit the gospel? What does Paul here teach about (a) the motive for unity, and (b) the power by which it may be achieved?

Note. 2: 6–11. It is generally thought that these verses are here quoted by Paul from an early Christian credal hymn. It is worth committing this section to memory and exploring it in depth.

☐ STUDY 4 Philippians 2: 19–30

1 What is said here or can be inferred about the character and career of Epaphroditus? Note carefully how the two workers here mentioned personally exemplified the virtues considered under the previous study, *i.e.*, they had the mind of Christ. Compare verses 20, 21 with 4, 5; and verses 29, 30 with 5–8. Examine your own life in relation to these standards.

2 What phrase occurs three times in this passage and several other times in the letter? What clue does 4: 2 give as to one reason for this repeated emphasis? Are our hopes for the future and our relationships under the same sway as Paul's?

□ STUDY 5 Philippians 3: 1–11

Paul now turns to another subject—possibly, as some think, resuming his writing after a break. His subject now is the essential character of the Christian life from its beginning in justification by faith to its glorious consummation at the coming of the Lord; and he illustrates the theme from his own life.

1 What three characteristics of the true people of God are given in verse 3? How far are they true of me?

2 Examine carefully the reasons for 'confidence in the flesh' which Paul enumerates in verses 4–6. Are there not many church-goers today who are relying for salvation on just such grounds as these? What, in contrast to all this, is the position of the true Christian? What choice does Paul show needs to be made in order to become one?

3 Faith in Christ as the sole ground for acceptance with God led, in Paul's case, to intense desire to know Christ; nothing else seemed to him of any value (verses 8, 9). Along what two lines in particular did he want a deeper knowledge (verse 10), and to what end (verse 11)?

Notes

1 Verse 2. Note the emphatic 'Look out', repeated three times. A word meaning 'incision' or 'mutilation' is here used instead of 'circumcision', because the circumcision on which they insisted was harmful rather than helpful to spiritual well-being. *Cf.* Gal. 5: 2–4; 6: 12–15.

2 Verses 3, 4. 'Confidence in the flesh': *i.e.*, reliance upon outward privilege and personal merit. 'We are the true circumcision': *i.e.*, the true people of God. *Cf.* Rom. 2: 17, 23, 28, 29.

□ STUDY 6 Philippians 3: 12–21

1 Verses 12–17. Once a person knows he is 'saved' or 'justified', what attitude should he adopt to life? Even after he has 'grown up' as a Christian and become 'mature', what concern should still dominate his thoughts? What is he never justified in doing? How in consequence ought I to be acting?

2 Verses 18–21. What kind of outlook, interest and expectation should a Christian have, and why? By contrast, what kind of appetite and interest dominates some? What difference should the cross of Christ make to my daily life? *Cf.* Gal. 5: 24; 6: 14.

Notes

1 Verses 12, 15. 'Perfect' or 'mature': the Greek word means 'having reached its end'. It was used of persons who were full-grown or mature.

2 Verse 20. The thought here is that Christians here on earth are a colony of heavenly citizens, just as the Philippians were proud to think of themselves as a colony of Roman citizens. *Cf.* Acts 16: 12, 21.

☐ STUDY 7 Philippians 4

1 Note in detail how the believer's relationship to the Lord should make a difference (a) to his own condition, (b) to his attitude to circumstances, and (c) to his relationship to people. Note the importance of the mind and its right use; and note what God can do for our minds. *Cf.* Is. 26: 3. Examine your own life to discover ways in which you may trust Christ to make you 'different'.

2 What teaching is implicit in this passage about (a) the bond effected by Christian giving; (b) the need for regularity in it; (c) the way God looks at it; and (d) the way in which He repays it? *Cf.* Lk. 6: 38.

Notes

1 Verse 5. 'The Lord is at hand': this may mean either that the Lord is close by, at their side (*cf.* Ps. 119: 151), or that His coming is imminent.

2 Verse 18. 'A fragrant offering' (RSV), or 'an odour of a sweet smell' (AV, RV): a phrase used in the Old Testament of acceptable offerings. *Cf.* Gn. 8: 21; Lv. 1: 9, 13; Eph. 5: 2.

EZEKIEL 1 - 32

Introduction

Ezekiel was one of the many taken captive by Nebuchadrezzar in the first captivity, commonly referred to as the captivity of King Jehoiachin (*e.g.*, 1: 2), because this king himself was among those carried away. This occurred in 597 BC, eleven years before the actual destruction of Jerusalem.

Ezekiel was a priest as well as a prophet. He began prophesying in 592 BC and continued till at least 570 BC. See 1: 2 and 29: 17. His ministry was divided into two distinct periods by the destruction of Jerusalem (586 BC). Before this event it was his painful task to disillusion his fellow-exiles, to proclaim that all hopes of the early deliverance of the city and speedy return of the exiles were vain. Jerusalem must fall. After this event the character of his ministry completely changed. He sought to rebuke despair and to afford comfort and hope by promises of future deliverance and restoration.

To witness with the object first of overthrowing men's natural hopes, and then of overcoming men's inevitable despair, is a work that can be undertaken and carried through only under the constraint and by the inspiration of a divine commission. Such a commission was Ezekiel's compelling urge. He was a man whose whole life was dominated by his sense of vocation and responsibility as a prophet—as God's messenger to his fellows. Similar necessity is laid upon us to be God's witnesses, and the essential truth of Ezekiel's message should be the unchanging truth of our own. Because God is righteous, sin must be punished; old things must pass away. But because God is gracious, and has provided a salvation for sinners, there is a gospel of hope for the hopeless; in Christ all things can become new.

Analysis

- 1:1 – 3:21 Ezekiel's call and commission.
- 3:22 – 24:27 Prophecies concerning the destruction of the city and nation (uttered before the fall of Jerusalem).
  - 3:22 – 7:27 Symbolic representations foretelling Jerusalem's overthrow, and their interpretation.
  - 8 – 11 Symbolic departure of the Lord from the Temple because of idolatry.
  - 12 – 23 Specific proofs of the necessity of judgment.
  - 24 Final symbol of the scattering of the people and their purification through exile.
- 25 – 32 Predictions against seven heathen nations—Ammon, Moab, Edom, Philistia, Tyre, Sidon, Egypt.
- 33 – 39 Prophecies concerning the restoration of the nation (uttered after the fall of Jerusalem).
  - 33, 34 The moral conditions of entering the new kingdom.
  - 35:1 – 36:15 The land to be rescued from its enemies.
  - 36:16 – 37:28 The nation to be restored, purified, revitalized, and re-united.
  - 38, 39 The Lord's final victory.
- 40 – 48 A vision symbolizing the ideal state of Israel as the Lord's people.

☐ STUDY 1 Ezekiel 1

The vision of this chapter was of supreme importance in Ezekiel's life. Not only was it the occasion of his call to be a prophet, but it was also the medium through which a new conception of God was revealed to him which was to mould his prophetic ministry.

1 As the vision of God's chariot-throne is outlined, follow the prophet's description of it, part by part: first the living creatures (verses 5–14), then the wheels (verses 15–21), with the throne on top, and finally the One who sat there. How is God described, and what is this meant to teach about the nature of God?

2 What do you find symbolized by the other features of the vision: the living creatures, the wheels, the throne, *etc.*?

Notes

1 Verse 1. 'In the thirtieth year . . .': probably of Ezekiel's age, *i.e.*, the year when he would have begun to function as a priest had he remained in Jerusalem.

2 Verse 3. 'The hand of the Lord was upon him there': a phrase used elsewhere in the book to signify a prophetic trance or ecstasy. See 3: 22; 8: 1; 33: 22; 37: 1.
3 Verse 5. 'Four living creatures': heavenly beings, yet representing the highest forms of life on earth (among birds, domestic animals, wild animals and the whole creation respectively), and indicating perhaps that all created things are under God's control.
4 Verses 19–21. Observe that there was no mechanical framework to the chariot. All was spiritual, and responsive to the Spirit.

☐ STUDY 2 Ezekiel 2: 1 – 3: 21

1 To whom was Ezekiel sent, and how are they described? What was to be the theme of his message to them? See 2: 3–7; 3: 4–11.

2 What two meanings are symbolized by the eating of the scroll one having reference to the prophet himself (2: 8), and the other to his ministry (3: 4)? Consider the application of these things to all who would be God's messengers.

3 What consolations are there in these verses for one called to witness for the Lord among those who are obstinately opposed to the gospel? Why is such opposition no excuse for ceasing to witness (2: 5b)? What are the four possible cases which are cited in 3: 17–21? What relevance do these have for the work of Christian ministers today?

Notes
1 2: 1, 3. 'Son of man': a phrase occurring over ninety times in Ezekiel. It is used to draw attention to the prophet's insignificance and mere humanity.
2 2: 6. 'Briers and thorns . . . scorpions': symbols of the trials he would suffer.

☐ STUDY 3 Ezekiel 3: 22 – 5: 17

Jerusalem, under King Zedekiah, had recovered a measure of strength after its capture by Nebuchadrezzar in 597 BC, and false prophets were prophesying a period of divine favour (see Je. 28: 1–4). These reports reached the exiles in Babylon, and the burden of Ezekiel's message at this time was that, on the contrary, Jerusalem was about to experience God's judgments.

The closing verses of chapter 3 are best regarded as an introduction to the prophecies of chapters 4–24, which all relate to the approaching judgment on Jerusalem. During this time the prophet was commanded to live in seclusion, as if bound and dumb, except when God gave him some message to deliver (3: 25–27).

1 In chapters 4: 1 – 5: 4 the prophet is directed to show by four symbolic actions the impending siege of Jerusalem, with its privations and sufferings, and also the plight of those who would be carried into exile after the city's fall. What were these actions?

Which of them refer to the siege, and which to the sufferings of those who would be carried into captivity? With 4: 13, *cf.* Ho. 9: 3, 4; and note the explanation of 5: 1–4 in 5: 12.

2 What is said in 5: 5–17 of (a) the reasons, (b) the nature, and (c) the purposes of the terrible judgment that was about to fall upon Jerusalem? Some Christians are less Christian in their lives than many who reject or ignore Christ. In the light of these verses what may we infer to be God's attitude to this sad fact?

Notes

1 4: 10, 11. Food restricted to eight ounces, and water to two pints or less. *Cf.* 4: 16.

2 4: 15. Animal dung was, and still is, a recognized form of fuel in the East.

☐ STUDY 4 Ezekiel 6 and 7

1 Chapter 6. Against what sin is the Lord's anger particularly directed? In what forms is it found today?

2 What refrain frequently recurs in these two chapters? What does it teach us about the purpose behind Ezekiel's prophesying?

3 Contrast the phrase 'I will punish you according to your ways' (7: 9) with Ps. 103: 10; and see Pr. 1: 24, 29–31; 2 Cor. 6: 1, 2. What warning for the careless and indifferent does this contrast suggest?

4 What can be learnt from 7: 14–27 about the right and wrong uses of money? In what ways can it become a stumbling-block to the follower of Christ?

Notes

1 6: 3. 'Your high places': the word originally meant a height or eminence, but as these were used as the sites of temples and shrines, the word came to mean 'sanctuaries', as here. *Cf.* Dt. 12: 2, 3.

2 7: 20. 'They prided themselves upon the beauty of their silver and their gold, and made out of them . . . idols' (Moffatt). *Cf.* Ho. 2: 8.

☐ STUDY 5 Ezekiel 8

Chapters 8–11 describe what Ezekiel was shown in a prophetic trance fourteen months after his first vision. *Cf.* 8: 1 and 1: 1, 2.

1 The prophet is carried 'in visions of God' (verse 3) to Jerusalem, and is there shown four forms of idolatry, practised in or at the gate of the Temple. If you were asked what these practices were, how would you describe them? Observe also what classes of the community are seen engaging in them.

2 The idol-worshipping elders said, 'The Lord has forsaken the land' (verse 12). In what sense were their words true (*cf.* verse 6), and in what sense false? How does this chapter show that all that was happening was under the eyes and under the judgment of God?

Notes

1 Verse 3. 'Image of jealousy': *i.e.*, which provoked God's jealous anger. *Cf.* Dt. 32: 21.

2 Verse 14. 'Women weeping for Tammuz': *i.e.*, taking part in the heathen festival of mourning the death of the vegetation god, Tammuz, later known in Greek mythology as Adonis.

3 Verse 16. 'Between the porch and the altar': these men must therefore have been priests. *Cf.* Joel 2: 17.

☐ STUDY 6 Ezekiel 9 and 10

Following the prophecy of judgment, which Ezekiel recorded in chapters 6 and 7, and the vision of chapter 8, which illustrated in detail why such a judgment was justified, the prophet here gives a picture of God acting in judgment in the destruction of both the people (chapter 9) and the city (chapter 10) according to His word in 8: 18.

1 Chapter 9. What was God's answer to the prophet's cry of distress? *Cf.* Je. 14: 19; 15: 1. Who alone were spared, and why? How were they distinguished from others? Compare the distinguishing marks which similarly brought men salvation, described in Ex. 12: 13; Rev. 7: 1–3; 14: 1.

2 Chapter 10. To what use were the burning coals put, and what did they symbolize? How does this differ from their function in Isaiah's vision (Is. 6: 6, 7)?

Notes

1 'The cherubim' of chapter 10 are the same as the 'living creatures' which featured in the vision of chapter 1.

2 10: 14. We would expect to find the word 'ox' instead of 'cherub', and this should probably be understood.

☐ STUDY 7 Ezekiel 11

1 The political leaders in Jerusalem thought they were safe within the fortification of Jerusalem, as flesh in a pot is safe from the fire (verse 3). What does God say concerning them? For the fulfilment of the prophecy, see 2 Ki. 25: 18–21.

2 The people of Jerusalem thought that they were the favoured of the Lord, and would be given possession of the land, while those in exile would be cut off (verse 15). But what was God's purpose concerning those in exile (verses 16–20)?

3 Trace the steps by which the glory of God withdrew from His Temple. See 8: 3, 4; 9: 3; 10: 4; 10: 19; 11: 1, 23. What hint is given in chapter 11 as to the possibility of the return of the glory and under what conditions? *Cf.* 43: 1–4, 9.

Notes
1 Verse 1. 'Jaazaniah the son of Azzur': a different man from the Jaazaniah of 8: 11.
2 Verse 23b. 'The mountain': *i.e.*, the Mount of Olives.

☐ STUDY 8 Ezekiel 12 and 13

1 12: 1–20 declares by two vivid symbolic actions on the part of the prophet the doom that was in store both for the people of Jerusalem (verses 3, 4, 18, 19) and for the king (verses 5, 6, 10–16). Having grasped the significance of the prophecy, turn to 2 Ki. 25: 1–7 to see how exactly it was fulfilled.

2 Note the two scoffing remarks in 12: 22 and 27. What do these signify? How are they paralleled in modern attitudes to the second coming of Christ? *Cf.* 2 Pet. 3: 8–10.

3 Chapter 13. Condemnation of false prophets. By what two vivid images are they described (see verses 4 and 10, 11), and what is the effect of their prophesying (verses 6, 10a, 22)? What phrase differentiating them from true prophets occurs twice in the chapter?

Note. 13: 18–21. The magic armbands and veils were devices used by soothsayers and clairvoyants to deceive gullible victims. A useful section on the interpretation of this passage is to be found in *NBD* (article 'Magic and Sorcery', p. 767). The handfuls of barley and pieces of bread were probably used in forms of divination, forecasting life or death to inquirers.

☐ STUDY 9 Ezekiel 14 and 15

1 14: 1–11. (a) If men whose hearts are inwardly alienated from God come professing to seek guidance from Him, will God answer them? What must they first do? If they do not so do, what will be their end? (b) If a prophet should fail to follow this rule, and attempt to give guidance, how will God deal with him?

2 People might ask, 'Will not the presence of righteous men among a sinful nation save it from destruction?' *Cf.*, *e.g.*, Gn. 18: 23–26. How does God in reply show that in the present instance the righteous will be saved out of the destruction, but will not be able to save others? *Cf.* 9: 4–6; Je. 15: 1. If any should escape, what purpose will this accomplish (see 14: 22, 23)?

Notes

1 Noah, Daniel and Job are probably all three patriarchal characters. It is not likely that Ezekiel would be thinking of his contemporary in exile, Daniel the prophet. We know of a Daniel from the Ras Shamra tablets of 1400 BC, and this is a more likely identification.

2 15: 2. For another example of Israel as God's vine, see Is. 5: 1–7.

☐ STUDY 10 Ezekiel 16

In this vivid allegory the prophet seeks to break down the pride of Jerusalem. She appears as the bride of the Lord God, who loved her from infancy, and did everything for her, but whose love she had requited with persistent and shameful idolatry. The chapter falls into four sections: (i) Jerusalem as a child and as a bride (verses 1–14); (ii) her sin (verses 15–34); (iii) her judgment (verses 35–52); (iv) her restoration (verses 53–63).

1 What was God's complaint against Jerusalem? With verses 22 and 32, *cf.* Dt. 32: 15–18. Notice also that God regards her sin as greater than that of Samaria and of Sodom. See verses 46–52 and *cf.* Mt. 11: 23, 24.

2 How may the teaching of this chapter be applied to one who has been truly converted, but has backslidden? What can we learn here for our warning of the peril and folly of the sin of unfaithfulness? *Cf.* Je. 2: 13, 19; Jas. 4: 4–10.

☐ STUDY 11 Ezekiel 17

In 588 BC Zedekiah rebelled against Nebuchadrezzar who, nine years previously, had installed him as puppet-king of Judah, at the time when Jehoiachin had been taken captive to Babylon. His rebellion encouraged false hopes among the exiles of a speedy end to their captivity, but Ezekiel silenced these with this parable about the eagle, the cedar and the vine. The first eagle (verse 3) was Nebuchadrezzar, removing the Davidic King Jehoiachin (the cedar twig, verse 4). Those who remained in Jerusalem under Zedekiah (the vine, verse 6) flourished for a time, but then turned towards the king of Egypt (the second eagle, verse 7), whose influence caused them to wither away.

1 What sin is the prophet specifically rebuking here? With verses 13–16, *cf.* 2 Ch. 36: 13; and with verses 7 and 15, *cf.* Je. 37: 5–8.

2 How do verses 22–24 show that neither the ambitious designs nor the perfidies of men can frustrate the purposes of God? Notice the emphatic and repeated 'I'. *Cf.* Pr. 19: 21; Is. 46: 8–13.

☐ STUDY 12 Ezekiel 18 and 19

The teaching of national retribution in chapter 16 and other passages seems to have raised doubts as to the justice of God's dealings with individuals (18: 2, 29). This is the subject of chapter 18. Chapter 19 is a lament.

1 Two fundamental principles are stated in 18: 4 in answer to the people's complaint in 18: 2. How would you express these in your own words? What verses in the New Testament can you think of which emphasize the same ideas?

2 In the remainder of chapter 18 two questions are answered: (a) Is each man responsible to God for his own acts, and for these alone (see verses 5–20)? (b) If a man turn from his past way of life, will that past affect God's judgment upon him (see verses 21–29)? How does this teaching reveal not only God's justice, but also His mercy? Why does it lead on immediately to the call to repentance of verses 30–32?

3 Chapter 19 is a lament over three of the kings of Judah. Try to identify these by comparing verses 3 and 4 with 2 Ki. 23: 31–34; verses 5–9 with 2 Ki. 24: 8–15; and verses 10–14 with 2 Ki. 25: 4–11. What did they all have in common?

Notes

1 18: 6, 11, 15. 'Eat upon the mountains': *i.e.*, join in idolatrous forms of worship. *Cf.* 6: 1–4.

2 19: 14. The fire which brought destruction sprang from the ruler himself, *i.e.*, Zedekiah. See 17: 19–21.

☐ STUDY 13 Ezekiel 20: 1–44

This section is a review of Israel's history (verses 5–31), with a prophecy of what God will yet do (verses 32–44). The review of history covers (a) the time in Egypt (verses 5–9); (b) in the wilderness (verses 10–17 and 18–26); and (c) in the land of Canaan (verses 27–31). With verses 1–3, *cf.* 14: 1, 2.

1 Analyse the repeated poetical pattern found in verses 5–9, 10–14, 15–17, 18–22. What restrained God from pouring out His wrath? What does this reveal of God's character? How does it show what is the one and only guarantee of our salvation? *Cf.* 1 Sa. 12: 22.

2 To what two conclusions does God say He will ultimately bring His people Israel (verses 42–44)? Has a like conviction been wrought in us?

Notes

1 Verse 25 is a Hebrew way of saying, 'I gave them good statutes but they had a bad effect; I thereby condemned those who were disobedient and I defiled those who performed human sacrifices.' *Cf.* Rom. 5: 20.

2 Verse 37. 'Pass under the rod': the eastern shepherd makes his sheep pass one by one under his staff, held horizontally, to count and examine them.

☐ STUDY 14 Ezekiel 20: 45 – 21: 32

The prophet is bidden to prophesy (a) against the south (of Palestine) (20:

45–49), and (b) against Jerusalem and the land of Israel (21: 1–17). The sword of the Lord is drawn from its sheath (21: 1–7), sharpened and polished (21: 8–13), and smites repeatedly in its deadly work (21: 14–17). In 21: 18–27, the explanation is given. The king of Babylon is seen, standing at the parting of the ways, seeking guidance by divination—Ammon or Jerusalem? The decision falls for Jerusalem, the city is taken, and the king (Zedekiah) slain. The closing verses of the chapter (verses 28–32) are a short prophecy of utter doom upon Ammon as well.

1 Who kindles the fire? Whose sword is drawn? Yet it was by a heathen king that the judgment was effected. What does this teach us concerning God's methods of accomplishing His purposes of judgment in the world? *Cf.* Je. 25: 9 ('my servant'); Is. 25: 1–4.

2 When human leaders and confidences all fail and are overthrown, where can we still look for the establishment of a reign of peace? See 21: 25–27; *cf.* Ps. 2: 6–9; Lk. 21: 25–28.

Notes

1 21: 21 refers to three well-known forms of divination practised by the Babylonians: drawing marked arrows from a quiver (or throwing them in the air to see how they fall); consulting the teraphim, the ancestral household gods, in some form of necromancy; and studying the marks on the entrails of sacrificial victims.

2 21: 27. 'Whose right it is': *i.e.*, the Davidic Messiah who is entitled to the kingship. *Cf.* Gn. 49: 10.

☐ STUDY 15 Ezekiel 22

This chapter falls into three divisions: (a) a description of the sins committed within the city (verses 1–16); (b) the certainty of judgment (verses 17–22); and (c) an indictment of all classes of the community (verses 23–31).

1 Group the sins enumerated in verses 1–12 under the following two heads: (a) religious, and (b) social. Notice how, with the loss of a true conception of God, there follows the loss of filial piety, moral purity, and civic justice. How far are the sins mentioned here prevalent among us today?

2 What four classes are mentioned in verses 24–29, and what charges are made against them? What is the saddest feature of the situation, as stated in verse 30? *Cf.* verse 19 ('all become dross') and Je. 5: 1–5.

Notes

1 Verse 4. 'Your day': *i.e.*, the day of your judgment.

2 Verse 13. Striking the hands was an expression of horror. *Cf.* 21: 14, 17.

3 Verse 30. 'Build up the wall': *i.e.*, act as a bastion against the inroads of wickedness.

☐ STUDY 16 Ezekiel 23

This chapter resembles chapter 16. Samaria and Jerusalem are condemned for their unfaithfulness in seeking alliances with foreign nations and their gods. Their conduct is represented in unusually realistic figures to make it appear how loathsome and repulsive it has been.

1 What is the main content of each of the four divisions of this chapter, namely verses 1–10, 11–21, 22–35, and 36–49?

2 Trace how Jerusalem walked in the way of Samaria and even exceeded her in wickedness, and therefore must drain to the dregs the same cup of judgment. What were the origins of her idolatrous tendencies, both on the historical and on the religious level (verses 8, 19, 27, 35)? What warning does this contain for God's people today?

☐ STUDY 17 Ezekiel 24

A last picture of Jerusalem before its destruction—a rusted pot set on a fire, with flesh being boiled in it. The flesh is taken out and scattered, symbolizing the dispersion of the people of the city; and the pot is then left on the fire, a symbol of the city lying waste and burned.

1 Verses 1–14. Compare what the chief men of Jerusalem said in 11:3 (see Study 7, Question 1) with what God says here concerning the city and its people. What may we learn from this? *Cf.* 1 Thes. 5:3; 2 Pet. 3:4.

2 Verses 15–27. How is Ezekiel's wife described in verse 16? Yet God makes this painful experience also a means of ministry. What was it designed to demonstrate? See verses 24 and 27. Can you think of other instances where the sufferings of a servant of God have been made to serve God's design, no matter at what cost to the sufferer? *Cf.* Col. 1:24.

Notes

1 Verse 23. The people would be too stunned by the evil tidings to take any action.

2 Verse 27. *Cf.* 3:26, 27.

Introductory Note to Chapters 25–32

These chapters are a series of prophetic utterances against seven foreign nations. They are intended to show that the calamities which were falling on Judah were not arbitrary, nor an evidence of God's weakness, but that, on the contrary, He is supreme over all peoples and all His acts are governed by fixed moral principles which reveal His holy nature. By their position in the book they separate the prophecies that belong to the period of Ezekiel's ministry prior to the fall of Jerusalem from those that followed later. (See Introduction.)

☐ STUDY 18 Ezekiel 25 and 26

Chapter 25 contains four prophecies directed against Ammon, Moab, Edom and the Philistines respectively. Chapter 26 is a prophecy of the approaching destruction of Tyre through the armies of Nebuchadrezzar, together with a vivid description of the far-reaching effects of her overthrow.

1 In chapter 25, find four ways in which unbelievers and enemies of the truth act towards the people of God when the latter are brought low by calamity. How will such adversaries be dealt with, and why? *Cf.* Pss. 94: 1–5, 21–23; 46: 8–10; Is. 26: 9b.

2 What, according to 26: 2, was the ground of God's judgment upon Tyre? As we try to imagine the scenes described in 26: 7–14, and measure the fame and worldly greatness of Tyre by the dismay caused by her fall (15–18), what lessons may we learn? *Cf.* Je. 9: 23, 24; Lk. 12: 15–21.

Notes

1 25: 10. 'The people of the East' are the tribes of the desert. Moab and Ammon were before long overrun by the Nabataeans.

2 26: 2. Jerusalem had been as an open gate, by which commerce had been diverted from Tyre.

3 26: 6. 'Her daughters': *i.e.*, towns on the mainland dependent upon Tyre.

☐ STUDY 19 Ezekiel 27 and 28

Further prophecies concerning Tyre. In chapter 27 the city is pictured as a stately ship. Verses 5–11 give a description of the ship; verses 12–25 of her cargo; and verses 26–36 of her shipwreck and total loss, with the widespread mourning that ensued. In chapter 28 the prince of Tyre is regarded as personifying the genius or spirit of the city, and as incarnating in his person the principle of evil which animated it. The terms used concerning him (especially in verses 11–19) are such that the figure of the human ruler seems to merge into Satan himself, the originator of the sins of which Tyre was guilty.

1 Contrast men's judgment of Tyre (27: 4, 33) and Tyre's view of herself (27: 3) with God's judgment of her (28: 2–8). What was the pre-eminent sin of Tyre? *Cf.* Dn. 4: 29–32.

2 In what sense did Tyre become 'a terror' (AV 27: 35, 36)? See also 26: 21; 28: 19. To what kind of fear should such a catastrophe give rise in our own hearts? *Cf.* Dt. 17: 12, 13; Rom. 11: 20; 1 Tim. 5: 20.

3 28: 20–26 is a short prophecy against Sidon, which was closely linked with Tyre. What is said in verses 20–26 to be the twofold purpose of God's judgments (a) in relation to Himself, and (b) in relation to His people?

Notes

1 27: 36. Hissing expressed astonishment, rather like whistling today.
2 28: 3. 'Daniel': see Study 9, Note 1.

☐ STUDY 20 Ezekiel 29 and 30

The prophet's gaze is now directed towards Egypt, pictured in 29: 1–16 as a great dragon or crocodile, whose destruction is at hand. The remainder of today's portion consists of three further prophecies of similar import, namely 29: 17–20; 30: 1–19; and 30: 20–26.

1 Compare the explanation of the allegory in 29: 8–12 with the allegory itself in 29: 3–7. What are the two sins in particular which caused God's judgment to fall on Egypt? With 29: 7, *cf.* verse 16 and Is. 30: 5.

2 29: 17–21. This is a prophecy dated sixteen years after that of verses 1–16, *i.e.*, in 571 BC. It appears to indicate that Nebuchadrezzar had not gained the spoils of war at Tyre as he expected, and is now promised a recompense from the conquest of Egypt. What light does this passage throw on the way in which God treats heathen nations?

3 'Her proud might shall come down' (30: 6; *cf.* 30: 18). Why cannot anyone ultimately prosper who trusts, as Pharaoh did, in his own resources and achievements? *Cf.* Jb. 9: 4; Lk. 1: 51.

Notes

1 29: 14, 15. Egypt is not to be finally destroyed, like Tyre (26: 21; 27: 36; 28: 19), but reduced in status.
2 29: 18. A reference to the chafing of helmets and the carrying of packs.

☐ STUDY 21 Ezekiel 31 and 32

These chapters contain three more prophecies concerning Egypt. In chapter 31, Egypt is likened to a mighty cedar, whose fall causes the other trees to mourn. In 32: 1–6 the figure of the dragon or crocodile is resumed (*cf.* 29: 3–5), and in 32: 7, 8 Egypt is likened to a bright star. The imagery is very vivid, depicting the utter destruction of Pharaoh and his hosts. In 32: 17–32 the prophet in a vision follows Pharaoh and his armies into Sheol, and sees them there among others also slain by the sword who bear the shame of their lack of proper burial.

1 How does chapter 31 further enforce the lesson of chapter 30? What is the reason given for the tree's destruction, and what effect is this intended to have on other nations?

2 Observe how often in these chapters the personal pronoun 'I' occurs. Do we realize enough that God is the chief actor in the developments of history? Over what realms, in addition to that of Israel, is His dominion here asserted?

Note. 32: 17–32. This is not to be regarded as a literal description of the state of men after death, but as an imaginative picture intended to show that all who use violence and lawless might, causing terror on the earth (*cf.* verses 23ff.), shall alike meet with retribution. Pharaoh's only consolation will be in the multitude of his companions (verse 31).

For Studies 22–35 on Ezekiel see p. 385.

PSALMS 73 - 89

☐ STUDY 57 Psalm 73

Pss. 73–83 are all entitled 'of Asaph' (*cf.* 2 Ch. 35: 15; Ezr. 2: 41; 3: 10). These psalms are marked by certain characteristic features, among which may be mentioned the representation of God as Judge and also as the Shepherd of His people. They are, in the main, national psalms, and look back to the past history of Israel to draw from it encouragement and warning.

1 The problem of the prosperity of the ungodly oppressed the psalmist sorely. See verses 2, 13, 16. Real life seemed to mock the assertion of verse 1. What was the root of the psalmist's distress? See verses 3, 22; *cf.* Pr. 23: 17; Ps. 37: 1. What is the 'more excellent way'? *Cf.* 1 Cor. 13: 4; 1 Pet. 2: 1.

2 How did the psalmist discover the grossness of his error? What did he come to see with regard to the wicked (verses 17–20), and what did he find that he possessed in God (verses 23–26)? Can you honestly and enthusiastically make the confession of verse 25?

3 What may we learn from the psalmist's example (a) in verses 15–17 (for 'the sanctuary', *cf.* Pss. 63: 2, 3; 68: 35), and (b) in verse 28? Do you delight in being near to God, and in speaking not of doubts (verse 15), but of God's mighty works?

Notes
1 Verse 15. The psalmist realizes that to parade his doubt (verses 13, 14), or to speak like the wicked (verse 9), would be to betray the family of God.
2 Verse 20. The sense is, 'The wicked are like a dream when one awakes; and when you, O Lord, awake, you will despise their shadow.'

☐ STUDY 58 Psalm 74

The psalm starts in anguish, because of the ruined sanctuary. At verse 12 it changes completely into a resounding hymn of praise to God, Creator and Redeemer. But both sections contain earnest pleas for God to act on behalf of His name and of His own.

1 Consider (a) the psalmist's survey and summary of Israel's shattering defeat (verses 1–11); and (b) how he then reminds himself that God is Creator, Redeemer and King (verses 12–17). As a Christian, can you face disaster and discomfort with such an assurance about God? *Cf.* Rom. 8: 18, 28.

2 Note the boldness and the persistence of the psalmist's requests. See verses 2, 3, 10, 11, 18–23. What is the basis of his confidence? Have you learnt thus to plead in prayer both for church and nation? Note the reasons the psalmist gives why God should answer.

Note. Verses 4, 9. 'Our signs': *i.e.*, the outward signs of the worship of God had been replaced by heathen 'signs' set up by their enemies.

☐ STUDY 59 Psalms 75 and 76

Ps. 76 celebrates the deliverance of Jerusalem from the Assyrians in the reign of Hezekiah. Though we cannot say that Ps. 75 belongs to this same historical situation, its theme of thanksgiving to God is certainly relevant to the events of 701 BC.

1 In Ps. 75 what characteristics of God's judgment are mentioned? What is the psalmist's response?

2 Ps. 76 falls into four sections of three verses each. How would you summarize the contents of each section? What was God's purpose in acting in judgment?

3 How does the teaching of Christ illustrate Ps. 75: 4–7? *Cf.* Lk. 14: 7–11; Mt. 20: 20–28. Does your belief in such teaching control your ambition and your ideas about promotion?

Notes
1 75: 8. A picture of divine retribution; *cf.* Is. 51: 17; Rev. 14: 10.
2 76: 5, 6. A vivid picture of the enemy, silent and inactive in death.
3 76: 10. Even the violent acts of the wicked will be turned to God's praise.

☐ STUDY 60 Psalm 77

1 Observe in detail the depth of the psalmist's depression. What was the chief question underlying his distress? How did he find an answer to it?

2 What particular aspects of the character of God are mentioned in verses 11–20? How do these begin to resolve the psalmist's problem? Do we in times of depression similarly 'call to mind the deeds of the Lord' (*e.g.*, Rom. 5: 8)?

☐ STUDY 61 Psalm 78: 1–39

1 A nation's history may teach many different lessons. From verses 1–8 what do you consider this psalm's main purpose is? What light do these verses throw upon the necessity and importance of family religion? *Cf.* Dt. 6: 6–9, 20–25.

2 From verses 1–39 make a list of (a) God's saving acts for His people; (b) the nation's sins; (c) God's judgments. In particular, from verses 34–37, consider the difference between true and false repentance. *Cf.* Je. 29: 13. Is your life free from a similar monotonous cycle of relapses? How, according to verses 1–8, may we avoid such failure?

☐ STUDY 62 Psalm 78: 40–72

1 The detail of verses 43–51 sets the people's disobedience (verses 40–42) in bold relief. What other purpose do you think the verses had? *Cf.* Ps. 103: 2; 2 Pet. 1: 9, 12, 13.

2 What disasters did idolatry bring upon Israel? How did God in His grace come to their aid? Of what is such action a foreshadowing?

Notes

1 Verse 61. A reference to the capture of the ark; see 1 Sa. 4: 21.

2 Verses 67–69. The tent at Shiloh, in the territory of Ephraim, was not rebuilt (for the reason given in verses 58–60), but Zion was chosen instead, in the territory of Judah, as the place for God's sanctuary.

☐ STUDY 63 Psalms 79 and 80

These two psalms are national prayers in times of national disaster. In Jewish synagogue worship Ps. 79 was prescribed for use in commemoration of the destruction of the Temple in 586 BC and in AD 70. Try to recapture the sense of desolation which pervaded the nation (79: 1–4, 7, 11; 80: 12, 13), together with the feeling that exile brought dishonour to the Lord's name (79: 10; *cf.* Ezk. 36: 20).

1 Ps. 79. Note here the plea for vengeance, coupled with prayer for forgiveness and deliverance. *Cf.* Is. 35: 4; 59: 16–19; 63: 3, 4. The New Testament is no less concerned for God's glory, but its spirit is different. *Cf., e.g.,* Mk. 11: 25; Rom. 12: 19–21. How do you account for this difference?

2 Ps. 80. What do the Israelites here confess concerning God's attitude towards them and His treatment of them? Where does their only hope of salvation lie? What ought we to learn from this?

Notes

1 79: 3. 'There was none to bury them': a disgrace threatened in Dt. 28: 26; and repeatedly predicted by Jeremiah (7: 33; 8: 2; 9: 22).
2 80: 1, 2. The three tribes here mentioned camped west of the tabernacle in the wilderness, and immediately followed the ark when the people were on the march. See Nu. 2: 17–24.
3 80: 17. This verse points forward to the Messiah.

☐ STUDY 64 Psalms 81–83

1 Ps. 81. What does God here demand of His people (verses 1–4)? Of what does He remind them (verses 5–7, 10–12), and with what promises and practical challenge does He confront them (verses 8, 9, 13–16)?

2 Ps. 82 is a dramatic picture of the judgment and condemnation of divinely appointed judges who have failed to fulfil their office. What does God demand of such men (verses 2–4), and what is the effect upon society of their failure (verse 5)? In such circumstances, what hope is there of justice being done?

3 Ps. 83. A strong coalition of enemy nations is plotting against Israel to destroy it. On what grounds does the psalmist plead for God to act? What in particular does he ask of God, and to what end? Contrast this with the prayer of Acts 4: 29, 30. Is a prayer like the psalmist's still legitimate?

Notes

1 81: 7. 'The secret place of thunder': *i.e.,* from the midst of the thundercloud. *Cf.* Ex. 14: 10, 24.
2 82: 1, 6. From Jn. 10: 34, 35 it is clear that earthly judges are here referred to. They were called 'gods' and 'sons of the Most High' in virtue of their high office as dispersing the divine justice. *Cf.* Rom. 13: 3, 4.

☐ STUDY 65 Psalm 84

1 Verses 1–4. 'Blessed are those who dwell in thy house.' Consider the significance of the language which the psalmist uses. Note particularly the names he gives to God. What was the object of his deepest delight?

2 What characteristics of the pilgrim to Zion are mentioned in verses 5–9? Whence does he derive strength to continue his journey? What is the basis of his security? What self-discipline must he practise? What are his crowning rewards (verses 10–12)?

Notes

1 Verse 5b. The meaning seems to be 'those whose hearts are set on pilgrimage' (*i.e.*, to Zion).
2 Verse 6. 'The valley of Baca': some dry and barren valley where balsam trees (baca) grow, which the travellers approach with dread only to find that the God-given rain has transformed it.
3 Verse 7. Far from being wearied by their journey the pilgrims are also strengthened by the prospect of the vision of God in Zion.
4 Verse 9. A reference to the king, the Lord's anointed, *i.e.*, the Messiah.

☐ STUDY 66 Psalm 85

1 Verses 1–7. To what does the psalmist make appeal in his prayer, and for what does he pray? Note that his prayers are not for himself, but for God's people. Do you have any comparable conviction and concern?

2 Verses 8–13. In His answer, what blessings does God promise, and to whom? What is the guarantee of fulfilment?

Notes

1 Verse 8b. The mg. suggests that there is here an abrupt warning to God's pious ones not to 'turn back to folly'. For what is meant by 'folly', see Ps. 14: 1; Rom. 1: 21, 22.
2 Verse 9b. The 'glory' is that of the revealed presence of God. *Cf.* Ex. 40: 34; Zc. 2: 5.

☐ STUDY 67 Psalms 86 and 87

1 Ps. 86. List (a) the psalmist's petitions, and (b) the reasons for his confidence that his prayer will be heard. Note especially in verses 8–13 the concentration of his thought on God in worship and thanksgiving. Can you pray verse 11, and mean it?

2 Ps. 87 is a kind of prophetic expansion of Ps. 86: 9. Zion is seen as the city of God's special choice and sovereign purpose. Individuals from the nations that were Israel's enemies are to become citizens of Zion. Are you one? What is the significance of the birth register,

and of being 'born there'? *Cf.* Jn. 3: 3, 5; Heb. 12: 22–24; Rev. 21: 27.

Notes

1 86: 2. 'I am godly': the adjective speaks of devotion to God, and loyalty to His covenant.

2 86: 11. 'Unite my heart to fear thy name': *cf.* Dt. 6: 4, 5; Je. 32: 39. The psalmist desires in singleness of heart and harmony of purpose to be wholly and exclusively devoted to God's worship and service.

3 87: 7. The city resounds with joy, each worshipper declaring that the one source of all his blessings is Zion and Zion's Lord.

☐ STUDY 68 Psalm 88

In some respects this psalm depicts the sufferings of the Jewish nation in exile. The Christian may find in it a picture of the sufferings of Christ. But the language of the psalm is universal, and no one specific application exhausts it; hence its continuing relevance.

1 Summarize the main features of the sufferer's distress. The sufferer cleaves to God most passionately when God seems to have removed Himself most completely. How do you account for the persistence of his faith? *Cf.* Is. 50: 10; Hab. 3: 17, 18.

2 Verses 4–6, 10–12. With the psalmist's view of death and its sequel, *cf.* Ps. 6: 5; 30: 9; Is. 38: 18. Contrast it with that of the Christian and note whence light and hope come. See 2 Tim. 1: 10; Heb. 2: 14, 15; 1 Cor. 15: 17, 18, 51–57.

☐ STUDY 69 Psalm 89: 1–37

This psalm vividly depicts the conflict of faith. In the first part (verses 1–37) the psalmist praises the Lord, who is reverenced in heaven and on earth, as the Victor over chaos, and the covenant God and Father of Israel's king and people. In the second part (verses 38–52), however, it is clear that the king has suffered a serious military reverse.

1 Verses 5–18 expand verses 1 and 2. What attributes of God are extolled? How is the blessedness of God's people described?

2 Verses 19–37 expand verses 3 and 4 concerning God's covenant. Ponder the scope, the conditions and the generosity of God's promises.

Notes

1 Verse 3. The original occasion is described in 2 Sa. 7, recalled in 2 Sa. 23: 5, and celebrated in Ps. 132: 11ff.

2 In verses 9–14 the pronouns 'thou' and 'thine' are emphatic.

3 Verse 10. Rahab was originally used to refer to the forces of chaos subdued at creation (*cf.* Jb. 26: 12). But here in Is. 51: 9 (*cf.* Ps. 74: 12ff.) the imagery is used to refer to the exodus from Egypt, when God's mighty power was shown in redemption.

□ STUDY 70 Psalm 89: 38–52

1 Notice the repeated 'thou' in verses 38–46. It is the same God of steadfast love, faithfulness and power, extolled in the earlier part of the psalm, who has brought about the downfall of the king and the desolation of the land. This constitutes the psalmist's dilemma. What bold requests for God's speedy action does he make (verses 46–51), and on what does he base them?

2 What may we learn from the psalmist's example when circumstances seem to call God's character and promises into question? How does faith survive in such situations? *Cf.* Gn. 18: 25; Rom. 11: 29, 33; Phil. 1: 6.

Note. Verse 52 is a doxology to close Book III of the Psalms.

For Studies 71–84 on the Psalms see p. 409.

EZEKIEL 33–48

Introductory Note to Chapters 33–39

These chapters all belong to the second period of the prophet's ministry after the fall of Jerusalem (see Introduction and Analysis). The only mention of a date is 33: 21, but the prophecies all presuppose that God's judgment upon the guilty city and nation, long predicted, has come to pass.

□ STUDY 22 Ezekiel 33

The prophet had known from the first that part of his commission was to be a watchman (*cf.* 3: 16–21), but now the time had come to put it into practice; for in the new era that was dawning, only those who individually repented and returned to God would live.

1 In what terms does Ezekiel express the need for repentance? What kind of behaviour is expected of the wicked man when he repents? *Cf.* Acts 26: 20; Rev. 2: 5.

2 Compare the two current sayings quoted in verses 10 and 24. Observe *where* they were current, and how the one is despairing, the other confident. What is God's answer in each case?

3 Why did the prophet suddenly become more bold to speak, and the people more curious to hear his words? See verses 30–33. What, however, was lacking in their new interest? *Cf.* Mt. 7: 26, 27.

☐ STUDY 23 Ezekiel 34

The new era will be different from what has gone before, because of a change of shepherd, *i.e.*, ruler.

1 What, according to verses 1–10, was the inherent vice of the rulers of the past, which brought disaster upon the nation? Contrast their methods (verses 4–6) with those of God (verses 11–16). *Cf.* 1 Pet. 5: 1–4.

2 What blessings are declared in verses 23–31 as following the coming of the Messiah? Interpreting them spiritually, what may we learn from these verses concerning God's gifts to us in Christ? *Cf.* Ps. 23; Heb. 13: 20, 21.

☐ STUDY 24 Ezekiel 35: 1 – 36: 15

In this section the prophet declares that the new era will be better than the past, because of the greater fertility of the land. When he uttered this prophecy, the land of Israel seemed ruined. Edom (Mount Seir) was seeking to obtain possession (35: 10; 36: 5), and the mountains of Israel lay desolate (36: 4). The prophet declares, first a judgment upon Edom (chapter 35), and then a return of Israel to enjoy times of unprecedented prosperity (36: 1–15).

1 Chapter 35. What are the three sins of Edom, mentioned in verses 5 and 10, for which they will be judged? Notice how frequently the punishment foretold exactly matches the Edomites' sin, *e.g.*, verses 5 and 9; verse 6; verses 14, 15. How does Ezekiel show that even in their hour of judgment God still identifies Himself with His people, Israel?

2 Summarize the blessings promised to Israel in 36: 8–15. If you interpret the restored land as a picture of our inheritance in Christ, what spiritual blessings are typified in these verses?

☐ STUDY 25 Ezekiel 36: 16–38

1 Consider carefully in this remarkable passage the following points: (a) why the Lord cast the people into exile (verses 16–19); (b) why He brought them back (verses 20–24); (c) the change wrought in their moral and spiritual condition (verses 25–31). Reflect how closely the prophet's teaching here anticipates the New Testament revelation of the steps by which God transforms a sinner into a saint. See particularly Rom. 3, 5, 6 and 8.

2 How will the change in the people and their restored prosperity affect the surrounding nations? See verses 35, 36 and *cf.* Jn. 17: 21, 23.

Notes

1 Verse 20. 'They profaned my holy name': because the nations, seeing them cast out, concluded their God could not protect them. *Cf.* Ps. 42: 10.

2 Verse 26. 'Heart of stone': *cf.* 2: 4; 3: 7; Zc. 7: 12. 'A heart of flesh': *i.e.*, sensitive to the divine Word.

☐ STUDY 26 Ezekiel 37

1 Why were the people unable to believe Ezekiel's prophecies of restoration and blessing? See verse 11. Did the vision of verses 1–10 show that things were not so bad as or worse than they seemed? Yet what happened, and why?

2 Notice that the regeneration of Israel came in two stages (verses 7–10). What would this have signified to Ezekiel? What part did he have to play in the change that took place? Are the spiritually dead coming to life as a result of your witness and praying?

3 Verses 15–28 are a glorious picture of the purified, restored and reunited Israel. Note the five great features of the Messianic kingdom described in verses 24–27. What light does this passage throw upon the conditions and blessings of Christian unity?

☐ STUDY 27 Ezekiel 38

In this chapter and the next the prophet foresees in the far distant future an invasion of Israel by nations lying beyond the circle of those with which Israel hitherto has had to do. They, too, must learn that the God of Israel alone is God, and they will learn it through meeting His power as they seek to plunder His land, and through being brought by Him to total defeat. Read Rev. 20: 7–10 in conjunction with this chapter.

1 In what two different ways are the causes of Gog's invasion described? Contrast verses 4 and 16 with verses 10–12. And yet may not all these verses describe one and the same cause? *Cf.* Rom. 9: 17, 18.

2 *Cf.* verses 18–23 with 37: 25–28. In what two ways will God bring the nations to know that He is God alone? *Cf.* Rom. 1: 16–18; 9: 22, 23; 11: 17–22.

Notes

1 Verse 2. The name 'Gog' is probably Ezekiel's own invention, formed by removing the first letter from the place-name Magog. It is pointless to try to identify these nations with modern states: they were simply tribes on the fringe of the known world in Ezekiel's day which he uses for these apocalyptic pronouncements.

2 Verse 13. These are merchant nations, stirred to excitement by Gog's invasion.

☐ STUDY 28 Ezekiel 39

1 A further prophecy against Gog emphasizes the completeness of his overthrow. In what three ways is this brought out in verses 9–20, and what attributes of God's character are thereby revealed (verses 21–29)?

2 What is meant by the expression 'I hid my face from them' (verse 23)? *Cf.* Dt. 31: 17; Pss. 30: 7; 104: 29; Is. 8: 17; 64: 7. Consider the great blessing that is contained in the promise of verse 29.

Introductory Note to Chapters 40–48

These chapters describe a vision given to Ezekiel some twelve years after the prophecies of chapters 33–37 (*cf.* 40: 1 with 33: 21). In these earlier prophecies he had declared to the exiles in Babylon God's purpose to restore Israel to the holy land as a nation purified, redeemed and re-united. The question must have been much in the prophet's mind how this restored community would be fashioned in its religious and political life; and in these chapters God gives to the prophet the answer to his questionings. There is first a description of the sanctuary, to which Jehovah will come in glory, and in which He will take up His dwelling (40–43); second, regulations with regard to the ministers of the sanctuary, and to the 'prince' who shall rule over the people; and third, the boundaries of the land are defined, and the territories of the tribes.

The question is sometimes asked whether the vision will be literally fulfilled. Why, however, should we suppose this, any more than that the vision of chapter 1 is a literal portrait of the divine Being? It is true that the prophets generally associate great changes in nature with the advent of 'the day of the Lord', and this is affirmed also in the New Testament (see, *e.g.*, Rom. 8: 21), but this is not to say that the vision which Ezekiel saw will find literal

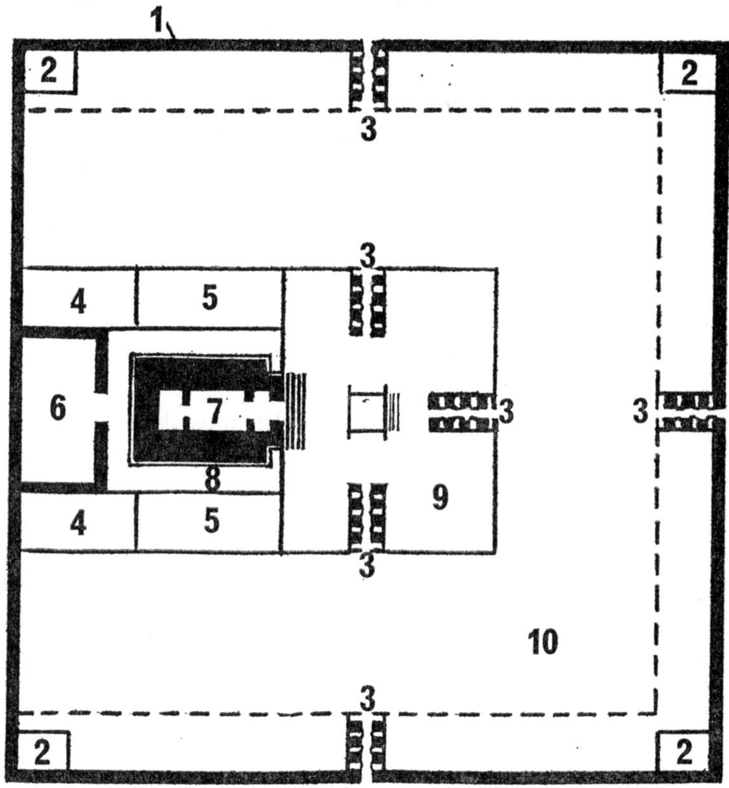

1 Surrounding wall
2 Kitchens
3 Gatehouses (see also diagram 3
4 Priests' kitchens
5 Priests' chambers
6 Building mentioned in 41: 12
7 Sanctuary (see also diagram 2)
8 Temple yard (see 41: 12–14)
9 Inner court
10 Outer court

DIAGRAM 1 Sketch Plan of the Temple Area

fulfilment. It is rather a setting forth, within the limits of Old Testament symbolism, of fundamental principles concerning God's relation to His redeemed and sanctified people when He dwells in their midst in His glory.

☐ STUDY 29 Ezekiel 40: 1–47

Having been cast into a trance and brought in spirit to the holy land, Ezekiel saw on the top of a high mountain what at first he thought to be a city but was in fact the Temple, with its courts and buildings. It was, however, a new Temple. While the sanctuary itself was similar to that of Solomon's Temple, the surroundings were very different. The prophet was met by a heavenly messenger, who had a measuring-tape of flax and a measuring-rod, and who acted as his guide.

1 What two responsibilities did the heavenly messenger place upon the prophet? See verse 4. When judged by these standards, how far is your own Bible study a success?

2 With the aid of diagram 1, follow the prophet's route as he was shown the outer gateway on the east (verses 6–16), the outer court (verses 17–19), and the gateways on the north and south (verses 20–27); then the inner court on a higher level, also with three gateways (verses 28–37). In the inner court, alongside the north gate, were a chamber and tables (verses 38–43), and there were two chambers for the priests, one near the north gate and another near the south gate (verses 44–47).

3 Note the symmetry of the ground plan of the Temple. Has this anything to teach us about God?

Notes

1 Verse 5. Two cubits were in use, one being eighteen inches long and the other twenty-one inches—a 'handbreadth' extra. The longer cubit was that used by Ezekiel. The measuring-reed would therefore have been 10 ft. 6 in.
2 Verse 12. 'A barrier': *i.e.*, a projecting wall.

☐ STUDY 30 Ezekiel 40: 48 – 41: 26

1 Follow with the aid of diagrams 1 and 2 the prophet's further examination of the Temple, as he comes first to the sanctuary itself, with its vestibule and two pillars (40: 48, 49), holy place ('nave', 41: 1), most holy place ('inner room', 41: 3, 4), and side chambers or cells built in three storeys (41: 5–11). The *interior* of the sanctuary is described in 41: 15b–26.

2 Note that Ezekiel, as a priest (1: 3; *cf.* 44: 16), entered into the

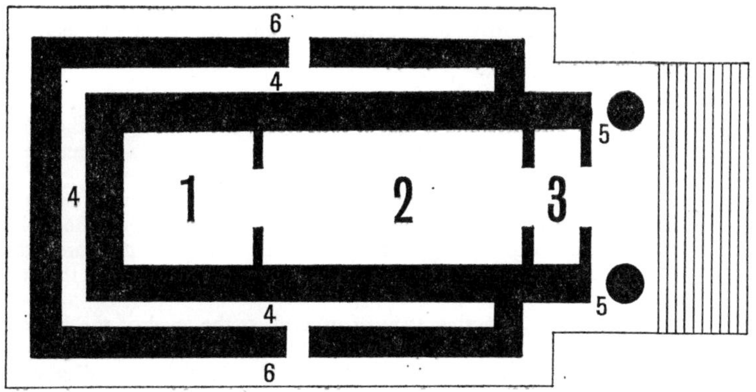

1 Most holy place
2 Holy place
3 Vestibule
4 Cells or side chambers (see 41: 5–11)
5 The pillars (see 40: 49)
6 The marginal area of the temple platform described in 41: 11

DIAGRAM 2 Sketch Plan of the Sanctuary

vestibule and the holy place, but not into the most holy place (41: 3, 4). Why did he not enter the most holy place? Contrast our privileges in Christ. See Heb. 9: 6–9, 24; 10: 19–22.

3 There were palm-trees both in the inner sanctuary (41: 18–20), and also on the gate-posts of the outer and inner courts (40: 16, 22, 31). So also in Solomon's Temple (see Ki. 6: 29; 7: 36). Applying this to the temple of our lives, what does it suggest both as to the hidden life of communion with God, and the outer life seen by all? *Cf.* Ps. 92: 12–14; Je. 17: 7, 8.

Notes

1 Verse 7. The meaning is that at each storey the walls facing the cells were made less thick, to leave a ledge for the beams to rest on, and thus the rooms on each floor were a little broader than the rooms below.

2 Verse 11b. The sanctuary stood upon a raised platform six cubits higher than the level of the inner court (verse 8), and occupied the whole platform except for a marginal strip running round three sides on the outer edge (see diagram 2). This narrow strip is what is here called 'the part that was left free'.

3 Verses 12–14. Another strip of ground, at the level of the inner court, encompassed the sanctuary platform, and is here called 'the temple yard'. It marked off the sanctuary from other buildings nearby (see diagram 1, 8). One of these buildings, on the west side, is mentioned in verse 12 (see diagram 1, 6), but its use is not specified. Other buildings are mentioned in 42: 1–14; 46: 19, 20.

4 Verse 22. The table here spoken of, which looked like an altar of wood, was probably the table of shewbread.

☐ STUDY 31 Ezekiel 42: 1 – 43: 12

This section opens with a description of other buildings in the inner court (42: 1–12), together with the purposes they are intended to serve (42: 13, 14). See diagram 1. The measurements of the outer wall, and of the whole Temple area are then stated (42: 15–20). In 43: 1–9 the prophet sees in a vision the glory of the Lord returning by the east gate, the gate by which, years before, he had seen Him depart (11: 1, 22, 23).

1 Observe the emphasis on the *holiness* of God. See especially 42: 13, 14; 43: 7–9, 11, 12. How was the holiness of the Temple to be safeguarded, in order to bear witness to this truth about the Lord?

2 How, for us, have the barriers been removed that separate us from the Holy One? And on what conditions may we draw nigh to God and render His acceptable service? *Cf.* 2 Cor. 1: 1; Heb. 7: 24; 10: 14; 1 Pet. 2: 5.

Note. 43: 7–9. In Solomon's Temple there was no walled-off outer court separating the Temple from the unconsecrated ground without (*cf.* 42: 20). The Temple, royal palace and other buildings all stood together in one great enclosure, and the burial-ground of the kings was not far distant.

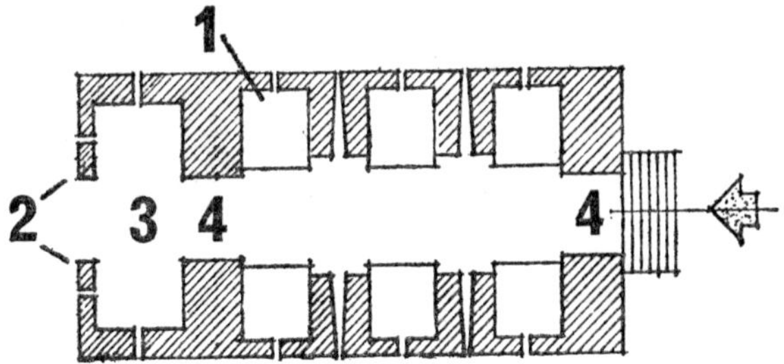

1 Side rooms (see 40: 7)
2 Side posts or jambs (see 40: 9, 16)
3 Vestibule
4 Thresholds

DIAGRAM 3 Sketch Plan of a Typical Gatehouse

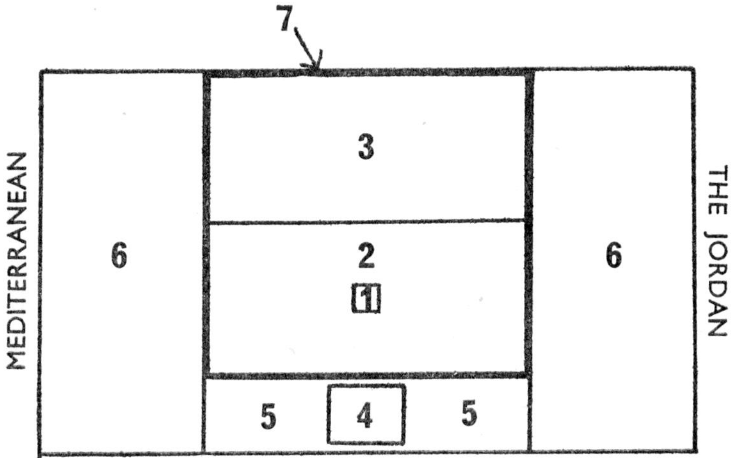

1 Sanctuary
2 Priests' territory
3 Levites' territory
4 City
5 City territory
6 Territory of the Prince
7 The Holy District

DIAGRAM 4

☐ STUDY 32 Ezekiel 43: 13 – 44: 31

This section opens with a description of the great altar in the centre of the inner court, together with the sacrifices by which it is to be cleansed and purified (43: 13–27). The altar rested upon a square base and was built of three square blocks of stone, each smaller than the one below, so as to leave at each level a projecting ledge. The uppermost block had four horns and was twelve cubits square. It was reached by steps on the east side. Chapter 44 lays down three ordinances, the first concerning the use of the east gate (verses 1–3), the second concerning the Levites (verses 4–14), and the third concerning the priests (verses 15–31).

1 Why had the altar to be cleansed before the offerings made upon it were acceptable to God? See 43: 27 and *cf.* Lv. 16: 18, 19; Col. 1: 19–22; Heb. 9: 23.

2 What lessons are taught in 44: 10–16 regarding God's judgments upon faithful and unfaithful service? *Cf.* Lk. 19: 17; 2 Cor. 5: 9, 10; 1 Tim. 1:12.

Notes

1 44: 7, 8. It had evidently been the custom before the exile to allow foreigners to officiate in the sanctuary and in its ministry, even though it may have been only in menial duties.

2 44: 19. They shall not bring their holy garments into contact with the people. *Cf.* Ex. 30: 29.

☐ STUDY 33 Ezekiel 45 and 46

Not only was the Temple different in many respects from that of Solomon, but the whole land was to be divided up in a new way. A broad strip of land, extending right across the country from the Mediterranean to the Jordan and including the Temple, was to be set apart for the Lord (45: 1–8). How it was to be used is shown in diagram 4. Verses 9–17 lay down regulations as regards weights and measures, and the dues to be paid by the people to the prince. The remainder is chiefly concerned with the feasts and offerings (45: 18 – 46: 15), but at the end are two notes, one about the right of the prince to bestow part of his territory upon his sons or servants (46: 16–18), and the other about rooms in the Temple courts to be used as kitchens for boiling the flesh of the sacrifices (46: 19–24).

1 How does 45: 8–12 show that the holiness which Jehovah requires is not only religious but moral? What light do these verses throw upon God's attitude to injustice and oppression, and to commercial dishonesty? *Cf.* 46: 18; Lv. 19: 35, 36; Pr. 11: 1; 1 Pet. 1: 14–16.

2 What is said three times in 45: 15–20 to be the purpose of the sacrifices? If they had not been offered, could the people have had any assurance in drawing nigh to God? What in the New Testament is revealed as the true ground of atonement? *Cf.* Heb. 10: 4–10; 1 Jn. 2: 1, 2.

Notes

1 45: 1. The holy district consisted of the area marked on diagram 4. 25,000 cubits was about eight miles.

2 45: 10–12. There was a vast amount of local variation in ancient Israel regarding weights and measures, and this was the cause of much commercial malpractice. Ezekiel is here demanding in God's name strict standardization.

3 46: 19 defines the positions of the priests' kitchens, as verses 21–24 do the position of the people's kitchens. See diagram 1.

☐ STUDY 34 Ezekiel 47: 1–12

The prophet is shown another aspect of what it means when God dwells in the midst of His redeemed and reconciled people.

1 Notice particularly where the river comes from. What may those who seek reform, whether it be social, political, or moral, learn from the revelation here given to Ezekiel? *Cf.* Ps. 46: 4; Is. 33: 21; Rev. 22: 1, 2.

2 What is symbolized by the increasing depth and extent of the waters? How long is it since you first came to Christ, and became a temple for His indwelling? Are the living waters flowing from your life in increasing measure? If not, what is wrong? *Cf.* Jn. 7: 37–39.

3 The river of life sought out the most desolate and seemingly irrecoverable region in all the land, and brought life and healing. Recall how this was also Christ's method. *Cf.* Mk. 2: 16, 17; Lk. 15: 1, 2; 19: 10; 23: 42, 43. What have these things to say to us?

Notes

1 Verse 1. The waters flowed from the sanctuary across the inner court, south of the altar, and appeared on the right-hand side of the outer east gate.

2 Verse 8. 'The sea': *i.e.*, the Dead Sea, in which nothing can live.

3 Verse 12. *Cf.* Ps. 1: 3; Je. 17: 8; Rev. 22: 2.

☐ STUDY 35 Ezekiel 47: 13 – 48: 35

Finally the prophet is shown in vision the boundaries of the land (47: 13–21) and the portions of the tribes (48: 1–29). The land was to be divided into parallel zones, running from the west coast to the Jordan.

1 What gospel principle is foreshadowed in 47: 22, 23? *Cf.* Eph. 2: 11–13, 19; Col. 3: 11.

2 How many tribes had their portion north of the broad zone assigned to the Lord in 45: 1 (see diagram 4, p. 393), and how many south of it? Which tribes had portions immediately adjacent to the central zone containing the sanctuary? What do you think was the reason for this privilege?

3 What does the new name of the city reveal about God's purpose in relation to His people? Looking back upon the vision as a whole, write down the main lessons which it teaches, and consider how these stand out still more clearly in the light of the revelation given us in Christ.

COLOSSIANS

Introduction

Colossae was one of a group of three cities (of which the other two were Laodicea and Hierapolis; *cf.* Col. 4: 13), situated in the Lycus valley about a hundred miles inland from Ephesus. Paul had not visited these cities himself (2: 1), but was given a full account of the situation at Colossae by Epaphras, who had founded these churches (1: 7; 2: 5; 4:12, 13).

While there was cause for thanksgiving (1: 3–5; 2: 5), yet there was ground also for deep concern because of the dissemination of a plausible false teaching, which, dressed in the garb of an enlightened philosophy (2: 8), claimed to be a higher form of Christianity. Would they have full emancipation from evil? Then they must observe circumcision and practise a strict discipline. Would they have access to the divine presence? Then they must worship angelic beings, by whose mediation they might draw nearer to the throne of God. No doubt these teachers gave Jesus a high place, but it was not the supreme place.

Paul's answer is to set forth Christ Jesus as pre-eminent in every sphere, and as all-sufficient for the believer's need. This is the main theme of the letter, which stands out among all Paul's Epistles for the fullness of its revelation about the Person and work of Christ. It contains also in brief compass a wealth of practical instruction for Christian living.

Analysis

1: 1–8	Greeting and thanksgiving.
1: 9–14	Petition.
1: 15–20	The pre-eminence of the Son of God.
1: 21–23	The Colossians share in the blessings of the gospel.
1: 24 – 2: 7	Paul's part in God's plan.
2: 8–23	Answer to the Colossian heresy: the all-sufficiency of Christ as Saviour.
3: 1 – 4: 6	A new pattern of life.
	3: 1–17 Practical implications of participation in Christ.
	3: 18 – 4: 1 Acting rightly in household relationships.
	4: 2–6 Prayer and witness.
4: 7–18	Personal references, greetings, *etc.*

□ STUDY 1 Colossians 1: 1–14

1 Of what blessings which God has made ours in Christ does the gospel speak? What results did this gospel produce in the experience of the Colossians who heard it? Have I made as much progress as they had?

2 In his prayer for the Colossians, for what further progress in the things of Christ does the apostle ask? Carefully note the items in Paul's prayer. In which of these directions do I most desire or need myself to make progress?

□ STUDY 2 Colossians 1: 15–23

1 What is revealed in verses 15–20 concerning our Lord's relation to God, to creation, and to the church? What practical effects should this revelation have on our Christian faith and life?

2 Verses 21–23. From what condition, at what cost, and with what goal in view has Christ rescued us? What is required of those who desire fully to enjoy these benefits?

□ STUDY 3 Colossians 1: 24 – 2: 7

1 In 1: 24–29 what does Paul say about (a) his sufferings (*cf.* Acts 9: 15, 16); (b) his commission; (c) his theme; and (d) the method, aim and inspiration of his ministry?

2 2: 1–7. What is essential if Christians are to stand firm in the faith and not be misled? How may they gain encouragement to continue and become more fully established? Do you (a) covet such progress for yourself; (b) pray like this for others?

Notes

1 1: 28. The false teaching suggested that full participation in knowledge and consequent maturity was restricted to a select few. The gospel makes it possible 'in Christ' for all alike—for 'every man'.

2 1: 29; 2: 1. 'Striving': a metaphor from the Greek games, a word used again in 4: 12. It describes here earnest conflict, straining every nerve, in prayer.

☐ STUDY 4 Colossians 2: 8–23

1 What four defects does Paul find in the false teaching (verse 8)? In what ways does he then set forth Christ as the one absolutely sufficient Saviour (verses 9–15)? List the treasures and the benefits which are ours in Him.

2 Verses 16–23. It is quite clear that the false teachers stressed (a) the observance of holy days, (b) the worship of angels, and (c) ascetic practices. On what grounds does the apostle show all these to be mistaken, useless and hurtful as a means of salvation?

3 Verses 11–15. How is the way in which Christians have been 'circumcised' distinguished from the rite practised by the Jews? By what ceremony has Jewish circumcision been replaced for Christians? How is its symbolism related to the death and resurrection of Christ? *Cf.* Rom. 6: 1–14.

Note. Verses 11, 12. 'By putting off the body of flesh': the false teachers advocated the rite of circumcision as a means of purification. Paul's answer is that in the believer's identification with Christ in His death and resurrection the whole body which has been governed by fleshly desires is put off, and a new man emerges. This far more than fulfils all that the rite of circumcision signified.

☐ STUDY 5 Colossians 3: 1–17

1 Verses 1–11. What results, (a) positive and (b) negative, should follow from being 'raised with Christ'; in other words, what should the experience make us (a) do, and (b) stop doing?

2 Verses 12–17. Make a list from these verses of the divinely-intended characteristics of active Christian living; and prayerfully examine your own living in the light of these standards.

☐ STUDY 6 Colossians 3: 18 – 4: 18

1 3: 18 – 4: 1. Observe how, in giving directions about the life of a Christian household, Paul urges 'upon each party its own duties and the other's rights'. What overriding concerns should influence all alike, and why?

2 4: 2–6. List the activities here demanded as essential (a) to prayer, and (b) to our relations with non-Christians. In my own practice of Christian self-discipline, to which of these points do I need to give more attention? Can I learn from verses 3, 4, 12 how to pray for others?

Note. 3: 21. 'Provoke': by excessive fault-finding and little or no praise.

PHILEMON

Introduction

The Epistle to Philemon contains no systematic presentation of doctrine. It has one avowed purpose—to ask Philemon to receive back a runaway slave who had been in his service and had absconded with his money. The man had come into contact with Paul in Rome and had been converted and transformed into a new man. It was not easy for Paul to let him go; it was harder still for Onesimus to face his former master. But it was hardest of all for Philemon to take him back. These men were Christians, however, and that made all the difference. The letter is one of great charm, tact, graciousness and love, and provides an unforgettable picture of Christianity in action. Though no place-names are mentioned, it is clear that the letter was written at the same time as that to the Colossians.

☐ **STUDY Philemon**

1 What light does this letter throw upon Paul himself? Is he puttins into practice Col. 3: 12–14? Consider closely the a ppeal he make and the arguments by which he reinforces it.

2 What had happened to Onesimus (whose name means 'useful' or 'profitable') to make him start living up to his name? Has acceptance of the Christian faith made us useful (a) to the person who led us to Christ; (b) to those who are our employers, or in a comparable position?

EZRA & NEHEMIAH

Introduction

The books of Ezra and Nehemiah continue the history of the Israelites from the point reached at the end of 2 Chronicles. The two books are closely linked together and cover between them a space of about one hundred years, from the first year of the reign of Cyrus, king of Persia (538 BC), to soon after the thirty-second year of Artaxerxes (432 BC). Other books of Scripture belonging to this period are Haggai, Zechariah, Malachi and Esther.

The events recorded in the books of Ezra and Nehemiah gather round three periods, as follows:

First Period (Ezr. 1–6), from the first return of exiles under Zerubbabel (or Sheshbazzar) and Jeshua the high priest (536 BC) to the completion of the Temple (515 BC). It is to be noted that, though these events are recorded in the book of Ezra, they occurred more than sixty years before Ezra himself appeared on the scene.

Second Period (Ezr. 7–10), describing the return of a second large company of exiles under Ezra, with some account of Ezra's ministry in Jerusalem (458 BC).

Third Period (Ne. 1–13), describing the arrival of Nehemiah as governor (444 BC), and his building of the city walls, together with his joint activity with Ezra.

Ezra and Nehemiah were men raised up of God to render invaluable service at a critical time in Israel's history. Ezra was a priest of the house of Aaron, a man of outstanding piety, a diligent student and capable teacher of the law of God, and a zealous reformer. Nehemiah was a public servant and a true patriot, who devoted himself to the improvement of the moral and material condition of his country. He combined watchfulness with prayerfulness, and energetic activity with conscious dependence upon God. While both men rendered notable service, the work of Ezra was the more enduring, for he gave to the law of God a place of supreme authority in the life of the people.

Analysis Ezra

1:1 – 2:70	The return of exiles to Jerusalem to rebuild the Temple.
3:1–13	The altar erected, and the Temple foundations laid.
4:1–24	The work opposed, and made to cease.
5:1–17	The resumption of the work, promoted by the prophets Haggai and Zechariah.
6:1–22	The completion of the Temple.
7:1 – 8:36	After an interval of nearly sixty years, Ezra's journey to Jerusalem in 458 BC.
9:1 – 10:44	Reformation, including expulsion of foreign wives, promoted by Ezra.

☐ STUDY 1 Ezra 1 and 2

1 First, what definite acts of God can be seen in bringing about this return to Jerusalem? With 1:1, *cf.* Je. 29:10. Then fill in the outline given here, by trying to imagine the feelings and actions of the people concerned. Note, *e.g.*, 1:5, 6; 1:7–11; the links with specific 'home towns' and positions; the claims in 2:59–63; the scene in 2:64–67; the generosity and contentment of 2:68–70.

2 In the light of these two chapters meditate on Jos. 23:14.

☐ STUDY 2 Ezra 3

1 As background to verses 1–6, see Lv. 23:23–43. What were the motives and purposes in the hearts of the returned exiles at this time?

2 In what further ways was the Lord put central in this settling-down period? Consider what challenge this study presents to you personally.

☐ STUDY 3 Ezra 4

1 Is not co-operation with others in work for God most desirable? Why then did the Jews refuse to co-operate with those who claimed to share their faith and who offered to help them to achieve their great spiritual objective? *Cf.* 2 Ki. 17: 24, 32, 33. See also Mt. 7: 15; and contrast 3 Jn. 8 with 2 Jn. 11.

2 What was the reaction of the frustrated adversaries? *Cf.* Am. 7: 10; Lk. 23: 2; Acts 17: 7 for similar incidents. What price did Zerubbabel and his fellow-Jews have to pay for their faithfulness? Do you know of any modern parallels? Note Eph. 6: 18–20.

Notes

1 Verses 1–3. 'The proposal to unite in building the temple was a political move; for in old-world ideas, co-operation in temple-building was incorporation in national unity. The calculation, no doubt, was that if the returning exiles could be united with the much more numerous Samaritans, they would soon be absorbed in them' (Maclaren).

2 Verse 5. 'Until the reign of Darius': *cf.* verse 24. It was a period of about sixteen years.

3 Verses 6–24. Ahasuerus and Artaxerxes are kings who succeeded Darius (*cf.* 7: 1). This indicates that these verses refer to a later period than do verses 1–5, and this is confirmed by the fact that the letters of verses 11–16 and 17–22 concern the rebuilding of the *city* of Jerusalem, not of the Temple. Some think the passage belongs chronologically to the time between Ezr. 10 and Ne. 1.

☐ STUDY 4 Ezra 5 and 6

1 When the work of rebuilding the Temple had ceased for many years (4: 24), by what various means did God cause it to begin again and bring about the fulfilment of His purpose? How does dedication strengthen faith and give guidance for prayer? *Cf.* Gn. 50: 20; Pr. 21: 1; Hg. 1: 14; 1 Tim. 2: 2.

2 Note the joy, dedication and worship when the task was completed (6: 16–22). *Cf.* Jn. 17: 4; Acts 14: 26; 20: 24; Col. 4: 17; 2 Tim. 4: 7; Rev. 3: 2.

☐ STUDY 5 Ezra 7

This chapter begins the second period covered by this book (see Introduction). Some sixty years have elapsed since the end of chapter 6.

1 What do we learn about Ezra from this chapter? Note particularly the order of the aims in verse 10, and consider the evidence which shows that he accomplished these aims. Have you any similar aims?

2 What called forth the doxology in verses 27 and 28? *Cf.* 2 Cor. 3: 5.

☐ STUDY 6 Ezra 8

1 How many males, all told, were with Ezra? These, with women and children (verse 21), would make a large company. They had also their goods and provision for the way, many precious vessels and much silver and gold. The journey was long (7: 9) and dangerous (8: 31). Would it have been wrong for Ezra to ask the king for an escort? *Cf.* Ne. 2: 9. Why did he not do so? Are we as careful as he to live out what we profess?

2 From Ezra's actions before setting out, what may we learn regarding undertaking work for God? See especially verses 15–20, 21–23, 24–30, 33–35, 36; and contrast Jos. 9: 14; Is. 31 : 1 ; Je. 48: 10a; Mt. 25: 3.

☐ STUDY 7 Ezra 9 and 10

1 For the background to this incident see Dt. 7: 1–4. In what ways had the people of God sinned? In what ways is it possible for Christians to commit similar sin today?

2 What can we learn from this chapter about (a) the responsibilities of leadership; (b) prayer and confession; (c) God's faithfulness; (d) the cost of repenting?

Analysis Nehemiah

1: 1–11	The distress of the Jews in Jerusalem. Nehemiah's prayer.
2: 1–10	Artaxerxes sends Nehemiah to Jerusalem.
2: 11–20	Nehemiah stirs up the people to rebuild the walls of Jerusalem.
3: 1–32	The apportionment of the work. List of helpers.
4: 1 – 6: 14	The work continued in spite of opposition and difficulties. Nehemiah's vigorous and exemplary leadership.

6:15–7:4	The completion of the walls. Provision for the protection of the city.
7:5–73	Register of those who returned with Zerubbabel.
8:1–18	Public reading and exposition of the law. Celebration of the Feast of Tabernacles.
9:1–38	Corporate repentance and confession.
10:1–39	A covenant to walk in God's law, publicly signed and sealed.
11:1–12:26	Lists of those who dwelt in Jerusalem.
12:27–47	Dedication of the city walls. Provision for the regular Temple services.
13:1–31	Separation from other nations. Reforms carried out by Nehemiah on the occasion of his second visit to Jerusalem.

☐ STUDY 1 Nehemiah 1

1 How long did Nehemiah brood over the news about Jerusalem before he took action (see Note 1 below)? Note the sequence of events—one which is often seen when God calls His servants to a particular task.

2 What can we learn from the example of Nehemiah's prayer? Note his attitude, his knowledge of the Scriptures, his grounds for expecting prayer to be answered. Dt. 7; 9–12; 29; 30 provide a background to the prayer.

Notes

1 Verse 1. The month Chislev corresponds to our November–December, and Nisan (2:1) to our March–April.

2 Verse 11. 'Cupbearer': a high official, who had the duty of tasting wine before it was handed to the king, lest it should have been poisoned.

☐ STUDY 2 Nehemiah 2

1 What is the order of events following Nehemiah's prayer? What difficulty did he have to face at each stage?

2 What light does the chapter throw on Nehemiah's secret communion with God? On what grounds was he confident that God would prosper him in his work? Are such communion and confidence lacking in your life?

Notes

1 Verse 3. Nehemiah had probably broken court etiquette in letting his grief be seen in the king's presence.

2 Verse 10. 'Sanballat': an important official, probably governor of Samaria. Tobiah may have been his secretary.

☐ STUDY 3 Nehemiah 3

1 Contrast the busy scenes of this chapter with the picture of the walls and gates lying desolate, broken and burned, in 2: 13, 14. What brought about the change? (Examine, if possible, a plan of the city at this time.)

2 Note how all classes in the city took part in the work, each being assigned his special place and task. What may we learn from this chapter of the value of (a) thorough organization, and (b) willing co-operation on the part of all?

Notes

1 Verse 5. The word 'Lord' should probably be 'lord', the reference being to Nehemiah. For the metaphor see Je. 27: 12.

2 The *Century Bible* divides the chapter as follows: verses 1–5, the north and north-west wall; verses 6–12, the west wall; verses 13, 14, the south wall and gates; verses 15–27, the south-east wall and gates; verses 28–32, the north-east wall.

☐ STUDY 4 Nehemiah 4

1 The successful progress of the work brought increasing opposition. Picture the characters concerned in the various scenes. What kinds of discouragement did Nehemiah meet, and how did he deal with each?

2 In verses 19–23 notice how Nehemiah shared in the hard work. Where did he plan to be if fighting broke out? What does this teach us about leadership?

☐ STUDY 5 Nehemiah 5

1 What social evil did Nehemiah put right (see verses 1–13)? And how did he do it?

2 What features of his conduct made Nehemiah an excellent governor? Are we developing similar characteristics?

3 What considerations ought to keep God's people from doing some things which others do as a matter of course? *Cf.* verse 15 and 1 Cor. 8: 13.

Note. Verses 1–5. The wealthier Jews were evidently demanding repayment at high interest of money lent by them to their poorer brethren, and were seizing the lands and property, and even the persons of the debtors whenever their demands were not met.

☐ STUDY 6 Nehemiah 6

1 Nehemiah's enemies now tried intrigue. The proposal to confer together is often an attractive one. What made Nehemiah persistently refuse it? Contrast Eve's folly in discussing the question raised by the serpent (Gn. 3: 1–5). Do you ever parley with questions that should never be allowed consideration?

2 What were the special subtleties of the attempts to ensnare Nehemiah? Notice how Nehemiah's singleness of purpose and loyalty to God were as a shield about him. What may we learn from this?

Note. Verse 5. 'An open letter': so that others besides Nehemiah might see its contents.

☐ STUDY 7 Nehemiah 7

1 What further steps did Nehemiah take in ensuring an orderly life in Jerusalem? Why was Hananiah put in charge of Jerusalem? Remembering that you may be called to responsibility in your work for God, what are you doing to develop these same qualities?

2 What makes a register of names so important? See verses 64, 65; and *cf.* Rev. 20: 15; 21: 27; Lk. 10: 20.

Notes
1 Verse 2. The 'he' refers to Hananiah. Possibly the appointment of two men in charge of the city means, as in 3: 9, 12, that each was ruler of half the district of Jerusalem.
2 Verses 64, 65; *cf.* Ezr. 2: 62, 63. The need was for a priest able to obtain guidance to decide whether these men were entitled to enjoy privileges as priests or not. For an example of the way in which Urim and Thummim were used, see 1 Sa. 14: 41.

☐ STUDY 8 Nehemiah 8

1 Chapters 8, 9 and 10 describe a remarkable revival. What was its first manifestation, and what further characteristics developed from this?

2 Consider how great a change of heart had taken place since before the exile. *Cf.* Je. 11: 6–8; 32: 36–40; Ne. 1: 5–11. How are these verses an illustration of Ps. 119: 71 and Heb. 12: 11?

Notes
1 Verse 10. 'Send portions . . .': *cf.* Dt. 16: 11, 14; Est. 9: 19–22.
2 Verse 17. The Feast of Tabernacles had been observed (see, *e.g.*, 2 Ch. 8: 13), but not, it seems, the making of booths.

☐ STUDY 9 Nehemiah 9: 1–21

1 What marks do you find here of a genuine repentance? *Cf.* 2 Cor. 7: 10, 11.

2 Meditate upon God's great kindness and many mercies, in spite of great provocation, as seen in this passage. How much cause have you for similar recollection, repentance and gratitude to God?

☐ STUDY 10 Nehemiah 9: 22–37

1 Analyse this summary (verses 6–37) of the history of God's people. What may we learn here about the heart of God, and the heart of man?

2 The Jews had learnt by bitter experience that disobedience brings penalty. Yet had God acted only in punishment? *Cf.* Ps. 130: 3, 4. What may we learn from this chapter about the principles of God's action towards His people when they sin? *Cf.* also Phil. 1: 6; 2 Jn. 8.

☐ STUDY 11 Nehemiah 9: 38 – 10: 39

1 Make a list of the seven specific ordinances included in the general covenant to walk in God's law (10: 29) and not neglect the house of God (10: 39).

2 What did the people agree (a) to give up, and (b) to give, that they might 'observe and do all the commandments of the Lord'? What does this teach us about the meaning of whole-hearted consecration? *Cf.* 2 Cor. 6: 14 – 7: 1; Pr. 3: 9, 10; Mal. 3: 10; 1 Cor. 16: 1, 2.

Notes

1 10: 29. 'Enter into a curse and an oath': *i.e.*, pledged themselves by an oath, invoking divine vengeance upon themselves, if they failed to observe it.

2 Verse 31b. *Cf.* Ex. 23: 10, 11; Dt. 15: 1–3.

3 Verses 35–39 give a general summary of such laws as Ex. 23: 19 and Nu. 18: 8–32.

☐ STUDY 12 Nehemiah 11

1 Though the Temple had been rebuilt and the city walls repaired, Jerusalem remained unattractive to dwell in (*cf.* 2: 3, 17), and the bulk of the people preferred to live in the country. By what two methods (verses 1, 2) were more inhabitants for the city secured? Are you willing to volunteer to serve in the place of greatest need? *Cf.* Is. 6: 8.

2 In verses 3–24 is given a list of those who dwelt in Jerusalem, in the following categories: (a) heads of families of the tribe of Judah (4–6); (b) of the tribe of Benjamin (7–9); (c) officials of the Temple—priests (10–14), Levites (15–19), other attendants, including singers (20–24). Try to picture the life of the city. Observe the prominence given to the house of God and its worship. Others helped in other ways, and some of them are described as 'valiant' or 'mighty men of valour' (literally 'men of strength and force'). Are you playing your part in the community to which you belong, helping it to become strong? *Cf.* Ec. 9:10a; 1 Cor. 15:58.

☐ STUDY 13 Nehemiah 12

1 How did the people celebrate the completion of the wall? See the further reminder in Lk. 17:15–18. As you read this passage, following in imagination the two companies as they marched in procession, remember Nehemiah's solitary journey as described in 2:12–15. Consider also how much you owe to God. *Cf.* 1 Cor. 15:10; Rom. 12:1.

2 'Nehemiah the governor' and 'Ezra the priest the scribe' (verse 26). Consider and contrast the office and character of these two great men, and how both alike were needed in this critical period of Jewish history. Have you discovered your gift and call of God or your variety of service for the common good? *Cf.* Rom. 11:29; 1 Cor. 12:4–7.

Note. Verse 30. 'Purified': by sprinkling the blood of sacrifices. *Cf.* Ezk. 43:19, 20.

☐ STUDY 14 Nehemiah 13

Nehemiah at some point in his governorship returned to King Artaxerxes, and later came again to Jerusalem (see verses 6 and 7), only to find that during his absence various abuses and backslidings had taken place.

1 Note in this chapter (a) five references to definite actions taken to deal with unsatisfactory features in the conduct and condition of the people; (b) the way in which Sanballat and Tobiah succeeded at last in gaining a footing in Jerusalem. What may we learn from these?

2 Have you the main sequence of events after the exile sorted out in your mind? In the light of 1 Cor. 10:11, what seem to you the main lessons to be learnt from this period in the history of God's chosen people?

PSALMS 90 - 106

☐ STUDY 71 Psalm 90

1 In verses 2–11 what is said about (a) man and (b) God? In view of these facts, what should be man's attitude (verses 11, 12)? What is meant by 'a heart of wisdom'? *Cf.* Pr. 9: 10; Je. 9: 23, 24; Jas. 4: 12–16.

2 Set down in your own words the petitions of verses 13–17. What convictions do they reveal concerning God's character and action? Can the petitions be transposed into a Christian key?

Note. Verse 11. It is only those who truly reverence the Lord who consider the reality of God's wrath against sin in all its intensity.

☐ STUDY 72 Psalm 91

The theme of this psalm is the security and blessedness of a life lived under God's protection. The change of pronouns has been variously explained. In verses 2 and 9a (see mg.) a solo voice declares its trust (in the first person singular), after which the choir respond with renewed assurances. Finally, in verses 14–16, God Himself speaks in words of gracious promise.

1 Life and health were insecure in ancient times. The world was haunted by unseen, malevolent powers. How does the psalmist's faith in God transform the situation? What comfort does the psalm bring to (a) the sufferer, and (b) one who anticipates suffering? *Cf.* the fuller statement in Rom. 8: 16–18, 28, 31, 35–37.

2 Verses 14–16. Note here seven gracious promises of God. Can you bear witness to their truth from your own experience and from the experience of other believers? *Cf.* 2 Pet. 1: 2–4.

Notes

1 The evils mentioned in verses 3, 5, 10, 13 refer to all kinds of adversity, insidious and hidden, or open and visible, explicable or inexplicable. Verse 13 refers not to Tarzan-like exploits, but to deliverance from dangers, natural and supernatural, not by magic (as in Egypt), but by faith.

2 Verse 14. 'I will protect': literally, 'I will set him inaccessibly high.'

☐ STUDY 73 Psalms 92 and 93

1 Ps. 92. The psalmist's eyes have been opened to discern the principles of God's working, which are hidden from those who have no spiritual understanding. What are these principles? How are both the emotions and the mind stirred?

2 Ps. 93. Might alone did not distinguish Israel's God from those of surrounding nations. What two unique features does this psalm mention? *Cf.* Ps. 90: 2c; Dt. 33: 27 and Ex. 15: 11b; Ps. 47: 8.

3 Consider the picture of the life of the godly, as described in 92: 12–14. What is the secret of their vigour and beauty? *Cf.* Ps. 1: 3; Je. 17: 7, 8; Is. 40: 29–31.

Notes

1 92: 1. 'To give thanks' means much more than 'to say "thank you"'. It involves public acknowledgment of God's grace by word, and probably with thank-offering.
2 92: 6. 'This' refers, as the colon shows, to the contents of verses 7 and 8.
3 92: 10. Horns symbolized power. *Cf.* Zc. 1: 18ff.; Ps. 75: 10. The figure is one of reinvigoration and reconsecration.
4 92: 12. 'Flourish': the same word as 'sprout' in verse 7.

☐ STUDY 74 Psalm 94

1 How does the psalmist find hope and comfort when oppressed by evil men? List carefully both the grounds and the content of his confidence.

2 What rebuke does the psalmist give to those in Israel who may have thought that evil men were right when they said (see verse 7) that God was indifferent to His people's need? What purpose does he see in the nation's present sufferings? See verses 8–15; *cf.* Pr. 3: 11, 12; Is. 49: 14–16.

Notes

1 Verses 1, 2. The fact that 'God of vengeance' is parallel to 'judge of the earth' shows that the former is not such an unpleasantly vindictive expression as the English might suggest. Both phrases indicate that God is concerned with the upholding of the moral order.
2 Verse 16. A court scene. 'Who is my counsel for the defence?' asks the psalmist. *Cf.* Rom. 8: 31, 33.

☐ STUDY 75 Psalms 95 and 96

These two psalms seem to have been associated with the new year festival. The renewal of the covenant was a special feature of this festival, and God was celebrated as Creator, King and Judge. Ps. 95 summons God's people to worship Him, a summons enforced by a grave warning against disobedience. Ps. 96 bids the whole creation join in worship of the Lord.

1 What is said in these two psalms to show that worship from all creation is the Lord's due? List the reasons why He ought to be worshipped. How should such worship find expression?

2 What special reasons are given in Ps. 95 why 'we' should worship God? Who constitute the 'we'? Of what danger are we warned to beware, and when, and why? *Cf.* Heb. 3: 7–15.

Notes

1 95: 3; 96: 4 (*cf.* 97: 9). The monotheism of the Old Testament is on the whole practical (*e.g.*, Ex. 20: 3) rather than theoretical. But 96: 5 expresses the logical conclusion of Old Testament as well as New Testament belief—that 'all the gods of the peoples are (literally) nothings'. *Cf.* 1 Cor. 8: 4–6.
2 95: 6. 'Our Maker': *i.e.*, the Maker of Israel as a nation—to be His people.

☐ STUDY 76 Psalms 97 and 98

1 Ps. 97. What aspects of the Lord's character are revealed here, and what are the several effects of this revelation? Do they characterize your reaction in the presence of God? *E.g.*, note verse 10a, mg.; *cf.* Rom. 12: 9.

2 Ps. 98. What acts of the Lord, past and future, cause the psalmist to praise Him? Does your worship begin and end with thoughts of God, and does it find similar vocal and audible expression? *Cf.* Eph. 5: 19, 20.

☐ STUDY 77 Psalms 99 and 100

1 Ps. 99. In what ways is the holiness or distinctive character of God here said to be demonstrated? What comfort and what warning can we take from the fact that God's holiness is not abstract but active? Do you share the psalmist's passion to see God publicly exalted in holiness? *Cf.* Rev. 15: 3, 4. Do you know what it means to call on His Name and to find that He answers (verses 6–8)?

2 Ps. 100. What does this psalm declare that we know about the Lord? And what should this knowledge make us do? In what spirit do you 'serve the Lord' (verse 2)?

Note. 99: 3. 'Terrible': *i.e.*, awe-inspiring. The same word is used in Dt. 10: 17; Ps. 76: 7, 12.

☐ STUDY 78 Psalm 101

Luther called this psalm 'David's mirror of a monarch'. Though the themes of the psalm are general, 2 Sa. 6: 9 may provide the clue to the historical situation—at the beginning of David's reign.

1 Verses 1–4. David could not sing to God without being aware that worship must have some effects upon his character and actions. Ponder the verbs of these verses. Is your Christian life as definite and decisive as this?

2 Verses 5–8. What company did David seek and shun? To what strenuous and sometimes violent action is the Christian similarly called? *Cf.* 2 Tim. 2: 14, 16, 19, 21–23.

☐ STUDY 79 Psalm 102

This psalm was probably written towards the close of the exile (see verse 13 and *cf.* Je. 29: 10; Dn. 9: 2). A description of the present distress (verses 1–11) is followed by a vision of a restored Zion (verses 12–22). The closing verses record the psalmist's assurance of the changeless character of God (verses 23–28).

1 What does this psalm teach us to do in time of trouble? See the title, and *cf.* Ps. 62: 8.

2 'For I . . . but thou' (verses 9, 12). Contrast with the extreme misery of verses 1–11 the vision of faith in verses 12–28. What has happened? Where is your gaze fixed—upon earth's sorrows, or upon God? *Cf.* 2 Cor. 4: 8, 9, 18.

Note. Verses 19, 20. *Cf.* Ex. 3: 7, 8. As then, so now.

☐ STUDY 80 Psalm 103

1 List the spiritual blessings mentioned in this psalm. Are you enjoying them yourself? Are you as mindful of their source, and as grateful to God, as the psalmist was?

2 What is emphasized by the mention of God's 'steadfast love' (verses 4, 8, 11, 17)? How is it demonstrated? What corresponding activity is demanded of those who would enjoy it? See verses 11, 13, 17, 18.

Notes

1 Verse 5. 'Like the eagle's': better, as in RV, 'like the eagle'. The meaning is 'made strong as an eagle'. *Cf.* Is. 40: 31.

2 Verses 11, 13, 17. The 'fear of the Lord' in the Bible does not refer to an abject, servile terror of the unknown or the terrifying. It is basically and consistently moral (see 20: 18–20), based on knowledge (see Pr. 9: 10), and means 'due reverence and awe'.

☐ STUDY 81 Psalm 104

This psalm has been described as a poetical version of Gn. 1. The two chapters may be compared with profit. Note the measure of agreement.

1 How is the dependence of the creature on the Creator brought out in verses 27–30? *Cf.* Ps. 145:15, 16; Gn. 1:29, 30. Ponder the beautiful picture of God which this affords. What ought it to make us do? *Cf.* Mt. 6:25–33.

2 Do we share the desires and resolves of the psalmist's heart, as expressed in verses 31–35?

Note. Verse 26. 'Leviathan' here refers to the sea monster. *Cf.* Gn. 1:21; Am. 9:3 for similar references.

☐ STUDY 82 Psalm 105

This psalm opens with a call to remember and recite the mighty deeds of the Lord. It is itself a historical retrospect, made, we may surmise from verse 45, with a view to encouraging obedience to the redeeming Lord. 'Remembering' was never a merely intellectual process in Israel's worship; it had a moral purpose.

1 Verses 1–5. List the imperatives used here. Think of appropriate times when you should obey them. *Cf.* Ps. 119:164. Might it be particularly helpful to turn to these verses and this psalm when depressed?

2 What reason is given in verses 7–10 and 42 for God's intervention on behalf of the Israelites? *Cf.* Lk. 1:72–74. For what similar reason do we know that He will not fail or forsake us? *Cf.* Heb. 13:5b, 6, 20, 21.

3 What may we learn from this psalm about the ways in which God protected, delivered, trained and provided for His chosen people? Will He do less for us? *Cf.* 1 Sa. 12:22.

Notes

1 Verse 2. 'Tell of': the meaning is 'meditate on'; but the Israelites seldom meditated silently.

2 Verse 28b. A difficult clause. The LXX omits 'not'; and this may be the original reading. Or the Hebrew (see mg.) may be a rhetorical question, 'Did they not rebel?'

☐ STUDY 83 Psalm 106:1–33

This section consists of a summons to praise the Lord, a prayer, and then (verses 7–33) a confession of seven instances of Israel's sin from the exodus to the entrance into Canaan.

1 What feature of Israel's failure is mentioned three times in these verses, and what were some of its consequences? *Cf.* Dt. 8:11–20.

2 Why did God, after delivering the Israelites, later overthrow them in the wilderness? Note the four things mentioned in verses 24, 25 which caused Him to change His attitude. With what awe and seriousness should the Christian take warning from this incident? *Cf.* Heb. 3:12, 17–19; 4:1.

3 The reference in verses 14, 15 is to Nu. 11 (see verses 4, 34). What inspired the Israelites' request, and what serious consequence followed? The New Testament indicates that we are involved in a war with fleshly lusts. How are we to fight them? *Cf.* 1 Cor. 10:6; 1 Pet. 2:11; Gal. 5:16.

☐ STUDY 84 Psalm 106: 34–48

The ending of this psalm, particularly verses 45–47, suggests that, whereas the function of Ps. 105 was to stimulate obedience, the purpose of the historical retrospect here, which, dismal though it is, is crowned by a reassertion of God's steadfast love, is to strengthen faith among an exiled people, tempted to despair.

1 A new generation entered Canaan (see Nu. 14:29–32; 26:64, 65), but the sinning continued. What was their first failure, and to what sins of ever deeper degradation did it lead (verses 34–39)? How are Christians to avoid similar entanglement? *Cf.* 2 Cor. 6:14 – 7:1; 1 Jn. 2:15–17.

2 What wonderful comfort can we take from the fact, which this psalm demonstrates, that man's rebellion did not exhaust the compassion of God? See verses 1–5, 45–47. What challenge do these verses bring?

Note. Verse 48. Probably a doxology to mark the end of Book IV of the Psalms.

For Studies 85–111 on the Psalms see p. 436.

HAGGAI

Introduction

The prophets Haggai and Zechariah are mentioned together in Ezra 5:1 as prophesying at that time in Jerusalem. Ezra 5 and 6 should be read in order to fit the ministry and God-given messages of these prophets into their historical setting.

The exact date of Haggai's prophesying is given in Hg. 1:1 as being the second year of Darius, king of Persia, *i.e.*, 520 BC (*cf.* Zc. 1:1). In 538 BC, the first company of exiles, under Zerubbabel, had returned from Babylon to Jerusalem, and had set about the work of rebuilding the Temple. But Samaritan opposition and intrigue proved too strong, and the work ceased (see Ezr. 4:1–5, 24). The people became occupied with their own concerns, and said with regard to the Temple, 'The time has not yet come to rebuild the house of the Lord' (Hg. 1:2).

The prophecies of Haggai consist of four utterances (see Analysis), which contain repeated promises of God's presence and blessing, if only the people will give themselves to the work of building the Lord's house. Haggai's words express for our instruction the abiding truth that God gives Himself and His best to those who fully honour Him and seek first His kingdom. There is no other hope of survival in the day of trouble and judgment, when God Himself will shake all things and reveal the worthlessness of every other boasted confidence (see Hg. 2:21–23; and *cf.* Heb. 12:25–27). Thus did Haggai, by the light of the Spirit of God, discern the truth about life's immediate circumstances, and foresee the similar, if greater, certainties of the final consummation in the day of the Lord.

Analysis

1:1–15 First utterance. A call to the people to recommence the building of the Temple. The work resumed.

2: 1–9	Second utterance. The builders encouraged. God is with them to prosper the work.
2: 10–19	Third utterance. The people and their offerings have been unclean in God's eyes. But now He will bless them.
2: 20–23	Fourth utterance. The kingdoms of this world shall be overthrown, and the Lord's elect servant exalted.

☐ STUDY 1 Haggai 1

1 How did the Jews of Haggai's day reckon their priorities? What was the consequence? And what was the Lord's command? What lesson did God wish them to learn? Is there a present-day application? *Cf.* Mt. 6: 33.

2 How had the people failed to live up to the purpose for which they had been allowed to return? *Cf.* Ezr. 1: 2–4. Contrast their first beginnings with the conditions described by Haggai. Is this at all your experience? *Cf.* Rev. 2: 4. What happened once they obeyed God's voice?

Note. Verse 1. 'The sixth month': corresponding to our August–September.

☐ STUDY 2 Haggai 2

1 Picture the desolate scene and the despondency of the people (verse 3). But how did the prospect appear to Haggai's eye of faith (verses 4–9)? On what grounds did he reassure them, and to what vision did he direct their eyes?

2 Verses 10–19. How does Haggai show that (a) in the sanctified life contact with unholy things must be avoided, and that (b) mere contact with holy things is not sufficient? Is it possible to deceive ourselves today, as the Jews of Haggai's day did? *Cf.* 2 Tim. 2: 19–22.

3 What will be the fate of all human activity and organization carried on without God, and what is the work that will stand, whose doers are blessed from the day they set their hand to it? *Cf.* 1 Jn. 2: 17. Why would Zerubbabel be safe when the Lord would shake the heavens and the earth?

Note. Verse 23. 'Like a signet': a symbol of honour and authority. *Cf.* Je. 22: 24.

ZECHARIAH

Introduction

Zechariah began his prophetic ministry two months after Haggai (see Zc. 1: 1; Hg. 1: 1). His book falls into two parts (chapters 1–8 and 9–14), and these are so different in character that many have thought that the second part must have been written by someone other than Zechariah. Such a supposition, however, is by no means necessary. The differences may be explained by the change of theme, and by the fact that the second part was written many years later than the first. A close study also reveals remarkable resemblances between the two parts.

The first part of the book has to do mainly with the rebuilding of the Temple, and contains Zechariah's words of encouragement and warning to the people and their rulers. After an opening call to repentance (1: 1–6) there follows a series of eight visions, which supply an answer to doubts and questionings in the people's minds. The first part closes with the prophet's reply to an enquiry from the people of Bethel (7: 1–3) about the continuance of the fasts which the Jews had been observing in mourning for the calamities that had overtaken them.

The second part of the book consists of two oracles (9–11 and 12–14). Both sections, as David Baron says in his valuable commentary, treat of war between the heathen world and Israel, but 'in the first the judgment through which *Gentile world power over Israel is finally destroyed*, and Israel is endowed with strength to *overcome all these enemies*', is the main theme; and, in the second, the judgment through which '*Israel itself is sifted and purged* in the final great conflict between the nations, and transformed into the holy nation of the Lord, forms the leading topic'.

Zechariah's writings foreshadow the appearance of Zion's King both in meekness and in majesty, and declare both His rejection and His dominion over the whole earth. They are therefore frequently quoted in the New Testament with reference either to Christ's first or to His second coming to the earth.

Analysis

1: 1–6	A call to pay heed to the Word of God.	
1:7 – 6: 8	Eight visions.	
	1: 7–17	The Angel of the Lord among the myrtle trees.
	1: 18–21	The horns and the four smiths.
	2: 1–13	The man with the measuring line.
	3: 1–10	Joshua the High Priest.
	4: 1–14	The golden lampstand.
	5: 1–4	The flying scroll.
	5: 5–11	The ephah and the woman.
	6: 1–8	The four chariots.
6: 9–15	The crowning of Joshua.	
7: 1 – 8: 23	Reply to the deputation from Bethel.	
9: 1–17	A Gentile conqueror and Zion's King.	
10: 1–12	What the shepherd king will bring to His people.	
11: 1–17	The rejection of the true shepherd and its tragic consequences.	
12: 1–9	The deliverance of Jerusalem.	
12: 10 – 13: 6	The penitence and purifying of the people.	
13: 7–9	The smiting of the shepherd and scattering of the flock.	
14: 1–21	Messiah's appearing, and the establishment of His kingdom on earth.	

☐ STUDY 1 Zechariah 1 and 2

1 What do we learn from Zc. 1: 1–6 about the Word of the Lord and the different consequences of obeying and rejecting it? What is and always will be true of it, whatever men do? With verse 6, *cf.* Mt. 5: 18.

2 In these chapters are three visions (1: 7–17; 1: 18–21; 2: 1–13). How do these answer the following questions? (a) What is God's real attitude towards Jerusalem? (b) How can the nations which oppress them be subdued? (c) Can the city, now desolate, have any future?

3 Consider how much that is said here of Jerusalem is true spiritually for us in Christ. See, *e.g.*, 2: 5, 8b, 10–12. Is there not the same call to us to believe, as there was to the people of Zechariah's day? *Cf.* 2 Cor. 1: 20.

Notes

1 1: 11. There was no sign of any stirring among the nations to fulfil God's purposes towards Israel.

2 1: 20, 21. 'Four smiths': agents appointed by God to destroy the 'horns' (*i.e.*, strength) of the nations.
3 2: 4, 5. The proposed measurement of Jerusalem is cancelled, for the reasons given here.
4 2: 6. 'The land of the north': Babylon (or Persia), where they had been exiled. See verse 7.

☐ STUDY 2 Zechariah 3 and 4

1 Joshua, as high priest, acts as the representative of the people. How is the people's guilt to be removed? By whose intervention is Satan rebuked and Joshua cleansed? *Cf.* Rom. 8: 31–34; Heb. 7: 25; 9: 26.

2 What is the meaning of the vision of chapter 4? What is its relevance today? *Cf.* Ho. 1: 7; 2 Cor. 10: 4, 5.

Note. 3: 8, 9. 'My servant', 'the Branch', 'the stone' are all titles of the Messiah. *Cf., e.g.*, Is. 28: 16; 42: 1; Je. 23: 5. The 'seven facets' may represent the omniscience of the Messiah. *Cf.* Rev. 5: 6.

☐ STUDY 3 Zechariah 5 and 6

1 Chapter 5 contains a vivid vision concerning those who practise wickedness, and of wickedness itself. What is to be the eventual fate of such? *Cf.* 2 Tim. 2: 19; 2 Thes. 1: 7–10; Rev. 21: 1–4, 8, 27.

2 What is foreshadowed in 6: 9–15 by the crowning of the high priest, and by the prophetic declaration that 'the man' (verse 12) thus signified shall be a priest *upon his throne*, and shall build the temple of the Lord? *Cf.* Jn. 2: 19–22; Eph. 2: 13, 19–22; Heb. 8: 1; 10: 11–13; 1 Pet. 2: 5.

Notes
1 5: 1–4. A vision of God's judgment pursuing the transgressor.
2 5: 6. 'The ephah': a barrel-shaped measure, having here a circular lid of lead.
3 5: 11. 'The land of Shinar': Babylonia.
4 6: 1–8. The vision in its details is difficult to interpret, but in general reveals the Lord ruling over the earth (verse 5), and exercising His judgmen by unseen agents. *Cf.* 2 Ki. 6: 15–17.
5 6: 10, 11. A deputation from the Jews in Babylon had come to Jerusalem. Zechariah is commanded to make 'a crown' from some of the silver and gold which they had brought, and to set it on the head of the high priest.

☐ STUDY 4 Zechariah 7

See Introduction. Zechariah's answer to the delegation from Bethel consists of four parts, each beginning 'And the word of the Lord came to me'. The first two parts of his reply are contained in this chapter and the last two in chapter 8.

1 With what did God find fault in these fasts? See verses 5, 6 and contrast 1 Cor. 10: 31. In the light of this part of the prophet's reply, is there not much in men's worship today that is not acceptable to God?

2 With verses 9 and 10, *cf.* Is. 58: 6, 7. Where does a man's enmity towards his brother take its rise? *Cf.* Mk. 7: 21, 22. What attitude of heart towards God had the Jews shown?

□ STUDY 5 Zechariah 8

1 Enumerate the blessings which God here promises concerning Jerusalem, noticing also the emphasis placed upon them by the number of times the phrase 'says the Lord' occurs. Is God less willing to fulfil to us the 'precious and very great promises' (2 Pet. 1: 4), which He has given us in Christ? *Cf.* Heb. 6: 11–18.

2 What, however, are the conditions for obtaining the promises of God? In the light of the evidence we have of God's willingness to give, where does the hindrance lie, if we are not enjoying in personal experience the things promised?

3 What will ultimately happen to the fasts about which the deputation from Bethel had enquired in 7: 2, 3?

Notes

1 Verses 4, 5. 'Old men . . . boys and girls playing . . .': these indicate and illustrate the security and peace which is promised.

2 Verse 10. Three evils are here spoken of from which the people suffered when God's house was neglected, namely, scarcity, absence of security and disunion.

□ STUDY 6 Zechariah 9 and 10

1 The opening verses (9: 1–8) are a prophecy of an invasion of Syria, Phoenicia and the country of the Philistines. The prophecy was historically fulfilled in the conquests of Alexander the Great. But to whom is the prophet's eye directed? How does this account, on the one hand, for the fall of Tyre, notwithstanding its wisdom, strong defences and wealth, and, on the other, for the preservation of Jerusalem? *Cf.* 9: 15a and 2: 5.

2 In 9: 9–12 a picture is presented of Zion's King, in which, as often in the Old Testament, His first and second advents are merged into one. What is said (a) of His character; (b) of the manner of His coming; (c) of the final extent of His rule; and (d) of the benefits He brings? *Cf.* Ps. 40: 2, 3; Joel 3: 16b; Is. 61: 7.

3 The remaining portion (9: 13 – 10: 12) has for its theme what God will yet do for His people Israel. Make a list of the things here promised, and reflect how they are symbols of spiritual blessings which are ours in Christ.

Notes

1 9: 1–6. Hadrach and Aram are probably Syrian towns; Hamath, Tyre and Sidon are Syrian neighbours; Ashkelon, Gaza, Ekron and Ashdod (verses 5, 6) are Philistine towns.

2 9: 7. A prophecy of the abolition of idolatrous sacrifices, and the incorporation of the remnant of the Philistines among God's people. The Jebusites were the original inhabitants of Jerusalem.

3 9: 8. When Alexander invaded these parts and swept through the coastal nations, nothing could stop his armies, but he was restrained from attacking Jerusalem.

4 9: 13–17. A prophecy of victory for Israel, when the enemy shall be trodden down like sling-stones and Israel lifted up like the jewels of a crown. In verse 15b is another figure, representing the Israelites as drinking the blood of their enemies, with which they will be as full as the bowls used in sacrifice, or like the corners of the altar that were drenched in blood.

□ STUDY 7 Zechariah 11

While plain in its main teaching, this chapter is obscure in many of its details. Its theme is grace and judgment. It opens with a vision of judgment sweeping over the land and making it desolate (verses 1–3). God shows to the prophet that the promises of the preceding chapter will not be realized without further uprisings of evil (*cf.* 10: 2, 3a). In verses 4–17 the prophet is bidden to impersonate first a good shepherd, and when he was rejected and despised, a worthless shepherd, under whom the flock will suffer many sorrows. The section is a vivid foreshadowing of the coming of Christ (verses 12, 13; *cf.* Mt. 26: 14, 15; 27: 9, 10).

1 Verse 7. The good shepherd's 'two staffs' (*cf.* 'rod' and 'staff' in Ps. 23: 4) were named 'Grace' and 'Union', indicating that He came in grace to bind the flock into one. How far is this a picture of Christ? *Cf.* Jn. 1: 14; 17: 20–22.

2 How is the lot of those who deliberately refuse the good described? *Cf.* Mt. 23: 37, 38; 2 Thes. 2: 8.

Notes

1 Verses 7, 11. 'Traffickers in the sheep': 'poor of the flock' (AV) fits the context better.

2 Verse 12. 'Thirty shekels of silver': the price of an injured slave (Ex. 21: 32). *Cf.* Mt. 26: 15; 27: 9.

□ STUDY 8 Zechariah 12 and 13

These chapters contain a prophecy of a combined attack of many peoples upon Jerusalem and of the deliverance God will give (12: 1–9), together with the repentance and cleansing which will be wrought within the nation by their vision and recognition of Him whom they pierced (12: 10 – 13: 9). The ultimate fulfilment of this prophecy will take place at the end of the present age (*cf.* Rom. 11: 25–27), but it has a present application spiritually to all who belong to Him.

1 What is to be the secret of Jerusalem's survival when threatened by so many enemies gathered together against it (12: 1–9; *cf.* 14: 3)? Has the Christian similar hope of overcoming the world, the flesh and the devil? *Cf.* Ps. 27: 1–5; 1 Jn. 4: 4; 5: 4.

2 What four experiences of God's people are set forth in 12: 10 – 13: 9? Do you know them in your experience? (a) With 12: 10–14, *cf.* Jn. 16: 8, 9; Acts 2: 37–40. (b) With 13: 1, *cf.* Heb. 9: 13, 14. (c) With 13: 2–5, *cf.* 2 Cor. 7: 1. (d) With 13: 7–9, *cf.* 1 Pet. 1: 5–7.

Notes

1 12: 11. Hadadrimmon is thought to be a city in the plain of Megiddo (or Jezreel), where King Josiah was killed, the darkest and saddest event in Jewish history (*cf.* 2 Ch. 35: 22–25).

2 12: 12–14. Both the intensity and the universality of Israel's repentance are here emphasized.

3 13: 2–6. The prophets, having been proved false, shall be ashamed, and will seek to disguise the fact that they prophesied. The wounds (verse 6) are either wounds self-inflicted in their prophetic frenzy (*cf.* 1 Ki. 18: 28), or more probably wounds received by them through the attacks of people upon them (*cf.* verse 3c).

□ STUDY 9 Zechariah 14

Verses 1–5 appear to be a prediction of the fall of Jerusalem in AD 70, together with a prediction of the Lord's return. In the Gospels (*e.g.*, Lk. 21: 20–28) these two events are also described as if they were one. Then follows an account of the blessings that will ensue.

1 Verses 1–5 describe the breaking in of the day of the Lord. Who will at that time be gathered against Jerusalem? What will happen to the city and its inhabitants? When and in what manner will the Lord appear?

2 In the day of the Lord what further results will come to pass as regards (a) Jerusalem (verses 6–11; *cf.* Rev. 22: 1–5; Jn. 4: 13, 14); (b) those who attacked Jerusalem (verses 12–15); and (c) the remnant of the nations that have escaped (verses 16–19)?

3 Picture the city as described in verses 20, 21. Are you aiming to see that your life is holy in every part? *Cf.* 2 Cor. 7: 1; 1 Thes. 3: 13; 1 Pet. 1: 15, 16.

Note. Verses 20, 21. Every aspect of the city's life will bear the mark of holiness —business life, religious life and domestic life. Verse 20b. The pots which were used for mundane purposes shall be as holy as the bowls which held the blood of sacrifice.

MALACHI

Introduction

Malachi (the name means 'my messenger'—see 3: 1) was doubtless a contemporary of Ezra and Nehemiah. He attacked the evils which arose at Jerusalem after the Temple was rebuilt and its services re-established, evils of which we have historical record in the book of Nehemiah. 'The religious spirit of Malachi is that of the prayers of Ezra and Nehemiah.' There is an ancient tradition which regarded 'Malachi' as a pen name, and assigned the authorship to Ezra himself.

This book is the more significant because it closes the Old Testament revelation. As a link between the law and the gospel, it combines severe insistence on the necessity of purity and sincerity of heart with the sure promise of the coming of a Deliverer to those who fear the Lord. Finally (4: 4–6), it appeals back to the law and the prophets (of whom Elijah is the chosen representative). The fuller revelation will not contradict its preparatory stages. The people are to find in the spiritual authorities they already know (*i.e.*, in the Old Testament) their assurance for accepting Him who should come. So, on the Mount of Transfiguration, when the Father called men to hear the Son, Moses and Elijah stood by to give their assent and to provide evidence that He was the fulfilment of all their anticipation. See Mt. 17: 3–5; Jn. 5: 46.

Analysis

1: 1–5	God's love for Israel.
1: 6 – 2: 9	The sins of the priests.
2: 10–17	The sins of the people.
3: 1–6	Warning that the Lord will come to judge and to purify.
3: 7–12	How to give practical expression to their repentance.
3: 13 – 4: 6	The future day of judgment.

☐ STUDY 1 Malachi 1: 1 – 2: 9

1 1: 1–5. The people of Judah, looking upon their condition and circumstances, were depressed and murmuring against God. What proof did the prophet adduce to show that God did love them as a nation? *Cf.* Pss. 34: 15, 16; 73: 26–28.

2 Of what particular sins were the priests guilty? With what will God punish them if they remain impenitent? What was the root of their failure?

3 What, by contrast, do we learn should be the quality and objectives of our service as messengers of the Lord of hosts? *Cf.* 2: 5–7, and *cf.* 2 Cor. 6: 3; 2 Tim. 2: 15; 1 Pet. 4: 10, 11.

Notes

1 1: 2–4. The Edomites were the descendants of Esau.

2 1: 5. 'Great is the Lord beyond the border of Israel': the people had too small a conception of their God, and this the prophet seeks to correct. *Cf.* verses 11, 14b.

3 1: 8. Perfect, unblemished sacrifices were demanded (Lv. 1: 3), and not the 'rejects' from the flock.

☐ STUDY 2 Malachi 2: 10 – 3: 6

1 2: 10–16. Although the people wept before the Lord, they found He would not regard their offerings. Why not? What particular sin was coming between them and God, and what 'heart condition' underlay it? *Cf.* Heb. 3: 12, 13.

2 How is 3: 1–6 an answer to the people's complaint in 2: 17? What similes are used to describe the day of the Lord's coming? What must be put away? And on what must my heart be set, if I am to be ready to welcome Him at His appearing? *Cf.* 1 Thes. 3: 12, 13; 1 Jn. 3: 2, 3.

Note. 2: 10, 11. 'Profaning the covenant of our fathers': *i.e.*, by marrying wives of other nations. *Cf.* Ex. 34: 10–12, 15, 16. 'The daughter of a foreign god' means a foreign woman of another religion.

☐ STUDY 3 Malachi 3: 7 – 4: 6

1 Of what are the people accused in 3: 7–15? What must we make our chief concern if we wish to obtain God's promised blessings? *Cf.* Pr. 3: 9, 10; Mt. 6: 30–33; 16: 25; Lk. 6: 38. In what practical ways ought I to respond to this call?

2 Two different classes of people are described in 3: 13–16. To which do you belong? The wicked may seem to have the best of it, but God says here that, in contrast to present circumstances, He is

going to make a day (3: 17 and 4: 3) in which the righteous and the wicked shall be openly distinguished and justly recompensed. How will this be effected? *Cf.* 4: 1, 2 with 2 Thes. 1: 7–10; 1 Jn. 2: 28; 3: 2; Rev. 6: 15–17.

Note. 3: 11. 'The devourer': *i.e.*, the locust.

JAMES

Introduction

It is generally believed that this letter was written by James, the brother of our Lord. During Christ's life on earth he was an unbeliever (Jn. 7: 5), but was converted when Jesus appeared to him after His resurrection (1 Cor. 15: 7). He was austere in disposition and practical in character. In the book of Acts (see 12: 17; 15: 13–21; 21: 18 and also Gal. 2: 9) he appears as leader of the church at Jerusalem. He was killed by the Jews about AD 61.

The letter is addressed 'to the twelve tribes in the dispersion' (1: 1), that is, to fellow-Jews living outside Palestine. It is terse and forceful, yet vivid and dramatic in style. It begins and ends abruptly, without any opening thanksgiving or final benediction. James seeks to encourage those who were passing through a period of trial and suffering; but at the same time rebukes such failings as profession of faith without the practice of it, sins of speech, strife and envying, eagerness to take the position of teachers, and a lack of steadfast endurance. He urges his readers to be 'doers of the word, and not hearers only', to express their Christian faith not in outward formality and barren profession, but by seeking to obey from the heart God's perfect law of liberty in the manifold relationships of life.

The central thought is that 'faith apart from works is barren' (2: 20). Justification is by faith, but the faith that justifies is a living faith which, by an inherent irrepressible necessity, must produce good works, or express itself in active self-committal and obedience.

Analysis

The letter is a homily rather than a treatise, and deals with practical religion; there is thus no continuous thread of argument through the book; rather, with sure touch, the author comments, encourages or chides on matters of doctrine and conduct as they arise, in vivid and energetic style.

1: 1–18	Dealing with temptation.
1: 19–27	Receiving God's word and doing God's will.
2: 1–13	Snobbishness and the royal law of love.
2: 14–26	Against an inactive faith.
3: 1–12	Control of the tongue.
3: 13–18	Earthbound and heavenly wisdom.
4: 1–12	Dealing with dissension and worldliness among Christians.
4: 13 – 5: 11	Warnings to the rashly confident and the callous rich; counsel and encouragement to the oppressed.
5: 12–20	Miscellaneous pastoral remarks; with emphasis on the place and power of prayer.

☐ STUDY 1 James 1: 1–18

A distinction is drawn in this passage between 'trials' (verse 2, 12), which may have positive effects (*cf.* 1 Pet. 1: 7), and 'temptation' (verses 13f.), which is the enticement to evil conceived within the human heart.

1 Verses 2–7, 12. What is our mental attitude to trials to be? What is their purpose and goal? In trying situations wisdom (*cf.* 3: 17) is necessary. How in particular is this wisdom to be obtained?

2 Verses 13–15. What is the origin of temptation, and what are the inevitable products of yielding to it? How can we avoid being deceived, and gain strength to overcome?

3 Verses 9–11, 16–18. Contrast the impermanence of men, poor and rich alike, with the changeless consistency of God our Father. What also is God's will for us, and what means does He use to fulfil it? How should these truths influence our attitude to life?

Notes

1 Verse 17b. The eternal Source of light is not, like the heavenly bodies, subject to variation or eclipse.

2 Verse 18. 'A kind of first fruits': the first fruits were evidence that the harvest had begun, and promise of more to follow.

☐ STUDY 2 James 1: 19–27

It is characteristic of James to pass from one paragraph to another by repetition of a key-word. Here, having spoken of God's word in regeneration (verse 18), he goes on to speak of the place God's word—as expressing His will—should have in the believer's life.

1 What are the possible hindrances and dangers which may prevent God's word from taking root and bearing fruit in our lives?

2 'Meekness' (verse 21) is not to be confused with inactivity. What lessons does James' illustration enforce concerning our reaction to God's word and His law? With verse 25, *cf.* Lk. 8: 15. How does your religion stand up to James' practical tests (verses 26f.)?

Notes

1 Verse 25. 'Looks into': literally 'peers closely at'; *cf.* Jn. 20: 5, 11; 1 Pet. 1: 12. 'The law of liberty': *cf.* Rom. 8: 2. The Christian gospel is a 'law of liberty' because God's Spirit creates within the hearts of those who receive it the will and power to obey God. So God's law becomes an inner constraint and is no longer chiefly an external restraint.

2 Verse 27. 'Religion': the word means the outward expression of faith. 'This is the ritualism which God loves,' says James, 'to visit orphans . . .'

☐ STUDY 3 James 2: 1–13

1 Verses 1–7. On what five grounds (three general and two particular) does James condemn the snobbish conduct described in verses 2, 3? With verse 4, *cf.* 4: 11. We, too, believe in the 'Lord of glory'. Are we free from the preoccupation with what people have rather than what they are? Do we love and learn from 'the rich in *faith*'?

2 Verses 8–13. 'This partiality business is just a minor matter.' How does James deal with this sterile objection? Why, in a life which may otherwise appear to be law-abiding, is one form of sin, like partiality, so serious?

Notes

1 Verse 12. Our freedom is not freedom *from* the obligations of moral law; if is freedom to *fulfil* (verse 18) the just requirements of the law.

2 Verse 13b. Mercy triumphs over (not justice but) judgment. The same word is translated 'condemnation' in 5: 12. Mercy will finally triumph because when the merciless are condemned, the merciful will be forgiven.

☐ STUDY 4 James 2: 14–26

James has already warned against an empty religion which is impure (1: 26, 27); here he warns against an inactive faith which is impotent.

1 Verses 14–20. Empty faith is words without action, profession without performance. *Cf.* 1 Jn. 3: 18 (NEB). How profitable is my faith by the test of James' illustration? How does my faith differ from that of the demons?

2 Verses 21–26. James illustrates his argument by reference to two very different people. How was the principle of verse 22 demonstrated in their lives? Is the principle at work in my own life?

Notes

1 Verse 14. The sense is: 'Can (that sort of) faith save him?' *i.e.*, from condemnation.

2 Verse 18. The objection that some have faith and some have works is specious, because without corresponding moral action faith is empty and barren, like that of the devils (verse 19).

3 Verse 25. 'Justified by works': *cf.* Rom. 3: 20, 28; Gal. 2: 16. Paul and James seem to contradict one another. But, in fact, Paul says, 'Faith can save apart from works of the law', and James says, 'Faith cannot save without the works of faith.' The two are therefore complementary.

☐ STUDY 5 James 3

In this chapter James returns to two subjects which he has already mentioned: the tongue (*cf.* 1: 19, 26) and wisdom (*cf.* 1: 5).

1 Verses 1–12. Why does James discourage undue eagerness to take up teaching? Ponder his vivid illustrations of the power, for good or evil, of the tongue. How is the malignity of the tongue most clearly shown, and why is it so serious? How does James also show that the tongue's inconsistency is monstrously unnatural?

2 Verses 13–18. What are the marks and results of the two kinds of wisdom described in these verses? Consider how the qualities of heavenly wisdom, described in verses 17, 18, were seen in the Lord Jesus. Are they evident in my life?

Notes

1 Verse 6. NEB translates: 'And the tongue is in effect a fire. It represents among our members the world with all its wickedness; it pollutes our whole being; it keeps the wheel of our existence red-hot, and its flames are fed by hell.'

2 Verse 13. 'Meekness': a word which today has lost much of its original nobility. For the Greeks it denoted a strong man's self-discipline and a wise man's humility. *Cf.* 1: 21.

3 Verse 14. 'Do not boast and be false to the truth': to boast of wisdom when the heart is full of envy and selfish ambition is mere sham. *Cf.* 1: 26.

4 Verse 18 is to be contrasted with verse 16. Disorder and vileness accompany envy and rivalry; but righteousness (or justice) is the seed and crop of the peacemakers.

☐ STUDY 6 James 4

1 Verses 1–10. How does James diagnose the condition of those to whom he is writing? Can you find in verses 4–10 seven steps to spiritual recovery? What cause is there for encouragement and gratitude in this often painful business?

2 Verses 11–17. The Christian community to which James was writing was further disfigured by evil speaking and rash confidence. What guidance does James give concerning our attitude (a) to our fellow-Christians, and (b) to tomorrow? What difference would it make to your life if you took seriously the definition of sin in verse 17?

Notes

1 Verse 4. 'Unfaithful creatures': literally 'adulteresses'. *Cf.* Ho. 3: 1. But the reference here is to apostasy, not immorality.

2 Verse 6. The quotation of Pr. 3: 34 is introduced to demonstrate the wonder of God's grace, which is able to overcome even the worldly spirit of James' readers, if they will humble themselves and respond to His Spirit's yearnings.

☐ STUDY 7 James 5

James denounces the callous rich in language which recalls that of the Old Testament prophets. *Cf.* 1: 9–11; 2: 1–7.

1 Verses 1–12. What is the outstanding fact underlying James' warnings to the rich, and his counsel to the oppressed? Do we, rich or poor, share this eternal perspective? What particular warnings should we take from verses 1–6? What reasons (verses 7–10) are there for self-control and what grounds for joyful peace of mind?

2 Verses 13–20. In what ways are we called upon to help others? In particular, what illustrations are here given of the power of prayer, and what conditions of effective prayer are laid down?

Notes

1 Verse 3b. NEB translates, 'You have piled up wealth in an age that is near its close.'

2 Verse 6. The reference is probably not to Christ, as some suppose (*cf.* Acts 7: 52), so much as to prevailing social conditions.

3 Verse 9. 'Do not grumble': the verse recalls 4: 11, 12, where open criticism is discouraged; notice the similar legal language.

4 Verse 11. 'The purpose of the Lord': literally 'The end of the Lord' (AV, RV), *i.e.*, what the Lord finally purposed for Job. See Jb. 42: 12.

5 Verse 12. It seems that James' readers were notoriously unable to control their tongues: *cf.* 1: 19, 26; 2: 12; 3: 5ff.; 4: 11; 5: 9.

6 Verse 16. 'Confess your sins': there must be no hushing up of sin if prayer is to prevail. *Cf.* Ps. 66: 18; Mt. 5: 23, 24.

1 CHRONICLES

Introduction

The two books of Chronicles, which are really one whole, were composed at a much later date than the other historical books, and frequent reference is made to former writings not now possessed by us. The date is after the carrying away to Babylon (1 Ch. 6: 15) and after the decree of Cyrus ordering the return (2 Ch. 36: 22, 23), which decree is found also in the first chapter of Ezra. The literary style is similar to the books of Ezra–Nehemiah, which suggests that all belong to the same period.

The books of Chronicles are placed last in the Hebrew Bible. They are separated from the other historical books, and form part of the section of the Hebrew Canon known as 'Hagiographa' or 'Writings'. The Hebrew title for the books of Chronicles is 'The Words of the Days', and the Greek title is 'Omissions'. The name 'Chronicles' comes from Jerome. The theme of the books is the need for God to be central in the life of the nation, and the frequent times in the history of the monarchy when the nation turned away from Him, with occasional times of reformation under such kings as Jehoshaphat, Hezekiah and Josiah. After the death of Solomon (2 Ch. 9) the story of the southern kingdom alone is told, with only occasional references to the northern kingdom. The work of the prophets as witnesses to the truth of God, when kings and even priests corrupted it, is shown again and again, as is the faithfulness of God to the people of His choice. The interest of the writer centres very largely in the Temple, its priesthood and its worship.

Analysis

1 – 9 Chiefly genealogies.

10 – 29 Events leading up to the building of the Temple. Reign of David.

10 – 12	Death of Saul and accession of David. The exploits of his mighty men.
13 – 16	The ark brought to Jerusalem—services arranged.
17	David's desire to build a Temple and the Lord's answer.
18 – 20	David conquers and subdues neighbouring peoples.
21	The numbering of the people.
22	David's preparation for Solomon's accession.
23 – 26	The ministry of the tribe of Levi.
27	Civil leaders of the nation under David.
28	David's address to the leaders of the people and to Solomon.
29	The people's response. David's death.

☐ STUDY 1 1 Chronicles 1–9

These chapters, which at first sight appear to be a mere wilderness of names, are seen on closer inspection to contain an orderly arrangement, like a garden divided into separate beds. The writer begins with the line of descent from Adam to Noah, and then gives the descendants of each of Noah's three sons (1: 1–27). Arriving thus at Abraham, he lists the sons of Ishmael, and of Keturah, and Isaac's two sons, Israel and Esau, with a list of the descendants of Esau (1: 28–54). With chapter 2 begins the list of Israel's sons, with their descendants. Judah comes first and is given the largest space (2: 3 – 4: 23); then Simeon (4: 24–43), Reuben, Gad and the half tribe of Manasseh (chapter 5), Levi (chapter 6), Issachar (7: 1–5), Benjamin (7: 6–12), Naphtali (7: 13), Manasseh (7: 14–19), Ephraim (7: 20–29), Asher (7: 30–40). It will be noticed that two tribes are omitted. In chapter 8 the descendants of Benjamin are given more fully, leading up to the family of Saul and his descendants; chapter 9 gives a list of inhabitants of Jerusalem, and repeats the genealogy of Saul as an introduction to the story of his death in chapter 10. Amidst these lists of names are a number of passages which may be spiritually applied with profit to ourselves.

1 Read 4: 9, 10 and 5: 18–22. What do you learn for your own life from the examples of (a) Jabez, and (b) Reuben, Gad and the half tribe of Manasseh about success and victory? *Cf.* Ps. 81: 10; Col. 4: 2; 1 Jn. 5: 4.

2 Build for yourself a mental picture of the lives and service of the Levites, as described in chapter 6. Are there lessons to be learned from this passage about the nature of true worship?

☐ STUDY 2 1 Chronicles 10 and 11

1 Chapter 10 is a sad story of failure. To what is Saul's failure ascribed? Are our own lives free from the sins which brought about Saul's downfall? *Cf.* Is. 8: 19, 20.

2 What instances are given in chapter 11 of the valour and loyalty of the men who followed David? What may we learn from the story concerning the nature of true fellowship, love and Christian service? *Cf.* Acts 20: 22–24.

Note. 11: 8. 'The Millo': probably the name of an ancient citadel in the city.

☐ STUDY 3 1 Chronicles 12

1 Observe the unity prevailing at this time among the followers of David—though drawn from so many different tribes—and also the diversity of gifts which were found among them. Make a list of these gifts and compare them with the gifts of the Spirit as set forth in 1 Cor. 12: 4–11. What was the secret of the unity that prevailed?

2 What qualities of character do you find commended in this chapter? Are they characteristic of the Christian church today? Are they true of you?

Note. Verse 18. 'Amasai': probably the same as Amasa of 2: 17; 2 Sa. 17: 25; 20: 10.

☐ STUDY 4 1 Chronicles 13 and 14

1 The story in chapter 13 will repay reflection. Was Uzzah alone guilty, or was the spirit of deep reverence lacking also in king and people? Was it too much like a heathen idol procession? What lesson would the judgment upon Uzzah impress upon the people? *Cf.* Heb. 12: 28, 29.

2 The Philistines were not willing to submit to the ascendancy of David, and three times made an all-out effort to regain the upper hand. What may we learn from the way David met the challenge?

Note. 13: 6. The power and majesty of God are emphasized, as also His presence. Note also the words 'before God' twice repeated in verses 8 and 10.

☐ STUDY 5 1 Chronicles 15: 1 – 16: 6

1 What reason does David assign for the failure of the first attempt to bring the ark to Jerusalem? Comparing chapter 15 with chapter 13, what was there common to both processions, and what peculiar to the second? What is the obvious lesson for us to learn?

2 'Sounds of joy' (15: 16; see also verses 25, 28, 29). What made David rejoice so greatly? What did the ark stand for in his eyes? What kind of activity should cause us similar joy?

☐ STUDY 6 I Chronicles 16: 7–43

1 Verses 8–22, 34–36. What should be the response of God's people in return for all His goodness? Make a list of all the things the psalm calls upon them to do. Note for what purpose Heman and Jeduthun were 'chosen and expressly named' (verses 41, 42).

2 Verses 23–33. Here the psalmist looks beyond Israel, and summons all nations to worship the Lord. What reasons does he give why they ought to do so? Can you use this hymn of praise as a thankful acknowledgment of all that the Lord means to you?

☐ STUDY 7 I Chronicles 17

1 From this chapter and other passages where Nathan is mentioned (2 Sa. 12: 1–15, 25; 1 Ki. 1 *passim*; 4: 5), work out what an important place he had in the lives of David and of Solomon. The revelation here made to him and through him to David is one of the chief Messianic prophecies in the Old Testament, and had a profound influence upon the development of the Messianic hope. *Cf.*, *e.g.*, Ps. 89: 26, 27; Lk. 1: 33; Heb. 1: 5.

2 In what sense did God deny David's desire, in what way modify it, and in what way answer it above all that David asked or thought? Note especially verses 4, 10b, 12a. Have you had any comparable experience of the Lord's dealing in your own life?

☐ STUDY 8 I Chronicles 18–20

1 What indications do you find in chapter 18 concerning (a) David's heart attitude towards God, and (b) the way in which he exercised authority as king? What in turn did God do for him? How may we enjoy similar God-given blessing?

2 How do chapters 19 and 20 show what grave consequences may arise out of a misunderstanding, and what retribution may result from an act of folly?

3 What good qualities are seen in Joab in these chapters? How? then, did he come to the sad end described in 1 Ki. 2: 31, 32, 34,

☐ STUDY 9 I Chronicles 21: 1 – 22: 1

1 What circumstances, do you imagine, may have left David particularly prone to temptation at this time? Why was the numbering

of the people displeasing to God? *Cf.* Je. 17: 5. What evidence do you find of the genuineness of David's repentance? *Cf.* 2 Cor. 7: 11.

2 What two proofs are there in this passage of God's forgiving mercy? Observe how God turned the incident into blessing by using it to show David the site of the Temple. *Cf.* 21: 18; 22: 1; 2 Ch. 3: 1.

☐ STUDY 10 1 Chronicles 22: 2–19

The thought of building a house for the Lord had been in David's mind, but now the way for action was open. This passage tells of (a) the abundance of what David prepared; (b) his charge to Solomon; and (c) his charge to the leaders of the tribes.

1 What may we learn from David's high conception of the kind of building that alone would be worthy (verse 5), and from the abundance of his preparations? Contrast the spirit of the people in Malachi's day (Mal. 1: 6–8). What may we learn also from David's willing acceptance of God's decision that not he, but Solomon, should build the Temple?

2 Study David's charge to Solomon and the people. What did he lay down as the all-important secrets of success? What were the people to do before undertaking the task of building (verse 19)? *Cf.* 2 Cor. 8: 5.

Introductory Note to Chapters 23–27

These five chapters describe how David and the leaders of the tribes organized before David's death the administration of the kingdom. The first matter taken in hand was the ministry of the priests and Levites, who had charge of the Temple and its worship and also administered judgment. This is set forth in chapters 23–26. Chapter 23 speaks of the Levites as a whole, chapter 24 of the priests (verses 1–19), and their attendants (verses 20–31); chapter 25 of the choirs; chapter 26 of the porters (verses 1–19), and of the officers and judges (verses 20–32). Then in chapter 27 are given in lesser detail the civil and military leaders of the nation other than Levites.

☐ STUDY 11 1 Chronicles 23 and 24

Chapter 23, after telling of the assembly at which these matters were decided (verse 2), first gives the division of the Levites according to their work (verses 3, 4), and then their divisions according to families or houses, as descended respectively from the three sons of Levi—from Gershom (verses 7–11), from Kohath (verses 12–20), and from Merari (verses 21–23). The remainder of the chapter defines their duties. Chapter 24 speaks of those who served within the Temple, distinguishing between the sons of Aaron, who were priests (verses

1–19), and the rest, who were attendants of the priests (verses 20–31). Together these made up the 24,000 of 23: 4a.

1 Compare the special duties of the priests (23: 13—see Note below) with those of the other Levites who were not sons of Aaron. What part of the Levites' former duties were now no longer necessary, and why (23: 25–32)?

2 Why has all this elaborate organization passed away? *Cf.* Heb. 7: 11–25. What has taken its place? *Cf.* Heb. 8: 1, 2; 1 Pet. 2: 4, 5, 9; Rev. 1: 6.

Note. 23: 13. 'To consecrate . . .': better, 'to sanctify as most holy him and his sons for ever', as in RV mg. The burning of incense implies also the sprinkling of the blood of the atonement. *Cf.* Ex. 30: 10; Lv. 16: 12–14.

☐ STUDY 12 1 Chronicles 25–27

These chapters record the family divisions and the work of (a) the 4,000 choristers mentioned in 23: 5 (see chapter 25), (b) the 4,000 doorkeepers (26: 1–19), and (c) the 6,000 officers and judges (26: 20–32). All these were Levites. Chapter 27 records the leaders of the tribes, the commanders of the monthly divisions, and the chief officers of state.

1 Who were the three chief leaders of praise? See 25: 1; also 6: 33, 39. 44; 15: 16, 17. Why is their ministry of praise called 'prophesying'? *Cf.* Eph. 5: 18, 19.

2 Amidst the many differences of function and service described in these chapters, notice the way in which all contribute to the worship and honour of the Lord. What developments of this lesson do you find in the teaching about Christian service in Eph. 4: 1–7, 11, 12; 1 Cor. 12: 18–21?

Notes

1 25: 1. 'The chiefs of the service': the phrase seems to refer here to those in charge of the Temple staff, 'the authorities of the temple' (Moffatt).
2 25: 3. 'Jeduthun': elsewhere called 'Ethan'. See 6: 44; 15: 17, 19.
3 26: 29. 'Officers and judges': the officers collected the tithes and other revenue and the judges gave judgment in matters of law.

☐ STUDY 13 1 Chronicles 28

When David had done all he could in his private and personal capacity in preparation for the building of the Temple, he summoned an assembly of the leaders in all departments of the nation's life to commend the scheme to them, and, as the next chapter shows, was greatly gratified by their response.

1 'I had it in my heart to . . . But God said to me, "You may not"' (verses 2 and 3). Have we known some such experience in our service of God? How does David bring out that God's plan was far better?

2 There are two charges to Solomon in this passage, in verses 9, 10 and 20, 21. Considering them together, (a) what was to be Solomon's first duty, (b) what the character of the God with whom he had to do, (c) what the two grounds of his confidence, and (d) what consequently the manner and spirit of his service? What lessons do you find in this for your life?

Note. Verse 19. Notice the distinct claim here made that the pattern of the Temple and of its service was given to David by revelation.

☐ **STUDY 14 1 Chronicles 29**

1 Study verses 1–9 as a lesson in giving to the Lord. What did David ask of the people, and on what grounds? What characteristics of their giving are specially emphasized? *Cf.* 2 Cor. 8: 3–5; 9: 7. Is our giving of similar quality?

2 Consider in David's prayer (verses 10–19) (a) what he says of God, (b) what he says of man and of his own attitude of heart, and (c) what he prayed for. Seek to learn how to enrich and enlarge your own praying.

PSALMS 107 - 138

☐ **STUDY 85 Psalm 107: 1–32**

This psalm has a general introduction (verses 1–3), then four examples showing God's steadfast love (verses 4–32), and a conclusion summarizing what is learnt about God from these experiences (verses 33–43).

1 What are the situations of difficulty from which God rescued His people? Study (a) the reasons for these difficulties, (b) the feelings of the people in them, and (c) the way in which they obtained relief.

2 What reactions are called for from those who have been delivered in these ways?

3 How do some of the acts of Jesus show the same pattern as God's acts here? *Cf.*, *e.g.*, verses 23–32 with Mk. 4: 35–41; Mt. 14: 22–33. What does this show us about Jesus?

☐ STUDY 86 Psalm 107: 33–43

1 What is shown about God Himself and His love by these great acts of deliverance? What was required of men to enter into these experiences?

2 Study the evidences given here of God's control of human experiences and circumstances. *Cf.* verse 34 with Joel 1: 19, 20; 2: 3; Dt. 29: 22–26; and verse 35 with Is. 43: 19, 20; 44: 3.

☐ STUDY 87 Psalm 108

The first five verses of this psalm are taken from Ps. 57: 7–11 and the remainder from Ps. 60: 5–12.

1 Verses 1–5. What moves the psalmist to such determined praise? How do these verses show us the way to appreciate and worship God, and to include praise as a vital part of our prayer?

2 Verses 6–13. In the agony of wondering whether God is helping them any longer, how does the psalmist anchor his faith? *Cf.* Heb. 6: 17; 10: 23; 13: 5, 6.

Note. Verses 7–9. The promise God gave in the Temple enforces His sovereign claim over these territories. The mention of Shechem and Succoth emphasizes God's claim over both sides of Jordan (*cf.* Gn. 33: 17, 18). Ephraim and Judah, paired, bind north and south. (For the sceptre see the promise of Gn. 49: 10.) Moab, Edom and Philistia are traditional enemies and hostile neighbours of Israel. A campaign against Edom seems to be in mind (verse 10).

☐ STUDY 88 Psalm 109

This psalm falls into three parts. Verses 1–5 are a prayer to God for deliverance from persecuting opponents. Retribution is then invoked by the psalmist (verses 6–20) upon the leader of his enemies and all that belongs to him. In the third section (verses 21–31) there is a return to prayer, culminating in thanksgiving and faith.

1 Verses 1–5. How does the writer show that he has a good conscience, and is not being opposed because of his own offensiveness or evil deeds? Compare Jesus' attitude in parallel circumstances (Lk. 23: 32–43; *cf.* also 1 Pet. 4: 12–19).

2 Verses 21–31. Instead of himself taking revenge, the psalmist takes refuge in prayer. Study the attitude of prayer in these circumstances.

Note. Verses 6–20. The retribution invoked includes the man himself, his person and office, his wife and children, his property, and also his prosperity. The place and significance of the imprecatory psalms (of which this is one), as part of the fullness of revealed truth, belong to the general subject of the progress of revelation. It is to be remembered that in pre-Christian days New Testament standards were not yet revealed. Old Testament believers lived in a dispensation in which retribution was a fundamental principle. Their very faith in a God of righteousness, who would reward the righteous and condemn the wicked, encouraged them to pray for His blessing upon themselves and for His vengeance upon their persecutors; and in this they had scriptural support (*e.g.*, Lv. 24: 19; Pr. 17: 13). Retribution was therefore prayed for as part of the practical vindication of God's actual and righteous sovereignty. Note here that the psalmist does not take vengeance himself, but leaves it to God. The New Testament teaches us also to love and pray for them that despitefully use us (Mt. 5: 43–45; Rom. 12: 19–21).

☐ STUDY 89 Psalm 110

This psalm speaks of the enthronement of a king (*cf.* Ps. 2), and of God's proclamation to that king. At morning time (verse 3b)—symbolizing the newness of the era about to begin—a solemn procession (verses 3, 7) moves by way of the spring (verse 7; *cf.* 1 Ki. 1: 33, 34, 45; 2 Ch. 32: 30) to the coronation in the holy city. There the king, as God's representative, begins his reign.

1 In detail, what hopes are expressed for this new epoch, with reference to (a) the rule of the king, and (b) the response from the people? Jesus applies this psalm to Himself in Mk. 12: 35–37. How then is all this realized in His Messianic kingship over us and the world?

2 Study the use of this psalm in the New Testament. No Old Testament verse is cited more often in the New Testament than Ps. 110: 1. *Cf.* Mk. 14: 62; 1 Cor. 15: 25ff.; Eph. 1: 20; Col. 3: 1; Heb. 1: 13; 10: 12, 13. Of what are we thereby assured?

3 The promised king is also to be a priest but not an Aaronic one. How does the writer to the Hebrews expound verse 4? *Cf.* Gn. 14: 17–24; Heb. 5: 7–11; 6: 20 – 7: 28.

☐ STUDY 90 Psalms 111 and 112

1 Ps. 111. What does the study of God's works reveal about Him to those who make it their delight to examine them? What response to God should follow?

2 Ps. 112. What social and ethical obligations are laid on the man who wants to please God? *Cf.* Mi. 3: 1–4; Je. 22: 1–4, 16; Mk. 10: 21. What blessings can such a man look for from God, in his own life and in his family's?

☐ STUDY 91 Psalms 113 and 114

Pss. 113–118 are psalms of redemption, the Hallel or hymn of praise that was sung at Jewish festivals in the time of Jesus. Looking back on God's past acts of redemption, particularly in the exodus, the people were encouraged to believe God would so act again. Jesus and His disciples may have sung these psalms at Passover as He Himself prepared for His act of redeeming us. (*Cf.* Mk. 14: 26.)

1 Ps. 113. What activities are here said to be characteristic of God? *Cf.* Lk. 1: 46–55. What kind of response, in terms of both time and place, should their acknowledgment secure from men?

2 Ps. 114. What features of the Israelites' journey from Egypt to Canaan are referred to? *Cf.* Ex. 14: 21, 22; 17: 5, 6; 19: 18; 33: 14; Nu. 20: 11; Jos. 3: 14–17. To what truths were these events a permanent witness?

☐ STUDY 92 Psalm 115

1 What answer is here given to idolaters who suppose that their gods are real, and that our God does not exist? Of what may we be sure concerning 'our God'?

2 What ought this psalm to stir us to do? What concern and what resolve ought it to prompt in us?

☐ STUDY 93 Psalm 116

While this psalm is written in the first person, there are indications that, like the other psalms of this group, it has a national character, and sets forth the reaction of the nation to the deliverance from exile. At the same time it echoes the personal experience of any believer.

1 How did trouble test the faith of the writer, and what new realization did his experience bring?

2 What is shown about his prayer during the trouble and afterwards? What resolves and dedication sprang from his experience?

Note. Verse 15. God sets a high value on the life of His people and does not regard their death lightly.

☐ STUDY 94 Psalms 117 and 118

Ps. 118 was used on a great Feast Day (verse 24). It opens with solemn liturgical exhortations and repeated responses. Then a kingly procession moves from outside the Temple (verse 19) to the interior (verse 26), culminating in a ceremony at the altar (verse 27). The king himself, entering into his victory celebration, has come through great struggles and opposition (verses 10–14, 18) to the gladness of victory and salvation (verse 21). This psalm, therefore, takes us to the centre of Israel's faith as a nation, and particularly to the triumph of her king.

1 In both psalms what truths about God particularly move the people, and how do they express their worship? What can we learn from their example?

2 Ps. 118: 5–21. Examine in detail the more personal testimony o the king. What has he been up against? What has the Lord done for him? Have you any comparable testimony?

3 Study the use of Ps. 118: 22–26 in its application to Jesus. *Cf.* Mt. 21: 9; Mk. 12: 6–11; Acts 4: 10–12; 1 Pet. 2: 7.

☐ STUDY 95 Psalm 119: 1–24

The psalm consists of twenty-two stanzas of eight verses each, and goes through the Hebrew alphabet letter by letter. Each stanza begins with a new letter, and each verse in that stanza begins with that letter.

1 How must God's Word be used so that a man may live a pure and sinless life? Conversely, what temptations have to be overcome so that our motives are right, both in coming to God and in living for Him? *Cf.* Jas. 1: 21–25.

2 What compelling reasons urge the writer to study God's law? In putting what we here read into practice, where is the responsibility for action ours, and in what matters must we look only to God?

☐ STUDY 96 Psalm 119: 25–48

1 In daily life the psalmist is confronted with many choices and subtle temptations. What are these, and how does the Word of God lead him (a) into the right choices, and (b) to victory in temptation?

2 For what motives and longings, described in this passage, do we particularly need to pray?

☐ STUDY 97 Psalm 119: 49–80

1 How have sufferings been used for good in the life of the psalmist? How does this lead us forward in understanding why suffering sometimes comes? *Cf.* Je. 2: 30; Heb. 12: 6–11; Am. 4: 6–11.

2 Each section begins with a statement about the Lord. How then is past experience of Him to be used in prayer, commitment and obedience?

3 What bearing have the commandments upon the relationships between God's servant and others who fear Him? See verses 63, 74, 79.

☐ STUDY 98 Psalm 119: 81–104

1 Study the various aspects of the psalmist's problems as described in verses 81–88. How is God's Word relevant in these troubles?

2 Verses 89–96. How is it helpful to know that the author of these commandments and promises is the God of creation?

3 How do verses 97–104 illustrate from the psalmist's experience that whole-hearted obedience is the practical condition for progress in knowing and understanding the truth? *Cf.* Jesus' words in Jn. 8:31, 32.

☐ STUDY 99 Psalm 119: 105–128

1 The psalmist has pledged himself to be God's servant (verse 106), but is tempted from several directions to go back on it. Which tests does he find hardest, and what is the way through them?

2 Verses 113–120. What does the psalmist say God is to him, and does for him? Can you make each of his statements your own?

3 Verses 121–128. In what matters is the psalmist conscious (a) of his dependence upon God only, and (b) of the importance of his own obedience?

☐ STUDY 100 Psalm 119: 129–152

1 List the terms in which the psalmist expresses his appreciation of God's Word. What tests and demands does he find that it can stand up to? What does this awareness mean (a) to him, and (b) to you?

2 When did the writer set himself to pray and study, and what may we learn from the way he prayed? Are your requests as personal, definite and comprehensive?

☐ STUDY 101 Psalm 119: 153–176

1 The writer continually prays for help and understanding (see verse 169), even though he has clearly been taught deep things already. What may we learn from this? See, *e.g.*, verse 176; *cf.* Rev. 3:17–19.

2 Why does the psalmist need God's help? On what grounds does he expect his prayers to be answered? What is his reason for continual praise?

3 In verses 161–168, find at least three characteristics of the psalmist's attitude to the Word of God, and three blessings which devotion to it bring into a man's life. *Cf.* Pr. 3: 1–4; 6: 20–24.

☐ STUDY 102 Psalms 120 and 121

In Pss. 120–134 we have a book of pilgrim songs, probably used on the way up to Jerusalem for the great national festivals. Gradually the pilgrim approaches Zion where God is, and where the people enter afresh into the blessings of His love and redemption.

1 What does Ps. 120 teach about the menace of the tongue and the way of control? *Cf.* Ps. 141: 3, and the very similar teaching in Jas. 3: 1–12; 4: 1–3.

2 In Ps. 121 the infinite concern and care of God is shown. How, when and where can a man look to this God? And what will He constantly do for us?

Note. 120: 5. Meshech is somewhere between the Black Sea and the Caspian Sea (Gn. 10: 2; Ezk. 27: 13; 32: 26); Kedar is a tribe of Bedouins in the Syrian-Arabian desert (Gn. 25: 13; Is. 42: 11). They are so far from one another that their significance here is probably as symbols of quarrelsome adversaries without any special reference to their geographical position.

☐ STUDY 103 Psalms 122 and 123

1 Ps. 122. What is this pilgrim's attitude to Jerusalem, and why does he obey the summons to come and to pray? *Cf.* Dt. 12: 5–7; Ps. 87.

2 According to Ps. 123, what is the best antidote to despondency? *Cf.* also Heb. 4: 16.

☐ STUDY 104 Psalms 124–126

1 Ps. 124. What salutary reflections does the psalmist draw from the narrow escape that is past? How do past experiences buoy up present faith? What ought we to learn from them?

2 Of what two things did the mountain beneath, and the mountains around, Jerusalem speak to God's people? With Ps. 125, *cf.* Dt. 33: 27–29a.

3 In Ps. 126, what are the effects of God's intervention? Note the significance of the illustrations used. What kind of hope does such recollection inspire?

☐ STUDY 105 Psalms 127–129

1 Ps. 127 and 128. What is the secret of true prosperity? *Cf.* Ps. 37: 5–7; Pr. 3: 5–8.

2 Ps. 129. What two permanent truths concerning the life of the servants of God in the world are here set forth? Compare the experience of the Servant in Is. 50: 4–10, and the example of Jesus as the Servant of God in 1 Pet. 2: 19–23.

☐ STUDY 106 Psalms 130 and 131

1 Study the psalmist's attitude in prayer. On what things does he particularly concentrate (a) about himself, and (b) about God? How does his renewed contact with the Lord enable him to encourage others?

2 What four things does the psalmist say about himself in Ps. 131? *Cf.* Mt. 11: 29; Phil. 4: 11–13, 17, 18.

☐ STUDY 107 Psalm 132

This is another psalm describing the procession into the Temple as the king enters for his coronation. With him he brings the ark, the symbol of God's presence, as David did on the first occasion of this sort.

1 What lessons do we learn about the presence of God among His people? What did it mean to the king as he looked at his responsibilities for his own life and for the life of the nation? *Cf.* 2 Sa. 7: 1–17.

2 How do failures to enjoy blessings and promises of this sort arise? See how some of the kings went astray (1 Ki. 11: 1–6; 15: 1–5; 2 Ki. 13: 1–6).

Note. Verse 6. 'Ephrathah' is the ancient name of Bethlehem, the home of David (see *NBD*, p. 383), and 'the fields of Jaar' mean Kiriath-jearim (1 Sa. 7: 1ff.; 1 Ch. 13: 5ff.), where the ark rested before David brought it to Jerusalem.

☐ STUDY 108 Psalms 133 and 134

1 Ps. 133. By what two similes does the psalmist depict the blessings of love and unity? What is the force of these similes? *Cf.* Jn. 13: 34, 35; 1 Jn. 2: 7–11.

2 Ps. 134. Note the 'two-way traffic' sustained in the house and from the city of the Lord. Where ought we to go to share in it? *Cf.* Heb. 10: 24, 25; 12: 22–24.

Notes

1 133: 2, 3. These similes both indicate copiousness. The oil was poured upon Aaron's head so plentifully that it reached even the collar of the robe. The dew of Hermon was also noted for its abundance.

2 Ps. 134 is a Temple song, consisting of the call of the worshippers as they left the Temple in the evening to priests who were to serve during the night, together with the priestly blessing in response. It forms an appropriate ending to the book of pilgrim songs.

☐ STUDY 109 Psalm 135

1 Who are summoned to praise the Lord? Why is it so reasonable to do so? See verses 1–5.

2 As is so often the case, the thought goes back to God both as the Creator and the Redeemer. Why are these two activities so significant? What does each reveal about God in contrast to idols, and what should contemplation of them move us to do?

☐ STUDY 110 Psalm 136

The psalm divides into a call to give thanks (verses 1–3), a description of God in His creative acts (verses 4–9), and then in His acts of salvation (verses 10–22), ending with a deduction and summary (verses 23–26).

1 By what titles is God described? See verses 1–3 and 26, and *cf.* Dt. 10: 17; Ne. 1: 4, 5. What acts demonstrate the appropriateness of these titles? And how do these acts show God's 'steadfast love'?

2 What permanent lessons does the psalmist draw out? Compare the same themes in Ps. 107.

☐ STUDY 111 Psalms 137 and 138

Ps. 137. The psalmist expresses the deep feeling of the exiles in Babylon, as the stinging experience of hostile surroundings and treatment, and the memory of the cherished city of Jerusalem, now a mass of rubble and ruin, overwhelm them.

1 Ps. 137. What interest and concern made the captives in Babylon weep rather than sing? Do you ever feel any similar constraint?

2 Whence does the writer of Ps. 138 gain the conviction that God is at work in his life? Examine the details of his confidence. How much of his confession can you make your own?

3 137: 6, 7. What place ought we to give in our thought, prayer and preaching to divine vengeance and just recompense? *Cf.* Ezk. 25: 12–14; Rom. 12: 19–21.

For Studies 112–119 on the final section of the Psalms see p. 478.

---

2 CHRONICLES

For Introduction, see p. 430.

Analysis

1: 1 – 9: 30	The building of the Temple. The reign of Solomon.	
9: 31 – 35: 27	The decline of the Temple.	
	9: 31 – 13: 22	First declension under Rehoboam. The kingdom divided and a rival worship established in the north.
	14: 1 – 20: 37	First reformation under Asa and Jehoshaphat.
	21: 1 – 22: 12	Second declension under Jehoram.
	23: 1 – 24: 16	Second reformation under Joash.
	24: 17–27	Third declension under Joash, after the death of Jehoiada the priest.
	25: 1 – 27: 9	Period of partial recovery under Amaziah, Uzziah and Jotham.
	28: 1–27	Fourth declension under Ahaz.
	29: 1– 32: 32	Third reformation under Hezekiah.
	32: 33 – 33: 25	Fifth declension under Manasseh and Amon.
	34: 1 – 35: 27	Fourth reformation under Josiah.
36: 1–21	The destruction of the Temple.	
36: 22, 23	The command of Cyrus concerning the rebuilding of the Temple.	

☐ STUDY 1 2 Chronicles 1 and 2

1 How did Solomon inaugurate his reign?

2 How do Solomon's request (1: 10) and God's response illustrate Mt. 6: 33? In my praying what do I 'seek first'?

3 What characterized the way in which Solomon went about the preparations for building the Temple? Is my service of God comparable?

Note. 1: 3. 'The tent of meeting': this was the Tabernacle used in the wilderness. After the Israelites entered Canaan, it was first pitched in Shiloh (Jos. 18: 1; 1 Sa. 2: 14b; 3: 21), then moved to Nob (1 Sa. 21: 1, 6), and then to Gibeon. Later Solomon brought it to Jerusalem (2 Ch. 5: 5), where it was probably stored and finally perished.

☐ STUDY 2 2 Chronicles 3: 1 – 5: 1

1 All that human skill and wealth could do (note how many times the word 'gold' occurs in these chapters) was done. Yet it was still inadequate. Why? See Heb. 9: 1–10, which, though spoken of the Tabernacle, is equally applicable to the Temple.

2 Solomon's Temple has long since passed away (see 36: 19), and the Temples that succeeded it also. Is there, then, today a place where men may draw near to God? See Heb. 10: 19–22, 'Let us draw near. . . .'

Note. 3: 3. 'The old standard': a reference to the cubit in use before the exile, which was a handbreadth larger than that used later.

☐ STUDY 3 2 Chronicles 5: 2 – 6: 11

1 This was one of the great days in Israel's history. How does Solomon interpret its significance in 6: 1–11?

2 We, who belong to the new covenant, are ourselves the temple of God (1 Cor. 3: 16; 6: 19). Is there any parallel between the place given here to the ark and the place we should give to Christ in our hearts? What is the ground of Christian praise, and what corresponds to the glory which 'filled the house'?

Note. 5: 5. See Note on 1: 3.

☐ STUDY 4 2 Chronicles 6: 12–42

1 On what grounds does Solomon base his prayer? See verses 14, 15 and 42. What three main petitions does he present in verses 16–21, and into what seven specific requests does he expand the third of these?

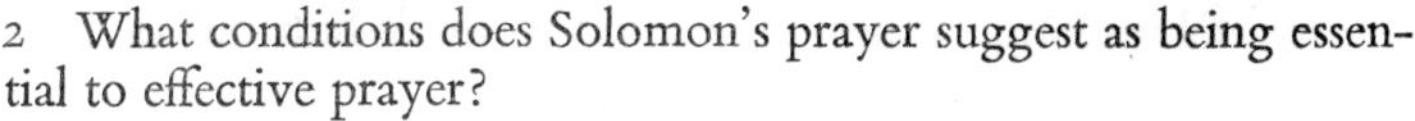

2 What conditions does Solomon's prayer suggest as being essential to effective prayer?

□ STUDY 5 2 Chronicles 7 and 8

1 God's immediate answer to Solomon's prayer is given in 7: 1–3. What effect had it upon the people? *Cf.* Lv. 9: 24. How far should God's mercies affect us?

2 God gave a further answer to Solomon privately in the form of a promise and a warning (7: 12–22). What were the conditions upon which Solomon's petitions were to be granted? Do I fear the fulfilment of God's warnings as I desire the fulfilment of His promises?

□ STUDY 6 2 Chronicles 9 and 10

1 What was the Queen of Sheba's testimony concerning Solomon? Has something similar been your experience of Christ? *Cf.* Phil. 3: 8.

2 What led Rehoboam to make such a disastrous mistake? What did he lack that Solomon possessed? *Cf.* 1 Ki. 3: 28.

Notes

1 Chapter 9. Another side to the portrait of Solomon is found in 1 Ki. 11: 1–13, and provides a background to the disruption. Note also 2 Ch. 10: 4.

2 From chapter 10 onwards students are advised to make a list of the kings of Judah as they work through the rest of the book, and to note the biblical assessment of each (*e.g.*, good or evil), with a brief mention of his contribution to the nation's religious life.

□ STUDY 7 2 Chronicles 11 and 12

1 Was Rehoboam good or evil? Was there a fundamental fault in his character? *Cf.* Jas. 1: 8.

2 What did Shemaiah achieve on the two occasions when he intervened in national life, and how was he able to do this? Is there a parallel between his work and that of a Christian today?

3 What lesson did God mean to teach through Shishak's invasion

□ STUDY 8 2 Chronicles 13 and 14

1 Chapter 13. Jeroboam had the advantages of numbers (verse 3) and of military skill (verse 13), and he, too, had received promises from God (*cf.* 1 Ki. 11: 29–39). What, then, gave Judah the victory? *Cf.* verse 18 with 1 Ki. 12: 28–33.

2 Chapter 14. What did Asa do to mark him out as 'good and right' in peace and war?

3 What is the connection between 14: 2–4 and 14: 11, 12? *Cf.* 1 Jn. 3: 21, 22; 5: 3, 4. If Asa had not set God and His commandments in the forefront of his endeavours, could he have prayed with such confidence or won so great a victory? What did Asa's faith provide him with besides the victory?

Note. 13: 5. 'By a covenant of salt': *i.e.*, a binding covenant, not to be broken. *Cf.* Nu. 18: 19.

☐ STUDY 9 2 Chronicles 15 and 16

1 Can you find in Azariah's message (15: 2–7) (a) a fundamental principle of divine government, (b) an illustration from Israel's past history, (c) an exhortation, and (d) a promise?

2 Chapter 15. How thoroughly and with what success were these lessons heeded by Asa (see especially verse 15)? *Cf.* Je. 29: 13; Mt. 11: 29.

3 In what ways did Asa backslide in his later years, and what were the consequences?

☐ STUDY 10 2 Chronicles 17 and 18

1 The chronicler gives four chapters to the reign of Jehoshaphat, who was one of the best of the kings of Judah. What, according to chapter 17, were the reasons for his prosperity? Note the word 'therefore' in verse 5. What method did Jehoshaphat introduce to give religious instruction to the people?

2 Chapter 18. How did Micaiah seek to proclaim the word of God, and what difficulties did he encounter? What may we learn from him concerning faithfulness in such ministry?

3 In what ways do the characters of Jehoshaphat and Ahab differ?

☐ STUDY 11 2 Chronicles 19 and 20

1 In the beginning of Jehoshaphat's reign he continued the policy of maintaining fortified cities for defence against Israel. But later he made peace with Israel through a marriage alliance (18: 1; 21: 6). How was this alliance with Ahab rebuked, and on what grounds? *Cf.* 2 Cor. 6: 14; see also 2 Ch. 20: 35–37.

2 After this rebuke, what further steps did Jehoshaphat take to establish true religion in the land?

3 When peril came, what did Jehoshaphat do first? What impresses you most in this story?

Note. 20: 2. 'Engedi': on the western shore of the Dead Sea, and therefore not far from Jerusalem.

☐ STUDY 12 2 Chronicles 21: 1 – 22: 9

1 Identify the sins here recorded of Jehoram. How did God deal with him, and why? To what did he owe his survival?

2 How far was the low state under Jehoram and Ahaziah directly traceable to the mistaken step of Jehoshaphat as recorded in 18: 1? What does this illustrate concerning the character and consequences of some sins?

☐ STUDY 13 2 Chronicles 22: 10 – 23: 21

1 *Planning.* Why had Jehoiada to wait seven years? What lessons may we learn from this for ourselves? *Cf.* Hab. 2: 3. Why did he have confidence that the plan would succeed?

2 *Action.* What lessons in careful planning and organization can we learn from Jehoiada in our service of Christ?

3 *Success.* Jehoiada was not content with half measures. How did he follow up his victory? See 23: 16–20.

Notes

1 23: 2, 3. This was the preliminary gathering, secretly convened in the Temple, in which all present pledged their loyalty to the boy king.

2 23: 11. 'The testimony': *i.e.*, the book of the law. *Cf.* Dt. 17: 18–20.

☐ STUDY 14 2 Chronicles 24

1 Joash was a weak character, who leant on others. To whom did he listen? What were the consequences? What lessons may we learn? *Cf.* 2 Tim. 2: 1.

2 Why was the stoning of Zechariah a peculiarly flagrant crime?

Note. Verse 16. This was a signal and unique honour. Contrast verse 25.

☐ STUDY 15 2 Chronicles 25

1 What would you say was the chief fault in Amaziah's character? How does the chapter illustrate the description of him in verse 2? See, on the one hand, verses 3, 4, 7–10; also 26: 4; and, on the other hand, 25: 14–16, 27. *Cf.* Je. 17: 9.

2 How does Amaziah's career, with its gradual drift away from God, show the peril of a half-hearted loyalty to Christ?

Note. Verse 10. The hired soldiers had been hoping for loot and plunder, hence their anger. See also verse 13.

☐ STUDY 16 2 Chronicles 26–28

1 How was it revealed that in Uzziah's heart, notwithstanding his piety (26: 5), there lurked the same evil tendency that had marred the life and reign of his father Amaziah before him? With 26: 16, *cf.* 25: 19; Dt. 17: 18–20. What forms might his sin take today?

2 How did the sin of Ahaz affect (a) God, (b) His people, and (c) himself?

3 In the midst of a godless age how did Oded, the prophet, and the men mentioned in 28: 12 stand out? What may we learn from their example? *Cf.* 1 Tim. 5: 20.

Notes

1 26: 5. 'Zechariah': not otherwise known, and not the prophet of the biblical book who lived at a later period.

2 26: 18. See Nu. 16: 40; 18: 7.

☐ STUDY 17 2 Chronicles 29: 1 – 31: 1

1 Hezekiah as king desired to reform the religious life of the nation, and worked urgently to a definite plan. What steps did he follow? Note his speed (29: 3; 30: 2) and his priorities (29: 16–21).

2 What evidence do you find that the Passover (chapter 30) was not merely an outward form, but betokened a genuine turning back to God? What signs were there of true spiritual revival?

Note. 30: 2, 3, 13, 15. The king availed himself of the provision in the law which allowed the Passover to be kept in the second month, instead of the first (see Nu. 9: 10, 11), and thus avoided having to wait almost a year.

☐ STUDY 18 2 Chronicles 31: 2 – 32: 33

1 How far was Hezekiah's thoroughness in all matters connected with religion the secret of his success? See especially 31: 20, 21. *Cf.* Rom. 12: 11; Col. 3: 23.

2 What lessons can we learn from the way in which Hezekiah met opposition?

3 How far did this spiritually-minded king fall short of perfection? How may we learn from him?

Notes

1 32: 1. This reference to Hezekiah's faithfulness (31: 20) is introduced to show that the coming of Sennacherib was not because he had sinned.
2 32: 5. Archaeologists think 'the Millo' at Jerusalem was probably part of the fortifications or the foundations for them.

☐ STUDY 19 2 Chronicles 33

1 Make a list of Manasseh's idolatrous deeds, as described in verses 3–9. It has been termed 'a very delirium of idolatry' and was done in the face of protest and rebuke (verses 10, 18).

2 What means did God use to bring Manasseh to his senses? And what may we learn from this as to one of the purposes of human suffering?

3 What marks of true repentance are seen in Manasseh after his restoration? In what ways could it have gone further?

Notes

1 Verse 6. A reference to human sacrifice in honour of the god Molech. *Cf.* 1 Ki. 23: 10; Je. 7: 31.
2 Verse 14. 'Ophel': a mound south of the Temple. *Cf.* 27: 3.

☐ STUDY 20 2 Chronicles 34 and 35

1 At what age did Josiah begin to seek the Lord? What effects did this have on his subsequent life both publicly and privately?

2 What was the effect of the finding of the book of the law (a) upon Josiah, and (b) through him upon the nation? *Cf.* Ps. 119: 59, 60. Is the Word of God having the same effect upon you, and through your life?

3 What does 34: 23–28 teach concerning (a) the inevitable consequences of sin (*cf.* Dt. 11: 26–28), and (b) God's attitude to the sincere penitent?

Notes

1 34: 14. 'The book of the law' was quite likely Deuteronomy (*cf.* Dt. 31: 26).
2 35: 3. It is usually assumed that the ark had been taken out of the holy of holies during the repairs, and that the Levites were now bidden to restore it, with the assurance that they would not again be asked to undertake this work. *Cf.* 1 Ch. 23: 26.

3 34: 28 and 35: 24. Josiah was spared from witnessing God's anger poured out upon Judah (34: 25) by his death, and thus may be said to have died 'in peace'.

☐ **STUDY 21 2 Chronicles 36**

1 Alongside the cataclysmic political happenings, what is the one outstanding event in this chapter which overshadows all else?

2 In the indictment of this chapter, on what sin does the emphasis lie (verses 12–16)? How would you describe the cause of Judah's downfall? *Cf.* 7: 19–22.

3 In what particular matters did Zedekiah fail?

4 What does this chapter reveal about the character of God?

Note. A summary of the kings and events of this chapter. (a) Jehoahaz was king for three months (verses 1–3). (b) Jehoiakim (Eliakim) reigned for eleven years (verses 4, 5). He was an Egyptian vassal until the Babylonians (or Chaldeans, verse 17) defeated them at the Battle of Carchemish (605 BC) and became the dominant power. The first Babylonian invasion occurred during this reign (verses 6, 7). (c) Jehoiachin was king for three months, until the second invasion (verse 10) terminated his reign; 10,000 leading citizens were taken into exile. (d) Zedekiah reigned for eleven years (verse 10, 11). He was a Babylonian vassal and his rebellion precipitated the third invasion, devastation and exile (verses 17, 18) in 586 BC.

ESTHER

Introduction

The book of Esther is a swiftly-moving story which repays reading at one sitting. Its author and date of composition cannot be identified with certainty. The wealth of detail and local colour, however, suggests that it was written in Persia not long after the events recorded in the book had taken place. Perhaps its Persian origin may account for the long time that elapsed before it was accepted as canonical by the Palestinian Jews.

Ahasuerus is usually identified with Xerxes (485–465 BC), and the action takes place in Susa, one of the three capitals of the Persian Empire. Chronologically this places the events some years before those recounted in Ezra and Nehemiah, which relate to the following reign—that of Artaxerxes (465–424 BC).

One of the most unusual features of the book is the absence of any mention of the name of God. There is, however, a strong undercurrent throughout of patriotism and a sense of overriding Providence, as the Jews in exile are saved from destruction. Their deliverance provides the origin of the Feast of Purim.

Analysis

1: 1–22	Queen Vashti disobeys King Ahasuerus and is deposed.
2: 1–20	Esther, a Jewess, is chosen by the king to replace Vashti.
2: 21–23	Mordecai exposes a plot against the king's life.
3: 1–15	Mordecai refuses to bow to Haman, the king's favourite, who thereupon plans to massacre the Jews.
4: 1–17	Esther is persuaded by Mordecai to intercede with the king.
5: 1–8	The king receives Esther.
5: 9–14	Haman schemes to secure Mordecai's death.
6: 1–14	The king makes Haman honour Mordecai publicly as a reward for revealing the plot against him.
7: 1–10	Esther's plea is granted and in consequence Haman is executed.
8: 1–17	Mordecai is honoured further and an edict is published allowing the Jews to defend themselves.
9: 1–19	The Jews slay their enemies.
9: 20–32	Their deliverance is commemorated in the Feast of Purim.
10: 1–3	Mordecai is given a position of great authority.

□ STUDY 1 Esther 1

1 Read this chapter in the light of 2 Cor. 4: 18 and 1 Jn. 2: 16, 17. What choice do such considerations force upon us?

2 What may we learn of the characters of Ahasuerus, Vashti and Memucan as seen in this chapter? *Cf.* Pr. 20: 2; Jas. 1: 19, 20; Eph. 4: 26, 27.

Notes

1 Verse 11. Persian women were usually present at feasts, so this would not be taken as a personal affront to Vashti.
2 Verse 14. 'Who saw the king's face . . .': *i.e.*, belonging to the inner circle of the king's counsellors.

□ STUDY 2 Esther 2: 1–18

1 By what steps did Esther become queen? Consider the events and the timing in terms of God's overruling care for His people. See Note on verse 16; *cf.* Rom. 8: 28; Is. 65: 24.

2 How far should a Christian conform to the laws and customs of his country? *Cf.* Dn. 1: 8; 1 Pet. 2: 13, 14.

Notes

1 Verses 5, 6. 'Who had been carried away . . .': this refers not to Mordecai, but to Kish his grandfather.
2 Verse 16. *Cf.* 1: 3. Four years had elapsed since Vashti was deposed.

□ STUDY 3 Esther 2: 19 – 3: 15

1 Mordecai made no secret of his Jewish faith, yet advised Esther to remain silent. What does this teach us for our own witness? Why did Mordecai not obey the king's command? *Cf.* Ec. 3: 1, 7b; Dn. 3: 8–12, 16–18; Acts 5: 28, 29.

2 What do we learn of Haman's character in chapter 3? See particularly verses 5–9 and 15. To what was he blind in the schemes that he made?

Notes

1 2: 19. 'Sitting at the king's gate': the phrase may imply that he was in the king's service in some way.
2 2: 21. 'Who guarded the threshold . . .': *i.e.*, of the king's sleeping apartments.

□ STUDY 4 Esther 4

1 The Jews mourn Haman's decree, but for Esther the situation requires personal action. Consider (a) what factors influenced the decision she reached (see particularly verses 4, 8, 13, 14, 16), and (b) whether verse 14 is relevant to your own immediate situation.

2 Esther made careful preparations to enter the king's presence. In our own approach to the King of kings, what parallels and contrasts can you find? See also 5: 1, 2; *cf.* Ps. 33: 8; Heb. 10: 19–22.

☐ STUDY 5 Esther 5 and 6

1 Mordecai could reasonably have expected a substantial reward for saving the king's life (2: 21–23). However, his service was acknowledged only after a long delay and by an apparent coincidence. In what ways does this help us to understand delays and disappointments in our own life? *Cf.* Ps. 37: 7; Is. 55: 8, 9.

2 Consider the developments in the story of Haman as illustrations of such verses as Ps. 34: 15, 16; Pr. 16: 18. What ought we to learn from such a record?

☐ STUDY 6 Esther 7 and 8

1 How does chapter 7 illustrate the theme of certain psalms? See, *e.g.*, Pss. 73: 17–19; 94: 1–7, 21–23. How should this influence our faith?

2 After the fall of Haman what did (a) Esther and (b) the Jews still have to do to obtain the deliverance promised by the king? See especially 8: 3–8, 11, 12. What parallel is there in Christian experience? *Cf.* Phil. 2: 12, 13.

Notes
1 7: 3. 'My life . . . and my people . . .': for the first time Esther acknowledges her nationality.
2 7: 9. Notice how often the king's decisions are influenced by those around him.

☐ STUDY 7 Esther 9 and 10

1 Select from these and earlier chapters the outstanding features o Mordecai's character. What was the source of his moral strength?

2 Notice here the severity of the judgment on the wicked. Are we in danger of underestimating this part of 'the whole counsel of God' (Acts 20: 27)? *Cf.* Heb. 10: 30, 31; 1 Pet. 4: 17, 18; Rev. 20: 12–15.

3 Why was the Feast of Purim instituted? See 9: 22; *cf.* Ex. 12: 14–17. Do we ever encourage and challenge ourselves by the remembrance of God's mercies to us? *Cf.* Dt. 8: 2; 1 Cor. 11: 24–26.

Note. 9: 26. 'Purim . . . Pur': these words are derived from the Assyrian *puru*, meaning a small stone, which was used to cast lots. See 3: 7; 9: 24.

ECCLESIASTES

Introduction

This book speaks through the mouth of Solomon, but does not in any way build on his authority. In the earlier part the writer describes human life as seen by a shrewd observer, who disputes the arguments of those who find a satisfactory aim in life either in intellectual labour, or in the gathering of riches, or in pleasure, or even in the attainment of an ethical ideal, seeing that death terminates all, and comes to all alike.

Man cannot by searching find out the deep things of God (3: 11) but must bow before His sovereignty (3: 14). Whatever appearances may indicate, God judges righteously, though judgment may be long delayed (8: 12, 13).

The recurring phrase 'under the sun' may be regarded as indicating the purely human standpoint adopted by the writer in the earlier chapters, and as roughly equivalent to 'in the world as man sees it'. It is salutary for the Christian to contrast the vanity and meaninglessness of this world, its business and pleasures, as set forth in Ecclesiastes, with our glorious heritage in Christ as set forth in the New Testament.

The book is the record of a spiritual pilgrimage, reaching its culmination in chapter 12 (*cf.* 12: 13, 14 with Rom. 2: 16). In Ecclesiastes, perhaps more than in any other book of the Old Testament, the standpoint of the writer should be borne in mind, and particularly the fact that he saw nothing for man beyond death save judgment. His attention is concentrated upon this life, for 'our Saviour Christ Jesus, who abolished death and brought life and immortality to light through the gospel' (2 Tim. 1: 10) had not yet appeared.

Analysis

1:1	The title.
1:2–11	The endless monotony of human life on earth.
1:12 – 2:26	The Preacher's experiences—wisdom, pleasure, labour alike fail to satisfy. 'There is nothing better for a man than to eat and drink and enjoy himself, as he does his work' (2:24, Moffatt).
3 – 6	Further illustration of the vanity of man's striving. His life is hemmed in by divine control, and ends in death. Various counsels. Riches do not satisfy.
7:1 – 11:8	The kind of life men should lead. Wisdom is better than folly. The fear of God brings a sure reward. God's works are unsearchable. Various counsels.
11:9 – 12:14	Childhood and youth pass; old age and death draw near. The ultimate conclusion: fear God and keep His commandments.

☐ STUDY 1 Ecclesiastes 1 and 2

1 In what ways does 1:1–11 show the monotony of life? Why is such pessimism unchristian?

2 How did the writer discover that neither the pursuit of wisdom (1:12–18) nor the enjoyment of pleasure (2:1–11) can satisfy man's heart?

3 Though wisdom is better than folly (2:13, 14a), what three facts rob even wisdom of its power to satisfy (2:14b, 17, 18 and 23, 24–26)?

☐ STUDY 2 Ecclesiastes 3:1 – 4:8

1 What, according to 3:1–15, is the best attitude to life? How does the Preacher illustrate his conviction? *Cf.* Mt. 10:29, 30. To what practical conclusion does he come?

2 In 3:16 – 4:8, what four instances are given of the futility of life, and what reflections do they arouse in the writer's mind?

Note. 3:1. 'Season . . . time': the two words express two thoughts, (a) tha everything happens at an appointed time; and (b) that the time is appropriate in relation to the working out of God's purpose.

☐ STUDY 3 Ecclesiastes 4:9 – 6:12

1 What are the blessings of friendship described in 4:9–12? How does this apply in the spiritual life? See, *e.g.*, Mt. 18:19, 20; Lk. 10:1.

2 What does 5: 1–7 teach concerning worship, in respect to (a) the right attitude of spirit, (b) words spoken in God's presence, and (c) the importance of fulfilling vows?

3 What is the teaching of 5: 8 – 6: 12 regarding money and the evils it brings?

Notes

1 5: 1. 'Guard your steps': *i.e.*, 'Never enter God's house carelessly' (Moffatt).

2 5: 3. As cares and labours cause a man to dream, so do many words in worship give rise to folly.

3 5: 20. 'Then he will never brood over the fewness of his days' (Moffatt).

4 6: 10, 11. 'Whatever happens has been determined long ago, and what man is has been ordained of old; he cannot argue with One mightier than himself' Moffatt). The meaning is that much talking against God's dealings is profitless.

☐ STUDY 4 Ecclesiastes 7 and 8

The Preacher has declared several times that man's best course in this present world is to enjoy the portion in life which God has given him, and the fruit of his labour. In these later chapters, while still holding to this view, he inquires more closely into the kind and quality of life which men should lead.

1 In the practical wisdom of chapter 7, what emerges as the guide-principle for life?

2 Though the future is hidden from man, what course of action is advocated in 8: 1–7? How is the problem of death approached in 8: 8–17?

☐ STUDY 5 Ecclesiastes 9: 1 – 10: 7

1 Why, from a Christian standpoint, is the view of life contained in 9: 1–10 untenable? *Cf.* Lk. 23: 39–43; and note how and why one of the criminals rebuked the other and found hope for himself.

2 What do 9: 11, 12 teach regarding a man's attitude to natural talents? In what way is the value of wisdom shown in 9: 13 – 10: 4?

☐ STUDY 6 Ecclesiastes 10: 8 – 11: 8

1 List the spheres in which the practical wisdom of 10: 8–20 apply, and deduce any general principles for your practical guidance.

2 11: 1–8. Since the future cannot be known, what advice does the writer give regarding an appropriate attitude in life? *Cf.* 9: 10.

Note. 11: 1, 2. 'Trust your goods far and wide at sea, till you get good returns after a while. Take shares in several ventures; you never know what will go wrong in this world' (Moffatt).

☐ **STUDY 7 Ecclesiastes 11: 9 – 12: 14**

1 In the Preacher's counsel to youth, (a) in what is youth to rejoice, (b) to what all-important fact must heed be given, and (c) who is to be remembered? What is the reason for this counsel?

2 Contrast the joyful hope of the Christian with the picture of death and old age given here. *Cf.* 2 Cor. 4: 16–18; 2 Tim. 4: 6–8; 1 Pet. 1: 3–5.

3 In summing up man's duty, what place is given to God? How, in consequence, ought we to live?

Notes

1 11: 10. 'Vanity' has here the meaning of 'transitory' or 'passing'.

2 12: 2. Old age is here compared to winter weather, when storm succeeds storm.

3 12: 3–6. A series of pictures of the failure of man's various bodily faculties in old age, such as strength of limb, number of teeth, keenness of sight, *etc.* 'When old age fears a height, and even a walk has its terrors, when his hair is almond white, and he drags his limbs along, as the spirit flags and fades' (verse 5, Moffatt).

SONG OF SOLOMON

Introduction

The Song of Solomon is unique not only for its exquisite literary charm, but also for its rich appreciation of human love and the beauty of nature, and its deep insight into the human heart. It has also appealed to Christians as a picture of the love of Christ for His church, and gives to them words in which to utter their hearts' devotion to Him.

It is uncertain who wrote it. The phrase 'which is Solomon's' in 1: 1 may equally mean 'which is for Solomon' (as in the title of Ps. 72) or 'which is about Solomon'; and there is no other clue to its authorship.

According to the earlier and more traditional interpretation, there are only two main characters—Solomon and his bride. Many commentaries of great devotional beauty and insight have made this interpretation familiar, in which the bride is regarded as a 'type' of the church, and Solomon of Christ.

Others, however, discern in the background of the story another figure, that of a shepherd, who is the girl's true lover. It is he whom she calls 'my beloved'. A girl from the village of Shulem, she had gone one day to visit her garden, when she fell in unexpectedly with some of Solomon's retinue, who took her captive to the palace (6: 11–13). There the king visits her, and struck by her great beauty seeks to win her for himself. But she has a shepherd lover to whom her heart is pledged, and to whom she remains faithful. Three times the king visits her, wooing her with growing ardour, until at last, finding all his efforts of no avail, he sets her free. At the close of the book she is seen leaning on the arm of her beloved, returning to her village home, where she is received by her family and friends as the shepherd lover's acknowledged bride. In this view, much of the book consists of reveries in which the girl communes in thought with her beloved; and of incidents and dreams connected with him, which with artless simplicity she tells to the ladies of the court.

With these different interpretations to choose from, we must obviously form our own view from a study of the book itself. If we take the Song as it stands it is clear that we must look at it first of all as a poem, or collection of poems, about human love between man and woman. The study questions are therefore designed primarily to discover the meaning of the Song of Solomon at this level.

Analysis

It is exceedingly difficult to analyse the Song. The following scheme is based on the three-character interpretation outlined above:

Section I

1: 2 – 2: 7	Scene in the private apartments of Solomon's palace.
1: 2–8	The girl, soliloquizing, expresses her longing for her absent lover (verses 2–4). Then, seeing the ladies of the court eyeing her, she explains to them the darkness of her complexion (verses 5, 6), and breaks out into a cry that she might know exactly where her lover is, to which the ladies of the court reply that she should go to seek him (verses 7, 8).
1: 9–11	The king enters, praises her beauty, and promises to adorn her with jewels.

1: 12 – 2: 6	The king having gone to his repast, the girl falls into a reverie, in which, in imagination, she communes with her beloved in some forest glade.
2: 7	She bids the ladies of the court not to seek to arouse love by artificial means.

Section II

2: 8 – 3: 5	The girl relates an incident of the past.
2: 8–15	Her beloved came one morning to call her to go with him, and to warn her of danger to love's fulfilment.
2: 16, 17	She bids her beloved return at the end of the day.
3: 1–4	When he did not return, she could not rest, but went out into the night to seek him.
3: 5	The same charge as in 2: 7.

Section III

3: 6 – 8: 4	The struggle is intensified, but ends in victory.
3: 6 – 4: 7	Solomon, appearing in royal splendour, makes a determined attempt to capture the girl's affections.
4: 8 – 5: 1	Alarmed, she flees in thought to her beloved, whose voice she hears, bidding her escape with him from the dangers of the palace (4: 8). He pours out his love for her (4: 9–15) in words far excelling the conventiona tributes just paid to her by the king. Her heart opens to her lover, and she sees their marriage day as if already come (4: 16 – 5: 1).
5: 2–16	The girl relates a disturbing dream which she has had; and in answer to a question from the ladies of the court gives an impassioned description of her beloved.
6: 1–3	The ladies of the court ask where he is, that they too may seek him, a suggestion that leads the girl to declare that no other can share her privilege ol possession.
6: 4–10	The king enters, and tells her in words of admiring praise that there is no-one who can compare with her, and that even his queens have sung her praises.
6: 11–13	The girl interrupts to explain how she came to be in the king's palace.
7: 1–9	The king continues to urge his desire.
7: 10 – 8: 3	The girl, refusing, turns in heart to her beloved to commune in spirit with him.
8: 4	The same charge as in 2: 7 and 3: 5.

Section IV

8: 5–14	The scene is the girl's village home.
8: 5	The girl, released, returns with her beloved to her home.
8: 6, 7	The girl's panegyric on true love.
8: 8–12	She recalls her brothers' words, and declares her faithfulness.
8: 13, 14	Her lover bids her speak and in the presence of his friends she calls him her beloved.

☐ STUDY 1 Song of Solomon 1: 1 – 2: 7

1 Much of this passage consists of conversation. The Analysis provides one answer to the problems of how many characters are speaking and where the break occurs. What do you think is the basic situation?

2 Can we learn anything from the different imagery used by the man (1: 15–17; 2: 2) and the woman to express their love and longing for one another? Does this suggest anything of the different qualities, or needs, of each?

Notes

1 1: 12–14. Women wore small bags of myrrh suspended from the neck under their dress. To the girl, her beloved was as the costliest perfume.
2 2: 1. The girl describes herself as an ordinary wild flower of the meadow.
3 2: 3. The apple tree affords both shade and fruit.
4 2: 4. 'The banqueting house': literally 'house of wine', signifying 'a place of delight'.
5 2: 7. A difficult verse. It seems to mean that love should awake or come to life of itself or in its own time, not by artificial stimulation and not before the beloved one is pleased to respond. Gazelles or hinds are noted for their timidity.

☐ STUDY 2 Song of Solomon 2: 8 – 3: 5

1 What purpose do the various pictures from nature serve in revealing the quality of love?

2 What characteristics of true love emerge in 2: 16, 17 and 3: 1–5?

Notes

1 2: 10–12. An appeal to respond to the approach of love, like nature to the return of summer.
2 2: 15. The enemies may be small—'little foxes'—but the mischief done great. If the blossom is spoiled, there will be no fruit.
3 2: 17. A picture of evening, not of early morning. The shadows flee away when the sun that causes them sets. The bride asked her beloved to wait until the evening. When it came, she 'sought him but found him not' (3: 1).

☐ STUDY 3 Song of Solomon 3: 6 – 5: 1

1 What do you make of Solomon's entrance here, and of his part in the whole of the Song? See also, *e.g.*, 1: 1, 12; 6: 8, 9, 12; 7: 1, 5; 8: 11, 12.

2 What do these frank expressions of a man's physical delight in his bride teach us about the place of sexual attraction in love and marriage? What is the significance of the private garden image?

3 Scripture uses marriage as a picture of God's relationship to His people and Christ's relationship to His church. See, *e.g.*, Is. 62: 56; Eph. 5: 21–33. Is there, therefore, a sense in which 4: 8–15 illustrates this relationship? *Cf.* Pss. 147: 10, 11; 149: 4. Is our heart reserved for Christ alone?

Notes

1 3: 7. 'Litter'; in verse 9, 'palanquin': a couch covered by a canopy borne by four or more men.

2 4: 4. The neck, decked with ornaments, is compared to a battlemented tower, hung with shields.

3 4: 8. On the three-character analysis the bride hears the voice of her beloved, calling her to himself, and the verse may be taken as a poetic description of the dangers to which she is exposed in the palace.

☐ STUDY 4 Song of Solomon 5: 2 – 6: 3

1 Is there any underlying reality in the disturbing dream of 5: 2–7? Would we be right to see in this passage teaching about, *e.g.*, the importance of response in love, or the likelihood of suffering if response is lacking?

2 How far is the bride's delight in, and praise of, her lover a feature also of our relationship to Christ? Do we meditate on Him as our 'beloved' and our 'friend' (5: 16)?

Notes

1 5: 2. 'I slept': these words indicate that the bride is relating a dream.

2 5: 4. The door was bolted—on the inside (see verse 5).

3 5: 10. 'Distinguished among ten thousand'; literally, 'marked out by a banner', *i.e.*, as outstanding among the rest as a standard bearer.

☐ STUDY 5 Song of Solomon 6: 4 – 8: 4

1 In 2: 16 the girl's first thought was of her claim upon her lover. Now (6: 3) she thinks first of his claim on her. In 7: 10 her claim is no longer mentioned. Her concern is to satisfy him by giving herself. The importance of this for human marriage relations is clear. But can these stages in love apply to our relation to Christ? If so, how?

2 8: 4. The warning is repeated here for the third time (see also 2: 7; 3: 5). Why do you think it was given, and with such emphasis?

Notes

1 6: 4. 'Tirzah': the name (meaning 'delight') of a beautiful town, which later became the royal residence of the kings of northern Israel.

2 6: 12, 13. A possible translation, in line with the three-character analysis, is 'My soul has unwittingly brought me to the chariots of the companions of my prince'; *i.e.*, she fell in with some of Solomon's retinue. She fled, but they called her back, and gazed upon her, as she put it, as if she were a company of dancers.

3 7: 1–6. These verses may be part of the song composed by the women (6: 9b, 10), or may be spoken by Solomon. In verses 7, 8 he is certainly the speaker.

☐ STUDY 6 Song of Solomon 8: 5–14

1 What does this passage add to all we have already learnt of the nature of love? What attacks may true love have to face?

2 What qualities are here shown to be characteristic of true love?

Notes

1 8: 6. 'Set me as a seal . . .': in ancient times men carried their seal fastened to breast or wrist for safe preservation. The girl desires to be thus held fast on the heart and arm of her beloved. 'Jealousy is cruel as the grave': better, 'Ardent love is unyielding as Sheol'.

2 8: 8–10. The girl recalls her brothers' earlier words. They had waited to see if she would be as a wall against temptation, or as an open door to give it entrance. Here she claims that she has shown herself as a wall.

3 8: 11, 12. Solomon appears to have offered her a vineyard of great wealth; but she put it aside in favour of the vineyard which was hers in her beloved.

☐ STUDY 7 The whole Song of Solomon: Revision

Most of the study questions have been concerned with the Song's meaning at the level of human love between the sexes. Re-reading the Song, draw out some of the lessons it can teach us about Christ's love for us, and our love for Him. How does our personal devotion to Christ measure up to these very high standards?

2 PETER

Introduction

The second Epistle of Peter was written just before his death (1: 14, 15). We may regard it as his last word, and this fact lends added significance to the final message, 'Grow in the grace and knowledge of our Lord and Saviour Jesus Christ' (3: 18).

Peter is obviously concerned about the heresies and moral evil which have crept into the church, and is writing to warn, to exhort and to comfort. In contrast with the gloomy picture which he draws is the prominence he gives to the hope of our Lord's return. He explains that this is delayed, not through any slackness on God's part, but through His forbearance (3: 9). He is afraid that the Christians, under the stress of persecution and temptation, will forget the commandments which have been delivered to them through the prophets and the apostles. He writes to remind them of their calling and to stir them up (1: 9, 12, 13, 15; 3: 1, 2).

Chapter 2 is strikingly similar in content to the Epistle of Jude. As Peter dwells on the evil which is rampant, he stresses more than ever the call to holiness which he had given in his first letter. 'You therefore, beloved, knowing this beforehand, beware lest you be carried away with the error of lawless men and lose your own stability' (3: 17). The essential antidote to error is the true knowledge of God and of the Lord Jesus Christ. This is the key to this Epistle. See 1: 2, 3, 8; 2: 20; 3: 18.

Analysis

1: 1, 2	Introduction.
1: 3–15	The call to progress in Christian character and fruitfulness.
1: 16–21	The veracity of the Christian message.
2: 1–22	Description and condemnation of evildoers and false prophets.
3: 1–7	Warnings for the last days.
3: 8–18	The longsuffering of the Lord, and the certainty of His coming.

☐ STUDY 1 2 Peter 1: 1–11

1 How do verses 1 and 10 describe the Christian's relation to God? What is meant by 'knowledge' in verses 2, 3, 8? What provision has God made for our present life, and what will be our final position (verses 3, 4, 11)?

2 If our salvation is the product of God's call and power (verses 10, 3), why are we urged to zealous effort (verses 5, 10)?

3 Analyse the picture of the fully developed Christian, given in verses 5–7, in relation to (a) his personal character; (b) his attitude to God; and (c) his dealings with others. Observe that all rests upon a basis of faith, but faith without these added qualities is not enough.

☐ STUDY 2 2 Peter 1: 12–21

1 Of what does Peter take such care to remind his readers? Does any Christian not need this kind of reminder? *Cf.* 3: 1, 2; Dt. 32: 18; Heb. 2: 1.

2 How do verses 16–21 provide an answer to theologians who claim that truth does not require a basis of historic fact?

3 Explain from verses 20, 21 the nature of the inspiration of Scripture. What gives it its authority, and what should govern its interpretation.

Note. Verse 19. 'The written word of prophecy has been confirmed by the vision of the Lord's glory . . . on the mount of Transfiguration, and Christians may well trust themselves to its guidance in this dark world, till light has dawned, which will render the lamp of an external revelation unnecessary' (Swete). This lamp of prophecy is referred to again in 3: 2.

☐ STUDY 3 2 Peter 2

1 Although we have the lamp of prophecy it is necessary to beware of *false* teachers. Note from today's passage the forms of evil in which the false teachers, of whom the apostle speaks, indulged. By which are you most liable to be snared? How far is this kind of behaviour seen in modern society? How would you meet the claim of those who profess to be free from the restraints of convention (verse 19, *cf.* Jn. 8: 34–36)? *Cf.* verse 20 with Mt. 12: 43–45; Heb. 6: 4–8.

Note. Verses 4–10 are parenthetical, interrupting the description of the false teachers, which is resumed in 10b.

□ STUDY 4 2 Peter 3: 1–10

1 What arguments do the scoffers of verse 3 use? What is the best defence against them (verse 2)?

2 In verses 5–7 Peter refutes the scoffers by reference to the unfailing fulfilment of God's word. Explain from these three verses how the words and actions of God in the past assure us that in the future He will again do what He has said. Is there a similarity between the people of Noah's day and our own (*cf.* Mt. 24: 37–39)?

3 Why is 'the day' so slow in coming (verse 9)? *Cf.* Ezk. 28: 23, 32.

Note. Verse 10. 'Elements': the material elements of the universe; but, as man think, with specific reference to the heavenly bodies.

□ STUDY 5 2 Peter 3: 11–18

1 Make a list of the practical conclusions which Peter draws from the certainty that the day of the Lord will come. How do these work out in the way you yourself live?

2 Verses 17, 18 sum up the theme of the whole Epistle. How are we to maintain stability in the Christian life? Show that to be stable is not to be static.

Note. Verse 12. 'Hastening' (RSV) is better than 'hasting unto' (AV). The day is being hastened as by our repentance and zeal we remove the need for God's forbearance (verses 9, 15). *Cf.* Rom. 2: 4.

JUDE

Introduction

The writer of this Epistle has been generally identified with Judas, one of the brothers of the Lord (Mt. 13: 55). The letter was probably written after the fall of Jerusalem, possibly between AD 75 and 80.

The message of the Epistle is very similar to that of 2 Peter. Both authors write out of a sense of deep urgency (*cf.* Jude 3, 'I found it necessary'). Evil men and evil ways had crept into the church, and were endangering its life. This evil must be fought; and the object of both Epistles is to stir up the Christians. Jude, like Peter, looks to the past for illustrations of divine judgment upon sin, and declares that judgment will fall as certainly as in the past upon those who are now turning their backs upon truth and righteousness. Finally, he exhorts his readers to keep themselves in the love of God, who will hold them fast, through Jesus Christ our Lord. Peter foretold the coming of false teachers, but they were already active when Jude wrote.

Analysis

1–4	Introduction, and purpose of the letter.
5–7	God's judgments in the past.
8–16	Description and condemnation of the evil which has crept in.
17–25	Exhortation and benediction.

☐ STUDY 1 Jude 1–16

1 Contrast, clause by clause, the threefold description in verse 1 of the faithful believers, to whom Jude is writing, with the description in verse 4 of the false intruders into the church, whom he condemns.

2 Compare Jude 4–16 with 2 Pet. 2: 1–18. What resemblances and differences do you find?

3 Verse 3. Are you contending for the faith? If it was once for all delivered to the saints, is there any scope for modification as the church develops?

Note. Refer to the *NBC* for explanation of verses 9, 14, 15.

☐ STUDY 2 Jude 17–25

1 Verses 17–21. When confronted by the adverse influences of the world, what are we to do, and what will God do, to maintain our spiritual development?

2 What should be our attitude as Christians to those around us who may be going astray, and what to the sin that has defiled them?

3 What may we learn from verses 24, 25 concerning the ground of our confidence, the source of our joy, and the object of our aspirations? What should such awareness move us to do?

DANIEL

Introduction

The book of Daniel is rich in spiritual instruction, and will reward prayerful study. It shows, first of all, how those who believe in God can take their place in the society where they find themselves, play their part in current affairs, and yet remain true to God, thereby bringing glory to Him and blessing to men. Such men and women are needed among the nations today.

The book of Daniel is also a tonic to faith. The overthrow and exile of the Jews raised the question 'Where is their God?' (Ps. 115:2). The book of Daniel reveals God as sovereign over the nations, watchful over those who trust in Him, and working all things 'according to the counsel of his will'. The earlier chapters helped to bring home to the Jews the great truth of the sole Deity of the Lord. This weaned them from idol-worship (*cf.* Ps. 115:3–11). The later chapters of the book, with their exact prediction of the course of events, were the means by which the faith of the remnant was sustained amid the troubles and persecutions that they endured. This book should help also to sustain our own faith in days o darkness.

The book of Daniel is also an integral part of Scripture in its revelation of things to come. This assumes that the book is a true record and prophecy belonging to the time of the exile. There has been a strong trend in recent times to dispute this, and to assign the composition of the book to a period 400 years later, when many of its predictions had already become facts of history. The older view is not without its difficulties, but the progress of archaeology has already removed some of these, and in holding to the authenticity of the book, we are in line with the New Testament, which bears witness to its miracles and predictions (see, *e.g.*, Heb. 11:33, 34; Mt. 24:15), and quotes from or alludes to it frequently, especially in the synoptic Gospels and the book of Revelation.

Analysis

History (chapters 1–6)

1 Daniel and three other youths selected, proved, educated.
2 Nebuchadnezzar's dream and its interpretation.
3 Nebuchadnezzar's golden image, and the fiery furnace.
4 Nebuchadnezzar's second dream, with its fulfilment, and his testimony.
5 Belshazzar's feast, the writing on the wall, the fall of Babylon.
6 Darius' edict. Daniel in the den of lions.

Prophecy (chapters 7–12)

7 Vision of the four great beasts, in the first year of Belshazzar.
8 Vision of the ram and he-goat, and of four kingdoms, and of the little horn, in the third year of Belshazzar.
9 The prayer of Daniel; the revelation concerning Messiah.
10–12 Vision of the future, and of 'the time of the end', in the third year of Cyrus.

☐ STUDY 1 Daniel 1

1 What were the motives which lay behind the resolve of Daniel and his three friends to avoid defilement? *Cf.* Lv. 3: 17; 20: 24–26. How did they set about achieving their aim? What Christian qualities did they display in their approach to authority? With what gifts did God reward them?

2 What light does the story throw upon what it means to be 'in the world' (Jn. 17: 11), but 'not of the world' (Jn. 17: 16)? Notice how firmness of conviction in youth laid the foundation for later steadfastness.

Notes

1 Verse 1. The year is probably 605 BC, and the reference is to a Babylonian foray immediately after their victory at Carchemish.

2 Verse 2. 'Shinar': an ancient name for Babylon.

☐ STUDY 2 Daniel 2: 1–30

1 Daniel and his companions were brought suddenly into great peril through no fault of their own. Note carefully what steps Daniel took. What may we learn from his example as to how to act in any such time of sudden danger? *Cf.* Acts 4: 23, 24; 12: 5.

2 Watch the four at prayer. They might have asked God to change the king's mind, for he was acting very unreasonably; but what did they ask? Consider the faith behind their petition, and how God answered them above what they had asked. See 2: 47–49; and *cf.* Eph. 3: 20, 21.

☐ STUDY 3 Daniel 2: 31–49

1 Observe that the four kingdoms, though historically appearing one after the other, are yet all parts of the one image. Also, it is not only the last kingdom of the four, but the whole image that is broken to pieces by the stone that smites it. What does the dream reveal as to God's final purpose? And what differences do you find between the kingdoms of the world that compose the image and the kingdom prefigured by the stone? *Cf.* Rev. 11: 15.

2 What divine purposes did the dream serve in relation to (a) Nebuchadnezzar, (b) Daniel and his friends, and (c) all who knew, or know of it?

Note. Verses 39, 40. Those who assign the book of Daniel to the Maccabean period take the four kingdoms to be those of Babylon, the Medes, the Persians and the Greeks. This, however, apart from other objections, seems to go contrary to the book itself, which regards Medo-Persia as one kingdom (see 5: 28; 6: 8; 8: 20, 21). The older interpretation, therefore, which takes the four kingdoms to be Babylon, Medo-Persia, Greece and Rome, is to be preferred.

☐ STUDY 4 Daniel 3

In the opening part of this chapter the king manifests a very different attitude towards the Lord from that of 2: 47. The probable reason is that between chapters 2 and 3 there is an interval of several years, during which Nebuchadnezzar had evidence that his own god was greater than the God of the Jews (*cf.* verse 15b). It accounts also for the enmity of the Chaldean officials against Shadrach, Meshach and Abednego. They would resent Jews continuing to hold rule over the province of Babylon.

1 What threefold accusation was brought against the three Hebrews? Consider how subtly it was worded to stir the king's anger.

2 How does this trial of faith differ from anything these men had had to meet hitherto? For similar instances of courage see Acts 4: 8–12; 5: 29–32; 2 Tim. 4: 16, 17. What purposes were served by the miracle of deliverance which God wrought?

☐ STUDY 5 Daniel 4

The theme of this chapter is pride. It takes the form of a decree by Nebuchadnezzar announcing the strange psychical affliction he has undergone, through which he has learnt the all-important lesson that 'the Most High rules the kingdom of men, and gives it to whom he will' (verse 25). It can be compared with Is. 14: 8–17 and Ezk. 28: 1–10, passages which in their turn look back to the basic sin of humanity (Gn. 3).

1 How effective was the king's experience in bringing him to humility? Contrast his attitude to God and confession of Him in this chapter with his previous utterances in 2: 47; 3: 29. How would you define the change?

2 What are the main themes of Daniel's teaching in this situation? With verse 27, *cf.* Mi. 6: 8.

Notes

1 Verse 13. 'A watcher, a holy one': *i.e.*, an angelic figure who acted with the authority of God.

2 Verse 33. The mental derangement, known as zoanthropy, lasted for a set period described as 'seven times' (verse 16). This could mean 'seven years' or simply 'a substantial period of time'. In the apocryphal 'Prayer of Nabonidus', found at Qumran, it is recorded that King Nabonidus, a successor of Nebuchadnezzar, spent seven years of his reign in isolation at Teima because of some strange illness. So this chapter is not without parallel in ancient traditions.

□ STUDY 6 Daniel 5

Babylon fell in 539 BC, twenty-three years after the death of Nebuchadnezzar. A quarter of a century, therefore, has elapsed since the events of chapter 4.

1 What four accusations did Daniel bring against Belshazzar? In what two ways was Belshazzar's sin aggravated and made more heinous?

2 Consider the judgment pronounced upon Belshazzar as symbolizing the divine judgment upon all ungodliness, whether in national or individual life. See verses 26–28, and *cf.* Pr. 15: 3, 9; Ec. 8: 11–13.

Notes

1 The identity of Belshazzar was for long unknown, but he is now known to have been the eldest son of King Nabonidus (556–539), and to have shared the duties of the throne with his father. While Nabonidus was away from Babylon, his son had supreme authority there.

2 Verse 10. 'The queen': probably the queen-mother, widow of Nebuchadnezzar.

3 Verses 25–28. The words represent three weights or coins, *viz.* mina, shekel, and peres or half-mina. But the interpretation conceals numerous plays on words, for the verbal roots mean 'to number, to weigh and to divide'. In the case of 'peres', 'to divide', a further similarity to the word for Persian has been used.

□ STUDY 7 Daniel 6

The identity of Darius the Mede is still a matter for debate, but the most likely candidates are Gobryas (Gubaru), the governor of Babylon, or Cyrus the king. This is one of many instances of biblical interpretation over which the reader has to admit that he simply does not know the answer until fresh evidence comes to light to help to solve the mystery.

1 Neither pressure of business nor the threat of death kept Daniel from prayer. How is it with you? Do you think that other qualities in Daniel's character revealed in this chapter were the outcome of his prayer life? What were those qualities? *Cf.* Is. 40: 29–31; Phil. 4: 5, 6.

2 Is your faith of such a kind that you can stand alone in obedience to God without external support? Are we so living that even our keenest critics take it for granted that the will of God comes first in our lives, come what may?

☐ STUDY 8 Daniel 7

The chapter records, first, the vision (verses 2–14); then the general interpretation (verses 15–18); then Daniel's enquiry concerning three features of the vision (verses 19, 20); and lastly, the answer given to these enquiries.

1 Assuming the four kingdoms to be the same as those which Nebuchadnezzar saw in his dream (chapter 2), what is there new in this vision which caused Daniel such distress and agitation of spirit (verses 15, 28)?

2 To Nebuchadnezzar the kingdoms of this world appeared in the glittering splendour of material wealth and power, whereas by Daniel they are seen as beasts of prey. What is the difference between these points of view, and which is the deeper and truer view? *Cf.* 1 Sa. 16: 7; Mt. 4: 8; 1 Jn. 2: 16, 17.

3 What is to be the final goal of history to which this vision looks forward? Who are meant by 'the saints of the Most High' (verse 18)? What privileges will they have in the days to come?

Notes

1 Verse 5. The bear represented the Medo-Persian Empire, noted for its greed for further conquest.

2 Verse 6. The wings on the leopard's back indicate the swiftness of Alexander's campaigns. After his death his empire was divided into four parts.

3 Verse 7. The fourth beast is either the Seleucid Empire, with its many kings (horns), of whom Antiochus Epiphanes was the most deadly, or Rome with its many emperors, under one of whom arose the Son of man.

☐ STUDY 9 Daniel 8

The vision of this chapter received historical fulfilment in the overthrow of Persia by Alexander the Great (330 BC), the division of Alexander's kingdom into four ('but not with his power', verse 22), and the rise of Antiochus Epiphanes, who did what is here foretold of him in verses 9–12 and 23–25 (170–164 BC). Gabriel's emphasis, however, upon the vision having to do with 'the time of the end' (see verses 17 and 19) suggests that its meaning is not exhausted in Antiochus, but that he is only a type of one greater than he, and yet to come, who will act in a similar way. *Cf.* 7: 24–26 and Mt. 24: 15; 2 Thes. 2: 8–10.

1 What expression is used both of the ram and of the he-goat in the time of their prosperity, and also of the king of verse 23? Yet what was the end of these kingdoms? Notice the repetition of the verb 'to break'.

2 Why was Daniel so deeply affected by this vision? Consider how the prophecies of Jeremiah and Ezekiel seemed to indicate that the return from exile would coincide with the advent of the kingdom of God (see, *e.g.*, Je. 32: 37–44; Ezk. 37: 21–28); but this vision shows long vistas of history stretching into the future, and *further suffering for the Jews.*

Notes

1 Verse 9. 'The glorious land': *i.e.*, Palestine.

2 Verse 10. 'The host of heaven . . . stars': used figuratively of Israel and her leaders.

3 Verse 11. 'The prince of the host': *i.e.*, God Himself. *Cf.* verse 25.

4 Verse 12. Israel was to be given over into the power of the 'horn' because of transgressions, and true religion was to be suppressed.

5 Verse 14. If the burnt offering ceased for 2,300 times, that would be 1,150 days, which is a little more than three years. It is known that Antiochus did suspend the burnt offering for three years and possibly a little longer.

☐ STUDY 10 Daniel 9: 1–19

1 Consider the effect of the fall of Babylon upon one who, like Daniel, saw in it a fulfilment of prophecy (verse 2; *cf.* Je. 25: 11; 29: 10–14; 50: 1–5). What did it lead him to do (*cf.* Ezk. 36: 37), and what light do verses 2 and 3 throw upon the use of Scripture in our praying?

2 As you read through Daniel's prayer, how would you describe his praying? See especially verses 3 and 19. In his confession, how does he speak of God? How of himself and his people? In his petition, on what does he base his plea for mercy, and for what does he ask?

☐ STUDY 11 Daniel 9: 20–27

Daniel had assumed that a period of seventy years would finish 'the desolations of Jerusalem' (verse 2), and in his prayer had pleaded with God for this (verse 18). God sends Gabriel to give him fuller understanding (verses 20–23), by conveying to him 'a word', which speaks not of seventy years, but of seventy weeks of years. The message is very condensed, and every clause is significant.

1 Verse 24. What are the six things here mentioned? Notice that they all concern the Jews and the holy city, and are to come to pass at the end of the full seventy weeks of years.

2 The seventy weeks of years are divided into three periods of seven weeks, sixty-two weeks and one week respectively. What the first period signifies is not certainly known, unless it is the time taken to build the city. What event, however, is stated as happening at the end of the second period?

3 The remainder of the passage has been variously interpreted, even by those who regard it as inspired prophecy. If verse 26a is a reference to the cross of Christ, then verse 26b seems to point to the destruction of Jerusalem and the Temple by the Romans in AD 70. But such questions as these arise: (a) Does the fall of Jerusalem in AD 70 exhaust the prophecy? (b) Who is the 'prince that shall come', and is he to be identified with the little horn of 7: 8, 24, 25? See Note 3 below.

Notes

1 Verse 24. 'To finish the transgression' and 'to put an end to sin' are parallel expressions meaning to bring Israel's sinning to an end. *Cf.* Rom. 11: 26, 27. 'To seal both vision and prophet': *i.e.*, to ratify them as being fulfilled. 'To anoint a most holy place': *i.e.*, the consecration of the Messianic Temple, fulfilled in the establishment of the church, the body of Christ.

2 From the decree of Artaxerxes I, referred to in Ezr. 7: 11ff. (458 BC), sixty-nine weeks of years bring us to the period of Christ's ministry. This prophecy of Daniel may account for the widespread expectation of a Messiah at the time Jesus appeared (*cf.* Mt. 2: 1, 2; Lk. 2: 25, 26; 3: 15), and may lie behind our Lord's own words in Mk. 1: 15a.

3 Verses 26, 27. Many hold that in this prophecy, as in other Old Testament passages, the beginning and end of the Christian era are telescoped together, and that the prophecy here leaps forward to the end of the age. If so, the last 'week' is separated from the first sixty-nine by the whole interval between Christ's first and second comings. With verse 27, *cf.* 2 Thes. 2: 8.

☐ STUDY 12 Daniel 10: 1 – 11: 1

1 This chapter is introductory to Daniel's last vision. Consider the date (10: 1) and trace out from Ezr. 1; 3; 4: 4, 5 what was happening at that time to the first contingent of those who returned from exile. What light does this throw upon the mourning of Daniel (verse 2) and upon the purpose of the vision?

2 What does this passage teach of the costliness of communion with God, and of true prayer?

3 Read Eph. 6: 10–13 in the light of this chapter; also 2 Ki. 6: 16–18; Ps. 34: 7. In the presence of the mysterious spirit-world, what comfort may we draw from the New Testament revelation that our Lord is supreme there also? *Cf.* Eph. 1: 20–23; Col. 1: 16; 2: 15.

Notes

1 Verses 5, 6. It is not said who this august being was. Some features of his appearance and person remind us of the visions of Ezekiel and John (Ezk. 1: 13–16; Rev. 1: 13–15).

2 Verse 8. 'No strength': 'Before God gives strength and power unto His people He makes them sensible of their own weakness.'

3 Verse 13. 'Prince': used here of guardian angels of the kingdoms.

4 Verses 16, 18. The angelic figure described in these verses is probably the same as the original being of verse 5, but the text is not very clear.

☐ STUDY 13 Daniel 11: 2–20

This passage is a forecast of history, not continuous, but selective. The period is one of nearly 400 years, from the time of Daniel's vision to the reign o Antiochus Epiphanes. Verses 2–4 are introductory, having reference (a) to the rulers of Persia, up to Xerxes (verse 2), and (b) to the rise of Alexander the Great nearly 150 years later, and to the division of his kingdom into four (verses 3, 4). From this point the prophecy confines itself to two of these four kingdoms: Egypt, whose ruler is called 'king of the south', and Syria, whose ruler is called 'king of the north'. The successive rulers of these kingdoms in historical succession were (a) *Egypt*: Ptolemy I (304–285 BC); Ptolemy II (285–246 BC); Ptolemy III (246–221 BC); Ptolemy IV (221–205 BC); Ptolemy V (205–180 BC); Ptolemy VI (180–145 BC); (b) *Syria*: Seleucus I (312–280 BC); Antiochus I (280–261 BC); Antiochus II (261–246 BC); Seleucus II (246–226 BC); Seleucus III (226–223 BC); Antiochus III, called the Great (223–187 BC); Seleucus IV (187–175 BC); Antiochus IV, called Epiphanes (175–163 BC).

Verse 5a of our chapter refers to Ptolemy I, and verse 5b to Seleucus I, who for a time was one of Ptolemy's generals, but became ruler of a wider empire then Ptolemy's. Verse 6 refers to Ptolemy II, who gave his daughter Berenice to Antiochus II in marriage upon certain conditions. The conditions were, however, broken and Berenice lost her life. Verses 7 and 8 refer to Ptolemy III, brother of Berenice, who successfully attacked the kingdom of Syria under Seleucus II and returned with great spoil. Seleucus II later invaded Egypt, but without success (verse 9). Verses 10–19 predict continued wars between the kings of Syria and Egypt in the reigns of Antiochus III, Ptolemy IV and Ptolemy V. The victory turned now to the north (verse 10), and now to the south (verses 11, 12). Then Antiochus brought Egypt low (verses 13–17), but, wishing to press westwards (verse 18), made an alliance with Egypt by giving Ptolemy V his daughter Cleopatra in marriage (verse 17). The plans for a conquest westward were, however, defeated by a Roman commander (verse 18), and Antiochus had to retire to his own kingdom, where he died (verse 19). Verse 20 refers to Seleucus IV, who imposed heavy taxes upon Palestine to build up his kingdom's finances. In all this time Palestine, named 'the glorious land' (verse 16) and 'the glory of the kingdom' (verse 20), was the pathway of marching armies, and a bone of contention between the warring nations. But it had not yet suffered what it was soon to suffer under Antiochus IV.

1 What was the purpose of this detailed prediction? In what way would it help the remnant during the persecution which was to come?

2 Ponder the words in verses 3 and 16 'shall do according to his own will'. See also verse 36, and contrast Jn. 4: 34; Rom. 12: 1, 2; 1 Jn. 2: 17. Are you learning to say with Christ Mt. 26: 42 and Heb. 10: 7?

Note. Verse 14. A party among the Jews will rise up, thinking by violence to bring to pass the fulfilment of prophecy.

☐ STUDY 14 Daniel 11: 21 – 12: 13

At chapter 11: 21 the predicted course of events as told in the vision reaches the reign of Antiochus Epiphanes, and the historical fulfilment can be traced with accuracy up to verse 35. The career of Antiochus is revealed in four main features: (a) the craft by which he obtained the throne and won his way to power (verses 21–23); (b) his love of munificent and lavish giving (verse 24a); (c) his plans for war (verse 24b), and especially his wars against Egypt (verses 25–30); and (d) his acts of sacrilege against the Temple in Jerusalem, and persecution of the Jews (verses 31–35).

The remainder of the passage (11: 36 – 12: 4) seems at first sight to be a continuation of the career of Antiochus, but on closer examination is seen to go beyond it, alike in its description of the king (verse 36; *cf.* 2 Thes. 2: 4), in the events which it records (*e.g.*, 12: 1, 2), and in the emphasis laid upon its being 'the time of the end' (11: 35, 40; 12: 4). The figure of Antiochus seems here to merge into the more sinister figure of the Antichrist. With 12: 2, 7, *cf.* 7: 25; 9: 27.

1 Gather out the evidence given here on the one hand of man's sinfulness and lust for power, and on the other of God's overruling control and purpose. *Cf.* Je. 17: 5–14.

2 What are the characteristics of those who will be glorified and of those who will be put to shame at the last?

Notes

1 11: 21. *I.e.*, he was not the recognized heir to the throne.
2 11: 22–24. 'The prince of the covenant' is probably Antiochus, the infant son and heir of Seleucus IV. 'The strongholds' are those of Egypt.
3 11: 27. Antiochus actually captured the king of Egypt, but they pretended to be friendly.
4 11: 30. 'Ships of Kittim': *i.e.*, Roman ships, which refused Antiochus liberty to proceed. He vented his anger, therefore, upon Palestine.
5 11: 31. 'The abomination that makes desolate': a small altar was placed upon the altar of burnt offering and sacrifices were offered to idols.
6 11: 37. 'The one beloved by women' refers to the god Tammuz. See Ezk. 8: 14.

PSALMS 139 - 150

☐ STUDY 112 Psalm 139

1 Verses 1–18 describe in three sections the psalmist's consciousness of God's scrutiny of his life. What departments of life are singled out as known by God in verses 1–6? What truths about God are emphasized in verses 7–12, and in verses 13–18?

2 Why is it that the psalmist can pray as he does in verses 23, 24, especially in the light of what he confesses in verses 1–4? Do you regularly pray this kind of prayer?

☐ STUDY 113 Psalms 140 and 141

1 In Ps. 140 note carefully the psalmist's description of his enemies: their character, their methods, their purpose. In these circumstances of intense danger, what does the psalmist do, what does he pray for, and how is his faith sustained?

2 Ps. 141 deals with some of the more insidious temptations which threaten to involve God's servant in evil. Note in detail what they are. Note also the kinds of help for which he prays. How does the influence of other people work here?

3 Both psalms mention the far-reaching significance of speech. Study how the things men say can do evil. How can greater control be gained over the tongue?

☐ STUDY 114 Psalms 142 and 143

1 Ps. 142 shows how God's servant is not immune from the depths of distress and despair. How does he describe how he feels? And then, what does he do? What does he believe? And what does he expect? *Cf.* Ps. 138: 7, 8; Jb. 23: 10; 2 Cor. 1: 8–11.

2 Ps. 143 consists of an invocation (verses 1, 2), a lament (verses

3, 4), a retrospect (verses 5, 6) and a petition (verses 7–12). Study how one important fact comes to mind in each of these first three sections. Note what reaction is caused each time in him. The petition itself falls into a pattern like this too. What solution does he now pray for in each aspect of his need? Note particularly his morning prayer in verse 8. Learn from such an example how to be more pointed in your praying.

☐ STUDY 115 Psalm 144

1 What does David confess (a) that he is in God's sight; and (b) that God can be to him and do for him? Have you similar cause to 'sing a new song' (verse 9)?

2 What special lessons for spiritual leaders of others can be learnt from this psalm? In particular, how do David's prayers express the special needs of a person with responsibility?

Note. Verses 8, 11. The meaning is that when they raised their right hand in solemn oath, they lied.

☐ STUDY 116 Psalm 145

1 How many different aspects of the character of God are mentioned in this psalm, and what kinds of appreciation and response should such contemplation of His character call forth?

2 How is the kindness of God shown to all, and how more specifically to those who fulfil certain conditions? *Cf.* and contrast Mt. 5: 4, 5; Rom. 3: 22; 8: 28.

☐ STUDY 117 Psalm 146

1 In verses 3 and 4 the psalmist is warning Israel against trust in alliances which are a substitute for trusting God. *Cf.* Is. 30: 1–5; 31: 1. Why is trusting in man such a mistake? *Cf.* Is. 2: 20–22; Je. 17: 5.

2 It was always important to Israel to be a remembering people. See how God's acts in their experience long before illustrate the statements about God in verses 6c, 7a, 7b, 7c. Look up Jos. 23: 14–16; Ex. 3: 7, 8; 16: 2–4; Ps. 126: 1, 2.

3 Jesus takes up these themes making them the programme of His whole ministry (see Lk. 4: 16–21), and explaining His miracles in these terms (see Mt. 11: 2–5, echoing Is. 29: 18, 19; 35: 5, 6). What does He mean to teach about Himself in this way?

☐ STUDY 118 Psalm 147

1 In each of the three sections of this psalm (verses 1–6, 7–11, 12–20) one attitude or attribute of God is being highlighted. Discover each of these. What are, then, the point and logic of the references in each section to God's control of the natural universe and of created things?

2 Faith and praise are here supported by concrete reasons. What do we thus learn to be the greatest reasons for trusting and praising God?

☐ STUDY 119 Psalms 148–150

These psalms again find their best setting in the gathering of Israel in the Temple, celebrating God's greatness particularly in terms of His works in creation and history.

1 Summarize as expressed here the psalmist's view of God in His cosmic magnificence and creative omnipotence. To what one end should everything be used, and all creation united?

2 How is God's special relation with His people shown, and of what things do they feel they can be assured as they dwell on what He is known to be?

REVELATION

Introduction

Many have been put off the study of the book of Revelation by fears of its difficulty, or the intricate nature of some interpretations. But no book of the Bible will more surely reward the student who approaches it for its present relevance rather than as an eschatological enigma. It is important to remember that the visions which occupy so large a part of it are not to be regarded as literal pictures: the book is written in the literary form known as 'apocalyptic', which expresses heavenly and spiritual realities by means of a conventional and elaborate symbolism.

It is generally agreed that it was written by John the apostle, and in days of persecution, as his exile proves (1:9). Some think that his exile was suffered under Nero, who died in AD 68; some under Domitian (81–96). The later date seems more probable. The struggle between the people of Christ and the power of Rome had now reached a state more advanced than that which is reflected in the Acts of the Apostles. Emperor worship became common from Nero's reign onward, and the outlook was dark and threatening.

The reference to Rome in chapter 17 is but thinly veiled. Some interpreters ('Preterist') regard all the references as being to contemporary events, so that for us the book speaks of things already past; some ('Historicist') have seen in chapters 2–19 references to Christian history before and after the fall of Rome, and to the conflict of evangelical religion with the Roman church, so leading on to the times of the end; others ('Futurist') regard chapters 2 and 3 as an epitome of Christian history, and the rest of the book as a prophecy looking forward to events at the time of the Lord's return.

A true interpretation may well find something of value in all these points of view. It is best to study the book with the assurance (1) that it had a real message for its own time; (2) that its lessons have been illustrated by the history of the church; and (3) that it contains prophetical references to the future. The reader should not be so troubled by the obscurities that he cannot rejoice in the message of what is clear. We can learn lessons of tremendous value about the place of Christ's people in the purposes of God and the glorious future awaiting them, the heavenly nature of our earthly conflict, which can be carried on only with divine aid, the need to overcome in the struggle, the eternal judgment of God upon Satan and sin, and the certainty of the complete victory, the lordship over history and second coming of Jesus Christ our Lord.

Analysis

1:1–8	Prologue.
1:9 – 3:22	Vision of Christ, alive for evermore, in the midst of the churches.
4:1 – 5:14	Vision of the throne of God, and of the Lamb in the midst of the throne, to whom is committed the sealed book of the judgments of God.
6:1 – 8:5	Vision of the 'seal' judgments, with two visions interposed for the comfort of Christ's people (7:1–8, 9–17).

8: 6 – 11: 19	Vision of the 'trumpet' judgments, with three visions for the comfort of Christ's people (10: 1–11; 11: 1, 2, 3–13).
12: 1 – 14: 20	Vision of the man-child, and of the dragon and the two beasts, with three visions for the comfort of Christ's people (14: 1–5, 6–13, 14–20).
15: 1 – 16: 21	Vision of the 'bowl' judgments.
17: 1 – 19: 10	Visions of Babylon, the harlot city, and her destruction.
19: 11 – 20: 15	Vision of Christ's return, of His triumph over all His enemies, and of the last judgment.
21: 1 – 22: 5	Vision of a new heaven and earth, and of the new Jerusalem.
22: 6–21	Epilogue.

☐ STUDY 1 Revelation 1: 1–8

1 Trace in verses 1 and 2 the course of the 'revelation' from its source in the mind of God by four successive steps to us who read and receive it. How is it described in its content, character and value, and what is required in those who read or hear? *Cf.* Lk. 11: 28.

2 Observe the place given to Jesus Christ in relation to God, and consider each title given to Him in verse 5a. *Cf.* Jn. 3: 11, 32, 33; 18: 37; Col. 1: 18; Rev. 19: 11–16. How does John describe His attitude to us, and what He has done for us? *Cf.* Jn. 13: 1; Eph. 1: 7; 1 Pet. 2: 9.

3 With 1: 7, *cf.* Dn. 7: 13 and Acts 1: 9–11. Is the thought of His coming a joy to you? *Cf.* 6: 15–17; 1 Thes. 4: 15–18; 5: 1–4; 2 Thes. 1: 7–10.

Notes

1 Verse 1. 'The revelation of Jesus Christ': *i.e.*, communicated by Him; and intended not to mystify but to disclose.

2 Verse 3. 'He who reads': *i.e.*, the one who reads this book aloud to his fellow-believers. 'The prophecy': a significant claim. *Cf.* 22: 7, 10, 18, 19.

3 Verse 4. 'The seven spirits': *i.e.*, the Spirit in His sevenfold fullness.

4 Verse 5. 'The faithful witness': this includes the thought of martyrdom. *Cf.* 1 Tim. 6: 13. Note the sequence—death, resurrection, enthronement.

☐ STUDY 2 Revelation 1: 9–20

1 What, according to verse 9, is the twofold experience in which all believers share, and what should characterize their lives? *Cf.* Jn. 16: 33; Acts 14: 22; 2 Tim. 2: 12a.

2 We are not for a moment to suppose that Christ is literally like this. What John sees is a vision, each feature of which is symbolic of some aspect of our glorified Lord. Write down against each feature here portrayed what trait in our Lord's character it suggests. What is the total impression left upon your mind?

3 What does Christ say of Himself and of His relation to the churches in verses 17–20? With verse 17, *cf.* Dn. 10: 8–11, 15–19, and with the figure of the 'lampstands', *cf.* Mt. 5: 14–16.

Notes

1 Verse 17: see also 22: 13. Note that Christ applies to Himself words spoken by God of Himself in verse 8. See also verses 17 and 22: 13.

2 Verse 18. 'The keys of Death and Hades': according to the teaching of the Rabbis these keys are in the hands of God alone.

3 Verse 20. 'Mystery': *i.e.*, something with a hidden meaning here explained. *Cf.* 17: 7; Mt. 13: 11. 'The angels of the seven churches': sometimes taken to mean the pastors or bishops of each church, but more probably denoting a guardian angel (*cf.* Dn. 10: 21; Mt. 18: 10).

☐ STUDY 3 Revelation 2: 1–7

The seven letters of chapters 2 and 3 are all similar in structure, beginning with titles descriptive of Christ, which have already occurred in the vision in 1: 9–20; then giving Christ's message to the church, and closing with a summons to hear and a promise to 'him who conquers'. In the last four letters the promise precedes the summons.

1 State in your own words what Christ found to commend in the church at Ephesus (verses 2, 3, 6).

2 What was the proof that their love had declined? How could this condition be remedied? What further danger otherwise beset them? How should we take such a warning to heart?

3 Verse 7a. Note the present tense 'says', and the combination of individual appeal and universal application. How does Christ still speak through these scriptures, and to whom? *Cf.* Mk. 4: 9, 23; 8: 18. How may the hearing ear be obtained?

Notes

1 Verse 6. 'Nicolaitans': see also verses 14, 15. '*Nicholaos*' may be meant as a Greek equivalent of 'Balaam', intended to describe a person who lays waste the people of God, as Balaam did through the introduction of idolatrous and immoral practices. *Cf.* 2 Pet. 2: 15, 16.

2 Verse 7. 'The tree of life': in contrast to the corrupt fruits of idolatrous and sensual self-indulgence. *Cf.* 22: 2.

☐ STUDY 4 Revelation 2: 8–17

1 Reconstruct from verses 8–11 the situation with which the believers in Smyrna were confronted. What does Christ declare

concerning (a) their immediate, and (b) their final future? In what ways were they already rich? How were they to conquer? To what result would such conquest lead?

2 Satan could not break the rocklike steadfastness of the church in Pergamum by frontal attack (verse 13), so he employed another method, tempting believers to ask, 'Is it necessary to be so uncompromising in our attitude towards idolatrous practices and pagan morals?' What is Christ's answer to this sort of question?

Notes

1 Verse 10. 'Ten days': *i.e.*, for a short period.
2 Verse 11. 'The second death': *cf.* 20: 14, 15; 21: 8.
3 Verse 13. 'Where Satan's throne is': Pergamum was the official residence of the Roman proconsul of the province, and the chief centre of the worship of the emperor.
4 Verse 17. 'The hidden manna': the Rabbis taught that the Messiah when He came would give the people manna to eat, now hidden in heaven. What is said here is that Christ is the true manna, the bread of life. *Cf.* Jn. 6: 48–51. 'A white stone': stones engraved with names supposed to possess magical qualities were highly valued in heathen circles. Christ gives privileges, personal to each recipient, which exceed all that can be found outside of Him.

☐ STUDY 5 Revelation 2: 18–29

1 In what ways is the description of Christ in verse 18 relevant to what follows? In what character is He here revealed? How should awareness of these truths affect our own behaviour?

2 The religious compromise and moral laxity that were creeping into the churches seem to have proceeded further in the case of Thyatira, and to have become a doctrine and almost a sect. What responsibility had the church as a whole towards the presence of such evil in its midst? What advice is given to the individual members who do not hold this teaching?

Note. Verse 20. 'The woman Jezebel': so called because of her moral likeness to Jezebel of old. *Cf.* 1 Ki. 21: 25, 26; 2 Ki. 9: 22, 30.

☐ STUDY 6 Revelation 3: 1–13

1 Verses 1–6. What was wrong with the Christians in Sardis, and what was needed to remedy the situation? Upon whose action did change and better living depend? Is our condition at all similar?

2 In verses 7–13 what Christian quality is shown to be essential? For how long ought it to be exhibited? To what rewards will its practice lead?

Note. Verse 8. 'An open door': *i.e.*, a missionary opportunity. *Cf.* 1 Cor. 16: 9; 2 Cor. 2: 12.

☐ STUDY 7 Revelation 3: 14–22

1 How do you think the church in Laodicea had become so blind to its true spiritual condition? *Cf.* Mt. 23: 25, 26; 2 Cor. 4: 18. Who undertakes to deal with them, and how?

2 What three qualities of Christian character are symbolized by 'gold refined by fire', 'white garments' and eye salve respectively? See for the first, 1 Pet. 1: 7; for the second, verses 4 and 19: 8; Ps. 51: 7; and for the third, Ps. 119: 18; 2 Pet. 1: 9; Eph. 1: 18, 19. How may these things be obtained?

3 How in its context is verse 20 to be understood? If a church as a whole is 'lukewarm', may individuals within it enjoy a close relationship with the Lord? What does the Lord promise to such? What are the conditions to be fulfilled in order to obtain what is promised? *Cf.* Jn. 14: 22, 23.

Note. Verse 17. Laodicea was prosperous and wealthy. After its overthrow by an earthquake in AD 61 it was rebuilt by its own citizens without imperial subsidy. 'We need nothing' was virtually what its inhabitants said.

Introductory Note to Chapters 4–11

We are now entering upon the main revelation of the book (see 1: 1 and 4: 1). We have seen the condition of the churches. Persecution had begun, and times of greater trial loomed ahead (see 2: 10, 13; 3: 10). The question, 'What of the future?' must have troubled every thoughtful Christian, and is now about to be answered. But first in chapters 4 and 5 God shows John a vision of the heavenly realities which abide unshaken behind and above the changes and uncertainties of earth.

☐ STUDY 8 Revelation 4

1 When John looked into heaven, what is the chief and outstanding sight which met his eyes? What may we also learn from this vision about the origin, the control and the purpose of the created universe? What kind of response ought this awareness to call forth from us?

2 What is here indicated or symbolized concerning the nature and character of God, and concerning the way in which He ought to be worshipped?

Notes

1 Verse 3. 'Like jasper': *i.e.*, radiant; *cf.* 21: 11. 'Like . . . carnelian': *i.e.*, red like fire or blood. The 'rainbow' suggests God's faithfulness. *Cf.* Gn. 9: 12–17.

2 Verse 4. These elders are normally taken to represent the church of Old and New Testaments.
3 Verses 6–8. 'Four living creatures': similar to those of Ezekiel's vision. See Ezk. 1: 5ff.; 10: 12. Their appearance suggests the characteristics of strength, service, intelligence and swiftness. For their song, *cf.* Is. 6: 3.

☐ STUDY 9 Revelation 5

1 Of what does this vision assure us concerning the purpose and the results of Christ's earthly sacrifice—as 'the Lamb who was slain'?

2 What is it that here prompts 'a new song' (verse 9)? How many ultimately join in the singing? What difference is there in qualification to sing on the part of those who do sing? See 14: 3. Have you discovered why you should sing?

Notes
1 Verse 1. 'A scroll': this is the book of destiny. It declares God's purposes of judgment and blessing for this world. Some regard it as the title-deed to the inheritance which Christ has procured for Himself and for His fellow-men by His redeeming work.
2 Verses 5, 6. Note the tense, 'has conquered'. The victory is already won. *Cf.* 3: 21. See also Jn. 12: 31, 32. The occasion here seen in vision is that of Christ's return from the cross to the throne of God as the Lamb that 'had been slain'. He is at once invested into His universal dominion. *Cf.* Mt. 28: 18; Heb. 2: 9; 10: 12, 13.

☐ STUDY 10 Revelation 6

1 As the book of future events is opened seal by seal, what points of correspondence do you find with Mt. 24: 4–14? *Cf.*, *e.g*, verses 4, 6 and 9 with Mt. 24: 6, 7 and 9. (For the meaning of the white horse, see Note 1 below.) What does this teach about the present course of world history?

2 To what climax of judgment do all these things mount up? See verses 12–17 and Note 3 below. *Cf.* Mt. 24: 29, 30. What is more to be dreaded than death? *Cf.* Is. 2: 19–21.

3 For what were the martyrs willing to lay down their lives? Are those right who think that God takes no action either for their reward or their vindication? May similar sacrifice still be called for?

Notes
1 Verse 2. Two principal interpretations have been given of the white horse and his rider. Many take it to be a picture of Christ going forth in the conquests of the gospel. *Cf.* Mt. 24: 14; Ps. 45: 3–5. Others regard it as a picture of invasion and lust of conquest, leading to the miseries of war, famine, pestilence and death. The latter seems more likely. The four horses, as in Zc. 6, form a series whose mission is to execute judgment.

2 Verse 6. Such was the scarcity that a day's wage (Mt. 20: 2) would suffice to buy only a small measure of wheat.
3 Verses 12–14. The imagery of these verses is such as is frequently used in the Old Testament to symbolize great upheavals among the nations. See, *e.g.*, Is. 13: 9–11, 13; Ezk. 32: 7–9; Na. 1: 5.

☐ STUDY 11 Revelation 7

Before the revelation of further judgments, two visions are interposed for the comfort of believers. In all that has been shown so far, nothing has been said of the church, except with regard to those who have been martyred. This passage shows the church first in this life, on earth, and so always limited in number (verses 1–8), and then, numberless in heaven, having life for evermore.

1 What assurance is given in verses 1–8 concerning God's watchful *care* over His people? *Cf.* Ezk. 9: 3–6; Jn. 6: 27; 10: 27–29; Rev. 9: 4.

2 In verses 9–17, who compose the great multitude, and where are they standing? How came they to be there, and what is now their occupation? Make a list of the blessings that they enjoy, translating the symbols into the realities which they represent.

Notes
1 Verse 1. It is a task given to angels to control forces of nature. *Cf.* 14: 18; 16: 5; Heb. 1: 7.
2 Verses 4–8. Some have thought that those who are 'sealed' represent believers from among the Jews, but in the light of 14: 1–4 it is better to regard the vision as including the whole 'Israel of God' (Gal. 6: 16).
3 Verse 14. 'The great tribulation': *cf.* 3: 10. Here both visions show that all who are the Lord's will be brought safely through this earthly trial.

☐ STUDY 12 Revelation 8 and 9

We are brought back, after the interlude of chapter 7, to the opening of the seventh seal. Will it usher in the final end? All heaven is silent, as if in suspense and expectancy (*cf.* Mk. 13: 32), but there follows a new series of judgments (*cf.* Mk. 13: 7, 8).

1 In 8: 3–5 we see, in the heavenly sanctuary, what happens to the prayers of Christ's people. What are we taught as to the efficacy of prayer when mingled with the incense of Christ's intercession and fire from the altar of His sacrifice? In this case what kind of answer is granted? *Cf.* 6: 9, 10; Rom. 8: 26; and see Note 5 below.

2 Contrast the first four trumpet judgments with the fifth and sixth, (a) in the objects affected, and (b) in the severity of their character and result. What was the purpose of these trumpet judgments? See 8: 13; 9: 20, 21. *Cf.* Lk. 13: 1–5.

3 What do we learn from these chapters concerning God's control over all that happens? See especially 8: 12; 9: 1, 4, 13–15.

Notes

1 8:3, 5. Two altars are to be distinguished, the 'golden altar' of incense, and the altar of sacrifice. See Ex. 37:25 – 38:7.

2 8:6. 'Trumpets': indicating that these judgments were sent in warning. *Cf.* Am. 3:6; Ezk. 33:1–5. The destruction wrought is therefore only partial—'a third'.

3 9:1. 'The bottomless pit': better, 'the abyss' (RV), the abode of the powers of evil. *Cf.* 11:7; 17:8.

4 9:11. 'Abaddon' and 'Apollyon': both mean 'destruction'.

5 9:13. 'The golden altar': indicating that the prayers of the saints were being answered.

☐ STUDY 13 Revelation 10

Rev. 10:1 – 11:13 is an interlude between the sixth and seventh trumpets, corresponding to chapter 7 (see Analysis). The seer first tells of his new commission (10:1–11), and then describes the church as God's sanctuary (11:1, 2), and as bearing witness in the world (11:3–13).

1 In what two ways does chapter 10 show that the revelation thus far given to John, though it extends to the end of the age (verses 6, 7), is by no means a complete disclosure of the hidden counsel of God? *Cf.* Dt. 29:29; Jb. 26:14. Of what was John now solemnly assured concerning truths which had been revealed?

2 What made God's Word sweet to taste, but bitter to digest? What responsibility did the reception of such revelation place upon John? *Cf.* Ezk. 2:8 – 3:4; 1 Sa. 3:15–18; 1 Cor. 9:16, 17. Have you any comparable privilege and responsibility?

Note. Verses 6, 7. The mysterious purpose of God, as revealed through the prophets and worked out in earthly history, is thus to be completed or finished.

☐ STUDY 14 Revelation 11

1 The question, 'Who are the two witnesses?' in 11:3–12 has received many answers. Assuming that they represent the witness of the church throughout the present age, what lessons may we learn from this passage concerning true witness for Christ, the authority of His witnesses, their preservation, their suffering to death, and their final triumph? *Cf.* Lk. 10:19; Jn. 16:2; Acts 7:54–60.

2 When God's purposes are completely fulfilled by the sounding of the seventh trumpet (see 11:7), who is seen to be triumphant at the last? What attributes and activities of God make certain His triumph over all opposition? What ought this prospect to make us do?

Notes

1 Verses 1, 2. The purpose of the measuring is to mark out what is to be preserved. If the Temple represents Christ's people (1 Cor. 3: 16), the outer court may represent the Jews in their unbelief (Lk. 21: 24).

2 Verses 2, 3. 'Forty-two months' is the same length of time as 'one thousand two hundred and sixty days' and as 'a time, and times, and half a time' (3½ years) of 12: 14. *Cf.* 12: 6. It appears here to be a conventional description of the duration of the present age. Note the contrast in verse 11—only 'three and a half days'.

Introductory Note to 12: 1 – 19: 10

At this point a new division of the book begins, and a new series of prophecies (*cf.* 10: 11). The earlier part of the book has been occupied mainly with outward events and acts of divine judgment, together with visions of the church and her sufferings; and it has been shown that behind all is God's throne, and that all that is happening is under His control, and in the hand of Christ. The present section of the book reveals another and graver aspect in the situation, namely, the enmity of powerful spiritual foes, of Satan and the world. This has so far only been hinted at (2: 9, 13, 24; 3: 9; 9: 11; 11: 7), but is now brought into full view, and it is shown that the sufferings of the church have their origin in the conflict between Satan and Christ.

☐ STUDY 15 Revelation 12

The chapter gives a symbolic picture of the birth of Christ, and of His return to the throne of God, but its main purpose is to show the power and malignity of Satan as the enemy of Christ and His people.

1 Gather out what is said about Christ. *Cf.* Ps. 2: 6–9; Lk. 10: 18; Jn. 12: 31; Eph. 1: 19–21. What is the significance of verse 10? *Cf.* Rom. 8: 33, 34.

2 Why, according to this chapter, is the lot of the church on earth one of constant conflict? *Cf.* Eph. 6: 10–13; 1 Pet. 5: 8. How is the fearful power of Satan depicted? How do or may we share in Christ's victory over him?

Notes

1 Verses 1, 2, 4–6, 13–17. The woman represents the true Israel, which, after Christ's ascension, forms the Christian church. For the imagery, see Gn. 37: 9; Ct. 6: 4, 10; Is. 66: 7–10.

2 Verses 3, 4a. 'Red': the colour of blood. *Cf.* Jn. 8: 44. The seven heads and diadems indicate far-reaching dominion, the ten horns, great power, and the tail, his vast size and strength. Note verse 9; and *cf.* Gn. 3: 15.

3 Verses 6, 14–16. The exact meaning of the symbolism is obscure, but the general sense is clear, that the church is under God's protection, and although Satan will seek to destroy her, his plans will be thwarted.

☐ STUDY 16 Revelation 13

Satan in his war against the saints uses two chief instruments: (a) totalitarian world power, hostile to the true God, subservient to Satan, and claiming worship for itself (verses 1–10); and (b) established religion, supporting the claims of the world power, by false miracles and signs (verses 11–18). Such 'beasts' were found in John's day in the Roman Empire and the cult of emperor worship. They have appeared also in later history, and may appear again.

1 Note how true Christians are here distinguished from others (verse 8; *cf.* 17: 8). What experience is inevitable for them in such a world situation as verses 1–10 depict? How is it appointed that they should show their faithfulness? *Cf.* Mk. 13: 13.

2 In what respects does the second beast differ in outward appearance from the first? *Cf.* 1 Pet. 5: 8 with 2 Cor. 11: 14. How does its aims and methods bring Christians into direct conflict with it? *Cf.* Dn. 3: 4–6; Jn. 15: 18–21.

Notes

1 Verse 2. Note a combination of the characteristics of the first three beasts in Daniel's vision. *Cf.* Dn. 7: 4–6.

2 Verse 3. This suggests a counterfeit to Christ's death and resurrection, intended to lead men to faith and worship.

3 Verse 4. The reason for worship is not moral greatness but brute force.

4 Verse 10 echoes words in Je. 15: 2. In the face of such treatment Christians are not to try to resist or retaliate.

5 Verse 12. This second beast completes the satanic trinity. It is called 'the false prophet' in 16: 13; 19: 20; 20: 10. He is the Lie dressed up like the Truth. *Cf.* Mt. 7: 15; Mk. 13: 22; 2 Thes. 2: 9–12.

6 Verse 18. Many take the number 666 to refer to 'Nero Caesar'. Others, because every digit falls short of the perfect number 7, regard 666 as a symbol of Antichrist.

☐ STUDY 17 Revelation 14

This chapter, like chapters 7 and 10: 1 – 11: 13, is an interlude introduced for the comfort of believers.

1 Verses 1–5 present a picture of the true followers of Christ. Although outwardly scattered, suffering and in danger of death, spiritually they are with the Lamb on the impregnable rock of Mount Zion, owned of God, not one missing (verse 1), and sharing in the worship of heaven (verses 2, 3). To what do they owe their position and what four characteristics mark their life? See verses 4 and 5, and *cf.* Mt. 5: 3; Lk. 14: 27; Eph. 4: 25; Phil. 2: 15. How does your own life appear in the light of these standards?

2 In verses 6–11 are shown three angels, each with a message for all who dwell upon the earth. Examine the contents of their threefold message. Verses 12 and 13 are addressed to believers. What

encouragement do they give to those who may have to die for Christ's sake?

3 In the twofold vision of verses 14–20 what are the differences between the two parts of it (verses 14–16 and 17–20)? *Cf.* Ps. 1; Mal. 3: 16 – 4: 3; Mt. 13: 39b–43.

Notes

1 Verse 3b. The song is 'from heaven' (verse 2); the saints on Mt. Zion are learning to sing it.

2 Verse 4. A symbol of purity of heart. *Cf.* 2 Cor. 11: 2.

3 Verse 6. 'An eternal gospel': *cf.* Ec. 12: 13, 14; Acts 14: 14–18; 17: 24–31.

4 Verses 9–11. The very marks, which once ensured benefits (see 13: 15–17), now single out individuals for judgment.

5 Verse 13b. The weariness of labour will be over, the reward of their deeds awaits them. *Cf.* Mt. 25: 34–40. Contrast verse 11: 'they have no rest'.

□ STUDY 18 Revelation 15 and 16

The series of judgments here described, though similar to those of the seals and trumpets, is seen as a separate 'portent' in heaven. What follow are no longer warnings but a final outpouring of the wrath of God.

1 John is looking at the seven angels, when his eye is caught by another vision, which he describes in 15: 2–4, no doubt for the comfort of believers, in face of the terrible judgments which are about to fall. What great truths are they thereby assured of, and encouraged to rejoice in? What should such awareness make them—and us—do? *Cf.* 16: 5–7.

2 In what respects are the 'bowl' judgments more severe than those of the seals and the trumpets? What was the reaction to them (a) of men, and (b) of the dragon and his allies? Before such a prospect, what ground have we for hope, and what reason for watchful concern? With 16: 15, *cf.* Mt. 24: 42–44.

Notes

1 15: 3, 4. 'The song of Moses': *cf.* and contrast Ex. 14: 30 – 15: 19.

2 16: 16. 'Armageddon': meaning 'the hill of Megiddo'; *i.e.*, the plain of Megiddo, where more than one famous battle was fought (Jdg. 5: 19; 2 Ch. 35: 22), and the hills around.

□ STUDY 19 Revelation 17

The people of Christ have another enemy—Babylon. Babylon is the name of a city, and John uses it to denote the Rome of his day, seated upon her seven hills (verse 9), and also upon many waters, *i.e.*, upon nations and kingdoms making up the Empire (verses 1, 15, 18). But Babylon, like the two beasts of chapter 13, is a symbol; not, like the first beast, a symbol of material power; nor, like the second beast, of false religion; but rather a symbol of the world's lust, love of gain, pride and corruption. Wherever these aspects of the worldly spirit find embodiment there is Babylon, and there God's judgment will fall, unless men repent.

1 John's wonder at the woman (verse 6) should lead us to examine her closely. What does each feature of the picture symbolize? Contrast the woman and her brood with the woman of chapter 12 and her seed (with 17: 14, *cf.* 12: 17). What, in the face of such a foe, is the prospect before those 'who follow the Lamb' (14: 4)?

2 Verses 7–13, as the interpreting angel himself admits, require for their understanding a mind that has wisdom (verse 9). Observe that two different meanings are assigned to the heads of the beast. Note carefully also the difference between the heads and the horns. The main lesson of the chapter is the certain 'doom' of Babylon. How is this brought about? What does this illustrate concerning God's judgments?

Notes

1 Verse 2. 'Committed fornication': a reference to the immoral practices which kings and rulers committed in response to the seductions of Rome.
2 Verse 8. It 'was, and is not, and is to ascend': the beast is a satanic counterpart of God Himself. See 1: 4.
3 Verses 10, 11. The Emperor Nero committed suicide, and the historian Tacitus says that a rumour spread abroad that he was not dead and would return. It is commonly thought that there is an allusion to this belief in verses 8a and 11. This is a satanic counterpart to the death and resurrection of Christ. Assuming that the seven kings of verse 10 were Roman emperors, the most probable theory sees in the five who 'have fallen', Augustus, Tiberius, Caligula, Claudius and Nero; in the one who 'is', Vespasian (AD 69–79), and in the one who 'has not yet come', Titus. After Titus came Domitian, who would be the 'eighth' (verse 11), and who resembled Nero so closely, especially in his persecution of the Christians, that he might well seem to be Nero come to life again.
4 Verses 15–17. The harlot city will eventually be brought down by a united revolt on the part of the provinces and their local rulers.

☐ STUDY 20 Revelation 18: 1–20

1 Consider first the messages of the angel and of the voice from heaven. What aspects of God's judgments do these emphasize? What urgent imperative does the Lord here speak to His own people? *Cf.* 2 Cor. 6: 14–18.

2 In contrast, listen to the voices of earth on Babylon's fall. Who are the speakers? To what fact about Babylon's fall do they refer, and for what reason did they thus mourn for Babylon? Observe the difference between the points of view of heaven and of the world. In such circumstances, in which would you join—mourning or joy?

3 When time permits, read Is. 13 and 47; Je. 50 and 51 and Ezk. 27 to see how deeply steeped is the mind of John in the visions and prophecies of the Old Testament.

☐ STUDY 21 Revelation 18: 21 – 19: 10

1 What thoughts does the action of the angel in 18: 21 suggest as to the purpose of God towards 'Babylon'? Notice especially how many times the words 'no more' occur in 18: 21–24. *Cf.* 19: 3. What truth is thus enforced concerning the whole system of godless luxury and lust which the name 'Babylon' represents? *Cf.* 1 Cor. 7: 31b; 1 Pet. 1: 24, 25; 1 Jn. 2: 17.

2 What calls forth the praises of 19: 1–3, 4, 5–8, and by whom respectively were they spoken? What truths about God's character and ways are here acknowledged? *Cf.* 19: 10; Is. 45: 21–25.

Notes

1 19: 3b. Symbolic of final destruction. *Cf.* Is. 34: 10.
2 19: 7. 'The marriage of the Lamb': the fulfilment of God's purpose as described in Eph. 5: 25b, 26. A final decisive contrast to the harlot and her impurities.

☐ STUDY 22 Revelation 19: 11–21

Following upon the destruction of 'Babylon', the beast, and the kings in alliance with him (*cf.* 17: 12–14), make war upon Christ, who comes forth from heaven in judgment to overthrow them. The end of the present age, prophesied throughout the book, has now come, and we have in today's portion Christ's second coming described, in its aspect of judgment upon His enemies, as in 2 Thes. 1: 6–10 and Ps. 2: 9.

1 Verses 11–16. In this symbolic picture of Christ seek to appreciate the suggestive significance of each descriptive phrase. Contrast some of the phrases of Zc. 9: 9, 10. In what ways will Christ's second coming be different from His first coming? Should this prospect fill us with fear or joy?

2 Verses 17–21. This is the battle of Armageddon, spoken of in 16: 14–16. Note the contrast between 'the great supper' of judgment and 'the marriage supper of the Lamb' (verse 9). *Cf.* the contrast in 14: 14–20 between the two harvests. See also Mt. 13: 30, 40–43. What truths are thus repeatedly emphasized concerning the final settlement and issue of world history?

Notes

1 Verses 13a, 15b. *Cf.* Is. 63: 2, 3.
2 Verse 14. These are armies of angels. *Cf.* Mt. 16: 27; 2 Thes. 1: 7–9.

3 Verse 20. 'The lake of fire'; so also in 20: 10, 14, 15; 21: 8; elsewhere called 'the eternal fire' or 'the Gehenna of fire' (Mt. 18: 8, 9; 25: 41); also 'the furnace of fire' (Mt. 13: 42, 50). It is the place of final destruction.

□ STUDY 23 Revelation 20: 1–10

Great differences exist among Christians concerning the interpretation of 'the thousand years' and 'the first resurrection'. Either the thousand years follow Christ's second coming, or this section is a fresh symbolic description of the period between Christ's first coming and His second coming. There does seem to be a parallel sequence in the main events of Rev. 11–14 and 20. It was through Christ's first coming that Satan was bound. *Cf.* Mk. 3: 23–27; Lk. 10: 17–19; Jn. 12: 31. Rev. 20: 7–9 can be understood as yet another reference to Armageddon. *Cf.* 16: 14–16; 19: 19. 'The first resurrection', however understood, is a privilege shared in only by faithful followers of the Lamb. Some think the phraseology symbolically predicts that the age of the martyrs would be followed by a far longer period of Christian supremacy during which the faith of Christ for which the martyrs died would live and reign. (See *NBC* and *More than Conquerors* by W. Hendriksen, Tyndale Press, 1962.)

1 What activity is particularly attributed to Satan? In what different ways is he dealt with? How is his activity made to serve God's purposes? *Cf.* 2 Thes. 2: 9–12. What will be his end? Who will share the same fate? *Cf.* Mt. 25: 41.

2 What are the rewards of the martyrs who are faithful to death? *Cf.* Lk. 22: 28–30; 2 Tim. 2: 12; Rev. 2: 10, 11; 5: 10. What grace should such awareness make us covet?

Notes

1 Verses 1–3. 'The bottomless pit': as the abode of evil spirits (*cf.* 9: 11) this is to be carefully distinguished from 'the lake of fire' (verse 10).
2 Verse 3. 'Must': for reasons hidden in the divine will.
3 Verse 8. 'Gog and Magog': the reference here is to Ezk. 38; 39, where the prophet conceived of a great invasion of the land of Israel.

□ STUDY 24 Revelation 20: 11 – 21: 8

1 20: 11–15. We have here depicted the final settlement of the destiny of the present world order and of all who belong to it. Who is to be the Judge? How is each man's destiny to be determined? What are the only alternatives? *Cf.* Mt. 16: 27; Jn. 5: 28, 29; Rom. 2: 6, 16; Rev. 21: 8; 22: 12.

2 21: 1–7. A revelation of the new world order is now given. *Cf.* Is. 65: 17; 2 Pet. 3: 13. What is its metropolis? Contrast Rev. 18: 10. Who are its citizens? What are their privileges? Of what blessings are they assured, and by whose word and deed?

☐ STUDY 25 Revelation 21: 9–21

This vision of the city of God is no more to be taken literally than was the vision of Christ in 1: 12–20. It is a symbolic picture, and we have to see in and through the symbols the spiritual realities which they represent.

1 For example, the size of the city (verse 16; see Note 2 below) expresses the same thought as the phrase 'which no man could number' in 7: 9; the shape of the city as a cube (21: 16) suggests its perfection of design and its permanence; the gold and precious stones its brilliance and perfection of quality, and so forth. What other spiritual realities does this passage suggest to you?

2 How is the contrast between this city and the harlot city Babylon brought to the mind of the reader? *Cf.* verse 9 with 17: 1. Work out this contrast in some of its features. What are the outstanding differences between Babylon and the New Jerusalem? *Cf.* Zc. 14: 20, 21; Lk. 16: 15; 1 Jn. 2: 16, 17.

Notes

1 Verses 12–14. The city, while offering entrance from all directions, is determined in character by the revelation given to Israel and through the apostles.

2 Verse 16. 'Twelve thousand stadia': about 1,500 miles.

3 Verse 18. 'Pure gold, clear as glass': see also verse 21. There is nothing not genuine, nothing not transparent.

☐ STUDY 26 Revelation 21: 22 – 22: 5

1 Make a list of all that is said not to be found in the perfected kingdom of God, *i.e.*, of all in 21: 1 – 22: 5 of which the words 'no' or 'no more' or 'nothing . . . nor any one who' are used. Over against these, set the positive blessings here spoken of. Comparing these blessings with those of the Garden of Eden (Gn. 1: 28, 29; 2: 8–25), how do they transcend them, and what is their chief glory? *Cf.* 1 Cor. 15: 46; Eph. 1: 3.

2 Would a non-Christian be able to enter the city (see 21: 27), and if he did enter would he find satisfaction in its blessings (*cf.* Eph. 2: 3; 1 Cor. 2: 14)? In the light of this, consider the absolute necessity of 'the blood of the Lamb' and of regeneration for every man. *Cf.* Jn. 3: 5; Lk. 10: 20.

Note. 22: 1, 2. Some interpret this to mean that there is one broad street which intersects the city, beside which the river flows, with trees on either bank. Others take 'street', 'river', and 'tree of life' as being collective nouns, and picture many streets and streams of the river flowing by them and many trees bearing fruit every month, all being symbolic of 'the superabundant character of God's provision'.

☐ STUDY 27 Revelation 22: 6–21

1 What word of Christ is repeated three times in these verses? See also 3: 11, and *cf.* 1: 7; 16: 15. How are we to reconcile this word with the fact that even now He has not come? What should be our attitude and response to this word of our Master? *Cf.* 2 Pet. 3; Mt. 24: 43–51; Heb. 10: 36–39. Can you join in the prayer of verses 17 and 20 as the spontaneous yearning of your heart?

2 How are the truth and the importance of the contents of this book confirmed to us in this passage? By what name is it four times described? What is its origin? Whence does it derive its authority? How ought we to express our regard for it and our response to it?

Notes

1 Verse 6. This book springs from the same divine source from which all the prophets have derived their inspiration.

2 Verses 8, 9. *Cf.* 19: 10; Col. 2: 18. John emphasizes both the attraction and the error of angel worship. The same might be said of the worship of the saints.

3 Verse 11. An emphatic warning that the time of the end is near, and the opportunity of a change of character is passing. *Cf.* Dn. 12: 10; 2 Tim. 3: 13. Yet see verse 17b below, and 21: 6.

4 Verse 16. 'The root and the offspring of David': *cf.* Mk. 12: 35–37.

☐ STUDY 28 Revelation 1–22: Revision

1 How would you sum up the chief message of this whole book? What abiding truths are we meant to learn from it for our instruction and encouragement? *Cf.* Jn. 16: 33; Acts 14: 22; Rev. 1: 9; 12: 10, 11. What are the things in which we are called to share 'in Jesus'?

2 Consider the seven beatitudes in this book. See 1: 3; 14: 13; 16: 15; 19: 9; 20: 6; 22: 7 and 14. Are you observing the conditions, and, in so far as is yet possible, are you beginning to know the wealth of the blessedness?